Dorothy Canfield Fisher

Dorothy Canfield Fisher

Dorothy Canfield Fisher

A Biography

Ida H. Washington

The New England Press
Shelburne, Vermont

The New England Press, Inc.
P.O. Box 525
Shelburne, Vermont 05482

Library of Congress Catalog Card Number: 81-83287
ISBN: 0-933050-08-9

Photographs courtesy of:
The Dorothy Canfield Fisher Papers
Special Collections
The Bailey/Howe Library
The University of Vermont
Burlington, Vermont

Printed by Queen City Printers Inc., Burlington, Vermont
PRINTED IN THE UNITED STATES OF AMERICA

Acknowledgments

There is no group of human beings more patient and helpful than those who work in the archives of our universities. Without them the fumbling attempts of absentminded scholars would founder long before reaching port. For help with the research behind this volume, I owe much to the library staff of Columbia, Princeton, and Brown universities and still more to the archivists of the University of Vermont, where the warm interest and encouragement of Dr. T. D. Seymour Bassett, Elizabeth Lovell, and Connell Gallagher have kept the project moving through seasons of discouragement and frustration.

In the academic world the support of an understanding administration is invaluable to all of us who teach and pursue research. I should like to express special appreciation to Dean Joseph P. Sauro of the College of Arts and Sciences of Southeastern Massachusetts University for his consistent support of my research and for providing time for this particular project.

My scholar husband's suggestions and criticisms have been much appreciated and sometimes followed, and my children have taken time from their own interests to search libraries for pertinent information and to run other errands in my behalf.

Special thanks for the typing go to Doris Nicholas, who has supported this last stage of creation, not only with her meticulous work but with her friendship and encouragement as well.

Contents

Introduction

Few authors are as difficult to place in the literary history of America as Dorothy Canfield Fisher. Her long life spanned the transition from the nineteenth to the twentieth century, and her writings paralleled the literary trend from Victorian optimism to naturalistic pessimism. To her, however, writing fiction was not a matter of current trends but an intensely personal and individual creative process.

In 1944 she answered with these words a friend's suggestion that she write another novel: "But fiction — that's more like falling in love, which can't be done by will-power or purpose, but concerns the *whole* personality, which includes vast areas of the unconscious and subconscious, as well as those processes within the control of purposefulness. This element of the unknown puts into the writing of fiction an element of the uncontrollable. And fiction written *without* the whole personality is not fiction (that is, recreated human life, interpreted), but only articles or statements in narrative *form*."[1]

These words hold the key to Dorothy Canfield Fisher's fiction, for woven into the novels and short stories that shocked and delighted generations of readers is the whole personality of the author who created them. A rich stream of heritage and experience had been poured into the formation of that personality, and many of its elements had settled into those hidden regions of the unconscious and subconscious where basic values are lodged. It is to the exploration of that whole author-personality that the present book is dedicated — to a study of the events of her life and their significance in her development as a writer of fiction.

Dorothy Canfield Fisher liked to say that human life is complex, and it would be difficult to find a better example of how complex life can be than her own experience. She was born and grew up in midwestern American university towns, where her father was a professor of economics and later a university president. She spent summers in the small, rural Vermont community that had been settled by her father's ancestors. She also made extended visits to Paris with her mother, who went there to study art. She studied

French language and literature in America and France, earning a bachelor's degree from Ohio State University and a doctorate from Columbia University. Although her training prepared her to teach, she never became a classroom teacher but turned instead to writing. She married, moved with her husband to Vermont, had two children, and lived with her family as an active participant in the life of a Vermont village.

During World War I, Dorothy and her husband, John Fisher, went to France. While he served as an ambulance driver, she organized a Braille press to produce books for the war blind and set up a refugee home in the Basque country for children evacuated from Paris. During World War II, she organized and led the Children's Crusade to raise money among American children for children who were the victims of war.

Her interest in education led her to visit the school of Maria Montessori in Italy, and she was one of the first to popularize the Montessori ideas and methods in America. Later, she served on local, state, and national educational boards and was a member of the boards of trustees of several different colleges. She wrote more than a dozen books and literally hundreds of articles on educational and historical topics. She belonged to the first board of selection of the Book-of-the-Month Club, influencing the reading taste of the American public for a quarter of a century, and she played a significant role in the early popularity of Pearl Buck, Isak Dinesen, and others.

She was much honored for her good works and received half a score of honorary doctoral degrees from American colleges and universities, as well as medals and citations from foreign governments. Her writings, both fiction and nonfiction, were immensely popular in America and were translated into many foreign languages.

Despite the important contributions she made in so many different fields, however, Dorothy Canfield Fisher wished to be remembered first of all as a writer of fiction. In 1957 she said about a proposed biography: "My efforts to be a good citizen, in my personal life, really should not be given so much attention that my books, to which I have given the very core of my heart and mind, should be pushed into the background."[2]

Her published fiction includes eleven novels and more than a hundred short stories. These works stand apart from the literary fashions of her time, both in the way they are written and in the subject matter they treat. In the narratives she creates a rich tapestry of environmental detail against which her characters move and act. The aspects of the environment conform neither to the standards of "the mid-Victorian period of hush-hush about the ugly and ignoble aspects of life" nor to those of the twentieth century, "a period when wormwood and vinegar are the fashionable flavorings,"[3] but are composed, like life itself, of both beautiful and ugly elements.

Her characters also differ from those of many of her contemporaries in possessing an element of inner strength. Although they suffer disappointment and even shattering defeat, her main characters exhibit a spark of indomitable human spirit that can survive disaster and rebuild for the future. She thus combines awareness of the precarious nature of existence with unshakable faith in the potential (though not always realized) capacity of human beings to live with its uncertainties and hazards.

Her novels attack materialism, social discrimination, religious and racial intolerance, and all forms of brutality and fraud. Far ahead of her times, she wrote of the waste of human resources implicit in consigning women to limited roles of social usefulness. The settings of her stories are ones familiar to her — midwest America, Vermont, and France — and the characters she has placed in these settings are three-dimensional personalities, composites drawn from qualities of people she knew.

Her fictional worlds are, however, not shallow pictures of a contemporary scene, but they have the timeless quality of work that rests on a heritage of slowly developed and firmly held values. We must therefore go back even before the birth of the author to find the first springs from which they came.

Part 1

The Writer's Heritage and Growth

"The basis of every tradition lies far back in past years. Events and attitudes of those long-ago years decide the shape and color of the institutions and of the attitudes which we call a way of life."

Vermont Tradition

1
Parents and Other Ancestors

It is one thing to admire creative artists and flaming crusaders from a distance. It is quite another matter to live in the same house with them.

At the head of the Canfield table sat James Hulme Canfield, dedicated educator and vigorous champion of equality and freedom, proud of his Vermont heritage and so consciously a part of it that he liked to say that he "had lived in Vermont since 1763."[1] Across from him was Flavia Camp Canfield, "an artist to her last irrational, charming, highly gifted, irresponsible fiber,"[2] "detesting regularity of any kind,"[3] consciously and vigorously opposing and rejecting the dead weight of those values and practices which she saw as "Vermont." Between them, two children completed the family circle, James A. Canfield (known as Jim) and Dorothy (christened Dorothea Frances and nicknamed Dolly).

To Dorothy's father, James Hulme Canfield, his Vermont ancestors and their standards were a constant source of inspiration and strength, symbolizing the best he could hope to attain, and he was eager to share this rich treasure with his beloved children. To his artistic wife, traditional patterns of behavior and ancestral expectations were an onerous burden, to be shaken off deliberately, because they interfered with the free pursuit of the best and highest goals. The ancestors Flavia liked to remember were those who had turned their backs on the stagnant past and had dared to strike out into new and unexplored paths. Three vivid ancestral personalities emerged from the often-repeated stories told by Dorothy's parents, moved into her own inner world, and appeared later in her literary works.

Dorothy's mother liked to tell about her adventurous father, Albert Camp, who grew up on a farm near Rutland, Vermont, and developed early the strength, resourcefulness, and marksmanship that were essential parts of a Vermont farm boy's equipment. When he reached the full vigor of early manhood, he set out into the western wilderness in search of new horizons, wandering freely, hunting and trapping, learning somewhere the art of surveying, and supporting himself by this and by his skill with ax and gun. In

Ohio he met Martha Barney, a Vermont girl from Rutland County who was visiting a married sister, and he followed her back to Vermont to court and finally to win her.

The grandmother's life was full of hardships, but they were the least important part of the picture that Flavia gave her little daughter. When Dorothy wrote of her grandparents, their struggles in the wilderness were only a background for their vital relationship:

> . . . log-cabin after log-cabin, rough clearing in the primeval forest, days when there was nothing but corn-meal in the pantry, long treks in covered wagons to escape from the fever-and-ague which burned and ravaged them; never more possessions than could be drawn by a team of lean horses, — and always unbroken love and devotion between the two wayfarers. Wherever their caravan halted for a few months was home to the woodsman's wife, because he was there; his vitality, his free-hearted zest in whatever came to them, bore her along like a tidal wave. And to the end of her days she worshipped the memory of his deep, never-wavering passion for her.[4]

For Dorothy's mother, who was the third of the five little girls born to the pioneer couple, life had been continually exciting and unpredictable. She and her sisters, Dorothy reported,

> never having known any other life, saw nothing unusual in the one they led, especially as their mother, her personality doubled and trebled by the exigencies of her life, stood, somehow, miraculously between them and the most impossible of the hardships to which their father so light-heartedly condemned them. They were always dressed in well-mended garments, they had shoes and stockings, they were clean and cherished, there was always cheer and loving-kindness between their father and mother, and when there was only corn-meal mush for supper, they scarcely noticed it, because of the old songs and stories of which their mother had such a store. . . . They adored their great, rollicking father, always in high spirits, and they preferred the deersteaks and squirrel stews which were the results of his wonderful marksmanship, to the tough, stringy beef and salt pork which was the diet of the other frontier children.[5]

In 1849 the news flamed across the country that gold had been discovered in California. New horizons and the chance for wealth were an irresistible combination for the born adventurer. Albert Camp moved his wife and children into the nearest town, leaving them with support for a year, and set out for California. Several months later word came that he had died of "mountain fever."[6]

The thirty-two-year-old widow married again; her second husband was a man as different as possible from her first husband. The Reverend Asa A. Allen was a Congregational minister in Black Earth, Wisconsin, a widower with eight children. Flavia and her four sisters moved into the Black Earth parsonage and grew up with the eight Allen children and with three younger ones from the second marriage.

The lively pioneer girls chafed under the restrictions of "Victorian housebound, genteel, young ladyhood."[7] They were all talented: musical, artistic, or literary. Flavia was an artist. As a girl she studied and taught at the University of Wisconsin, continuing her studies later with various artists in Paris and with the American artist William M. Chase. On a visit to her stepbrother Will, who had become a doctor in Clearwater, Iowa, she met James Canfield, an eager, adventurous young man, conquering the West with the building of railroads just as her exciting, gallant father had overcome it with his rifle and ax.

At about the same time Albert Camp shouldered his gun and set out into the western wilderness, Dorothy's other grandfather, Eli Canfield, was plowing the back pasture in Arlington, Vermont, with a book of poetry in his pocket. As an old man he recalled, "I plowed there . . . with a yoke of young steers who were not well matched nor well broke, one of which could not stand the heat. . . . While they were resting or cooling off I used to sit on the plow beam and read from a pocket edition of Milton's *Paradise Lost* or Young's *Night Thoughts.*"[8]

Eli Hawley Canfield early showed the keen interest in books and ideas that was to characterize him all his long life. His dream was to go to Williams College, and with a local friend he took and passed the entrance examinations. Yet there was no money in the Canfield household to send a boy to college. Through his friend he kept track of what was studied in the freshman year, however, and completed as much of the material as he could at home. Toward the end of this year of home study, he received a letter from a Reverend Mr. Perkins, who had gone from the Episcopal Church in Arlington to Pennsylvania, to a charge near Bristol College in Bucks County. There, in addition to pastoral duties, Perkins tutored young boys in Latin to prepare them for college. He found the tutoring a burdensome task and thought of the bright Canfield boy who had been a member of his parish in Vermont. Would he come to Pennsylvania to take over the tutoring work? For Eli it was a chance to teach and to study and "to break out of the place that held me."[9]

Bristol College was a new institution, established in 1834 by the Episcopal

Church.[10] Its emphasis was strongly religious and classical, and it had attracted an unusually distinguished faculty and student body. There Eli formed the acquaintance of many men who later rose to eminence in the church. When he arrived at Bristol, he found that his haphazard year of home study had prepared him beyond the freshman year at the college. "Comparing what I had gone over with the studies required at Bristol College, I found that I had some acquaintance with what was there required of the Sophomore class and bent all my energies to be equal to the class in October when they should begin the studies of their junior year . . . before the summer was past, in spite of a week's blindness, I was enrolled a member of the Junior Class."[11] The motivation and power of will that drove the young man from rural Vermont to read and study until he suffered "a week's blindness" were a prelude to one of the most interesting church careers of his time.

The college was only two years old when Eli enrolled as a member of the junior class, and it appeared to have a long and promising future ahead. Many people had pledged support, and the hopes of the faculty and students were high. However, the winter when Eli began his studies also ushered in the disastrous recession of 1837. The supporters of the college could not pay their pledges, and the college was literally without means. As Eli later reported, "to the amazement and horror of the entire public, the College which had been so prosperous and which gave such glowing promise of a great and glorious future was not only in debt but without means. . . . Nominally and actually extinct in 1837, it ceased to have a legal corporate existence in 1838 — 'Sic transit.'"[12]

The college buildings were turned to use as a boarding school for boys, where from 1838 to 1841 Eli was teacher and principal. From there he went to the theological seminary at Alexandria, Virginia, a stronghold of Low Church theology, to study for the ministry. The time he spent in Alexandria was the longest period in his life away from Vermont, a little more than three years.

Eli's first parish was in Delaware, Ohio, where he went with his bride, Martha Hulme of Burlington, New Jersey. An Easter letter to his Ohio parishioners in 1849 contains the exhortation: "Christians should be as careful of the books they read as of their companions, always selecting such as will invigorate the mind, prepare for the better discharge of the practical duties of life, or promote the growth of the spirit."[13] A close look at these qualities reveals that they not only set mental vigor in first place but omit completely any reference to sentimental morality.

The life of the intellect was only a part of Eli's vigorous existence, however. From Ohio he went to New York, first to Manhattan and then to Brooklyn, where he campaigned for the liberalism of the Low Church point of view as against High Church formalism, the "fol-de-rols (as he called them) of salvation by incense and candles and twiddling distinctions between green and blue and yellow stoles."[14] "He seems always to have been incandescent," his granddaughter wrote, "the whole six-feet-three of him, with motive-power which he could not, try as he might, use up fast enough to cool off."[15]

Eli's energies found outlets in writing and social action. He edited a church paper and wrote innumerable pamphlets, at the same time expanding his parish work into the surrounding slums, adding one mission chapel after another to the staid old parish where he was pastor. In 1863 he was sent to Europe with Henry Ward Beecher to try to explain to the Europeans what the Civil War was all about and to stir up sympathy for the Union and abolition causes.

With all his vigor, however, Eli was no match for his mother, Almera Hawley Canfield. Almera was Dorothy's favorite among her vigorous ancestors, and she often retold the stories about that diminutive woman with fiery convictions. One of the family favorites was about the time just before the Civil War when Eli returned home for a visit and was asked to preach in the local church. Dorothy's brother Jim reported what happened this way:

> He did, and in his sermon tried to pour a little oil on the troubled waters, to inject a note of Christian charity and forbearance in the discussions raging all around. He said that, after all, the Southern people were Americans too, our own blood brothers, that most of them were honest, decent folk like most of us, and that these tremendous issues should be, and could be, resolved without bloodshed if reason and forebearance, tolerance and patience were employed.
>
> He had barely reached this point when his mother Almera rose from the family pew, hissing violently, strode out of the pew into the aisle, stamped down the long aisle, still hissing at the top of her lungs — if you can hiss in such a manner — opened the big door at the rear of the church, stamped out, slamming it violently behind her and, hissing all the way, disappeared across the street to the Brick House.
>
> Poor grandfather faltered and stumbled and finally broke down completely and couldn't continue.[16]

Almera Hawley Canfield was a little woman, but one that her family or community would not soon forget. Dorothy's father often recalled her actions on the day of John Brown's death, for like many abolitionists Almera was a great admirer of the rebellious leader. Dorothy said once of her, "My great-grandmother Canfield, who was one of the most powerful and influential personalities in our family circle, dead or alive, for she died before I was born, brought us all up to believe that John Brown was really a saint as well as a fanatic."[17] Dorothy retold the story as one of the traditions that belonged not only to her but to the community as well, in her *Memories of Arlington, Vermont:*

> My father several times told me the story of his being waked up very early one morning when he was a lad in his middle 'teens, to see his grandmother, fully dressed, leaning over his bed and shaking his shoulder to wake him. She said, "Get up, Jim, this is the day John Brown is to be hanged. And I want you to go over and toll the bell for him."
>
> My father said he was so much startled by her gray face and trembling hands that he turned out of bed in a jiffy and got into his clothes. She sent him across the street (for the brick house which is now the Community House was my great-grandmother's home) and up into the belfry of St. James. There, obeying her because he didn't dare not to, he began to toll the bell very slowly, as it was always tolled to announce a death. He hadn't had any breakfast, and he got very tired doing it, but he didn't dream of stopping. About two hours later, another Arlington boy appeared climbing up the steps to the belfry roof. He, too, looked startled and round-eyed, and said as he took the bell rope from my father's hands, "It's my turn. Aunt Almera said toll." He began pulling the bell—one great strong stroke, and then a pause while you counted to get the strokes even. That was the way a funeral was always announced. My father went downstairs and across the street and had his breakfast. Nobody said a word to him about the bell ringing. His grandmother sat in the front parlor, listening to make sure the tolling was continuously done, and reading the Bible—the Old Testament part.
>
> In that way the bell was kept tolling all day long, one big boy after another being sent up by Great-grandmother. By the middle of the morning the people from out in the country districts, wondering what in the world could have happened, had one after another hitched up their horses and come into town to inquire from anybody out on the sidewalk, who was dead. They were told to go into the brick house and ask old Mrs. Canfield. When they did, they found Great-grandmother sitting in her little straight rocker, the big Bible on her knees, reading aloud the most awful texts from the Old Testament, the ones which called down vengeance on evildoers. She stopped long enough to tell them what the tolling meant, then went on reading aloud those savage expressions of hatred of evildoers.
>
> When night came she allowed the tolling to stop.
>
> But my father always said that for years afterward on still days, or

when he first woke up at dawn, he could hear that heart-shaking, Day-of-Wrath knell, solemnly filling with its deep resonance all our corner of the Vermont valley.[18]

In addition to her father's stories, Dorothy gathered other vivid impressions of her great-grandmother during summers in Arlington. "When I was about eight years old," she related,

> I went out one day to watch old Lemuel Hager, who came once a year to mow the grass in the orchard back of the house. As he clinked the whetstone over the ringing steel of his scythe, he looked down at me and remarked: "You favor the Hawley side of the family, don't you? There's a look around your mouth sort o' like Aunt Almera, your grandmother — no — my sakes, you must be her great-granddaughter? Wa'l — think of that? And it don't seem more'n yesterday I saw her come stepping out same's you did just now; not so much bigger'n you are this minute, for all she must have been sixty years old then. She always was the *littlest* woman. But she marched up to me, great lummox of a boy, and she said, 'Is it true, what I hear folks say, Lemuel, that you somehow got out of school without having learned how to read?' And I says, 'Why, Mis' Canfield, to tell the truth, I never did seem to get the hang of books, and I never could seem to git up no sort of interest in 'em.'
>
> And she says back, 'Well, no great boy of eighteen in the town *I* live in is a-goin' to grow up without he knows how to read the Declaration of Independence,' says she. And she made me stop work for an hour — she paid me just the same for it — took me into the house and started teaching me.
>
> Great land of love! If the teacher at school had 'a' taught me like that, I'd 'a' been a minister! I felt as though she'd cracked a hole in my head and was just pouring the l'arning in through a funnel. And 'twan't more'n ten minutes before she found out 'twas my eyes the trouble. I'm terrible nearsighted. Well, that was before the days when everybody wore specs. There wa'n't no way to get specs for me; but you couldn't stump Aunt Almera. She just grabbed up a sort of multiplying-glass that she used, she said, for her sewing, now her eyes were kind o' failing her, and she give it to me. 'I'll take bigger stitches,' says she, laughing: 'big stitches don't matter so much as reading for an American citizen.'
>
> Well, sir, she didn't forget me; she kept at me to practice to home with my multiplying-glass, and it was years before I could git by the house without Aunt Almera come out on the porch and hollered to me, that bossy way she had, 'Lemuel, you come in for a minute and let me hear you read.' Sometimes it kind o' madded me, she had such a way o' thinking she

could make everybody stand 'round. Sometimes it made me laugh, she was so old, and not much bigger'n my fist. But, by gol, I l'arned to read, and I have taken a sight of comfort out of it. I don't never set down in the evening and open up the Necronsett *Journal* without I think of Aunt Almera Canfield."[19]

From another neighbor Dorothy heard a story of Almera's butter making:

Whenever I begin to make the pats, I remember when I was a girl working for her. She kept you right up to the mark, I tell you, and you ought to have seen how she lit into me when she found out some of my butter pats were just a little over a pound and some a little less. It was when she happened to have too much cream and she was "trading in" the butter at the store. You'd have thought I'd stolen a fifty-cent piece to hear her go on! "I sell those for a pound; they've got to *be* a pound," says she, the way she always spoke, as though that ended it.

"But land sakes, Mis' Canfield," says I, all out o' patience with her, "an ounce or two one way or the other—it's as likely to be more as less, you know! What difference does it make? *Nobody* expects to make their pats just a pound! How could you?"

"How could you? How could you?" says she. "Why, just the way you make anything else the way it ought to be—by keeping at it till it *is* right. What other way is there?"

I didn't think you could do it. I *knew* you couldn't; but you always had to do the way Mis' Canfield said, and so I began grumbling under my breath about high-handed, fussy old women. But she never minded what you *said* about her, so long as you did your work right. So I fussed and fussed, clipping off a little, and adding on a little, and weighing it between times. It was the awfulest bother you ever saw, because it spoiled the shape of your pat to cut at it, and you had to start it over again every time.

Well, you wouldn't believe it, how soon I got the hang of it! She'd made me think about it so much, I got interested, and it wasn't any time at all before I could tell the heft of a pat to within a fraction of an ounce just by the feel of it in my hand. I never forgot it. You never do forget that kind of thing. I brought up my whole family on that story. "Now you do that spelling lesson just exactly *right*," I'd say to my Lucy, "just the way Aunt Almera made me do the butter pats!"[20]

A fearless adventurer, a dynamic preacher, and a civic-minded perfectionist—these were the three ancestors whose heritage came through to the young Dorothy with a clear call to follow. The particular path of her following, however, was formed by more immediate surroundings.

When Dorothy was born on February 17, 1879, her father was teaching political economy and sociology at the University of Kansas in Lawrence and crusading for the highly unpopular cause of "free trade." "At that time (the 1880s and '90s)," she recalled later,

> it caused about as much consternation in the people around him as if he had advocated free love. Opposition made him all the hotter an advocate. He wrote articles on the subject, gave lectures, taught it in his classes with passion. All through my little girlhood, there was an underlying current of mingled pride and apprehension in the family circle about this unorthodox conviction. We always felt (and so did he) that he might at any time lose his professional position because of it.[21]

James Hulme Canfield was born in Delaware, Ohio, on March 18, 1847, where his father had his first pastorate. His mother, Martha Hulme Canfield, was an unusually intellectual young woman for her day. She had read much, studied the classics, and wrote Sunday school stories, which were published anonymously for reasons of modesty and propriety. When James was still quite small, the family moved to New York, and when he was eight his mother died, leaving him and his younger sister to the care of their busy clergyman-father. At first James's grandmother and aunt came down from Arlington, Vermont, to keep house for their son and brother, but this arrangement proved unsatisfactory, and they took the children back to Arlington with them. A diary James kept in Vermont and his letters to his father tell of boyhood experiences typical for that time—school, fishing, sugaring. What they don't tell is what it was like to grow up under the influence of a grandmother like Almera Hawley Canfield.

A little boy takes his grandmother, and all his other relatives, for granted. However, the values and standards that James Hulme Canfield carried with him into the classroom and administrative office and bequeathed to his daughter Dorothy, the guiding principles he always thought of as "Vermont," were those of that "small spunky, fiery-hearted woman with impassioned convictions."[22] On the title page of one of his early publications stands a quotation that does credit to this heritage: "He that apprehendeth an evil, yet holdeth his peace, he doeth not rightly toward the common weal."[23] Through all James Canfield's vigorous and dangerous campaign for free trade, his grandmother's fearless, outspoken convictions clearly supported and stood beside him. Tolling the bell for John Brown had left its mark on Professor Canfield. His campaigns for free trade and free education left their mark on his daughter Dorothy.

When James reached the age to prepare for college, he went back to the parsonage in Brooklyn and studied at the nearby Polytechnic Institute before entering Williams College with the class of 1868. During a summer vacation he traveled with his father and Henry Ward Beecher on their goodwill mission to Europe. James must have been a rather typical college student, for when Dorothy's brother Jim was in his teens their father recalled:

When I was about your age I was travelling in Europe with my father and Mr. Henry Ward Beecher. One day in Geneva, Switzerland, Mr. Beecher and I were sitting on a bench in a little park near our hotel when he turned to me and said, "Jim, there's a little favor I'd like to ask of you. Of course I know, we all know, everyone knows, that while your father is only a poor simple-minded clergyman, with little or no knowledge of the great world — though for some inexplicable reason with some repute — you, his son, have had all the advantages of learning and society and are really a cultured and dashing man of the world, with all the savoir-faire that comes with wide experience in that world. In fact, we are ready to agree with you that in all matters of taste and manners you are infinitely superior to your father. We acknowledge this, we concede it, but don't you think for the sake of the poor old gentleman now withering into his forty-seventh year, and who is after all your father, that you might conceal this superiority somewhat, cloak it, hide it a bit, pretend a little. It wouldn't hurt you, much, and it would make it a little easier for him in these declining years of his and would embarrass us less. That's all Jim," he said, "It was just a passing thought of mine."[24]

The four years at Williams were happy ones, but as they drew to a close the letters of young James Canfield to his father were filled with an agony of indecision about a future career. Finally, he accepted an invitation from a college classmate to join in building the great western railroads. As he wrote later,

Horace Henry wired him to come to Calmar, Iowa, at once, and without knowing where the town was, and only finding out after he reached Chicago, he went. He promised to come home for Thanksgiving, but he was so busy that it was four years before he saw the East again. He went to work at once, for the firm of contractors with which Henry was connected; and with his headquarters in Minneapolis, remained in this business till the spring of 1871. He was bookkeeper, purchasing agent, and general utility man, with experiences which were of lasting helpfulness in all his later life.

In the spring of 1871 he took up the study of law, in the office of Hall and Gould, Jackson, Michigan. Mr. Hall being a one-time Bennington friend, the son of ex-Governor Hall, of Vermont. He was admitted to the Bar in the summer of 1872, and at once opened an office in St. Joseph, Michigan; where he remained till the summer of 1877. In June of 1873 he was married to Flavia A. Camp, at Clear Lake, Iowa, — where he had spent one of his railroading years.[25]

Just after Dorothy's father went west, he received a letter from an old Vermont friend, Jonas Wilder, then living in West Rupert. Mr. Wilder was for various intervals storekeeper, superintendent of the Rutland and Washington Railroad, and postmaster; he was also active in community affairs, served at one time as superintendent of the Congregational Sunday school, and instituted the West Rupert Fair.[26] The letter reads, in part:

> No matter what you do at first — if honorable — you can be reading up mankind, which enters largely into successful results — but — be sure and place your standard high and aim at something that in the end will benifit the world and your perseverance and determination will succeed. I feel as sure of it as ay one thing I ever calculated on. I have one thing to caution you about — I am not exactly compitent to give it a name, but opertunities will present that you can make a point, but naturly you will hold back fearing some might accuse you of a desire to show off — I tell you take all good oppertunity that you know you can sustain. I always made it a rule when asked to take a position of responsibility never say no. I tell you with a fair share of brains one can go through and acquit themselves with honour.
>
> "Never depend on being recommended, work your way. . . ." [all spelling *sic*][27]

It is surely no accident that this early letter has been preserved, whereas many contemporary to it are lost. There are echoes of it in the three mottoes James Hulme Canfield kept on his wall after he became a professor at the University of Kansas:

> All at it and all the time at it! that is what wins.
> What you can do, or dream you can do, begin it. Boldness hath genius, power and magic in it.
> The public business is the private business of every citizen.[28]

Of all the outstanding traits of his active career, none distinguished Dorothy's father more particularly than his willingness to take on "all good opportunity that you know you can sustain," and "when asked to take a position of responsibility never say no." In 1902, when he was asked to write a book of advice for college students, he recommended:

Whatever you may hold most desirable, most worthy of effort, you must remember that advancement and success always and necessarily mean increased responsibility. This is the unfailing result of every upward step which you take. There is no possible escape from this. No matter what may be the form of your ambition or of your activity, all growth simply means heavier burdens to be carried. These may not be increasingly burdensome — that is another matter; but the load is always increasing.[29]

In another statement from the same book, there is an echo of Jonas Wilder's suggestion about "reading up mankind." "No single habit or power will be more helpful to you in later life than the habit or power of grappling with men and holding them fast to you, with a sense of pleasure in their acquaintance with you."[30]

When James Canfield met Flavia Camp in Clearwater, Iowa, each saw in the other a vision of past blessings and future bliss. James had left behind the warmth of Vermont family ties; still further back in his memories was the lively young mother who had died when he was eight. Flavia's colorful, adventurous, exciting father had disappeared into the western wilderness when she was five; with her mother's remarriage she had been brought into a strict religious home that imposed restraints on her artistic temperament such that all her long life she harbored a distaste for formal religion.

James arrived in Clearwater with the building of the railroads, physically vigorous, intellectually alive, looking for new fields where he could put his talents to use. To Flavia he must have seemed like a reincarnation of her adventurous father. No one could have foreseen that his fields of conquest would not be on the open prairie but in the world of universities, where restraints on wives and families are almost as strict as those of the church. To James, away from home just long enough to be homesick, Flavia — of solid Vermont stock, charming, witty, original — must have seemed like a touch of home combined with the misty memories of the lively mother of his early childhood. Her quickness of speech and action were, however, to make problems for him as great as those his sense of social responsibility created for her. Their differences in temperament created a home in which a sensitive little daughter grew into a deeply perceptive novelist.

2
Home and School

In 1943, when she was sixty-five, Dorothy Canfield wrote to Pearl Buck: "The particular shadow which darkened my adolescent years was a complete lack of harmony between my father and mother. I've never spoken about this to anyone but you, this minute. But I remember very well how it seemed to be a burden greater than I could bear all the time when I was growing up. Yet there was no open quarreling or dissension — just a complete lack of the ability to make each other happy."[1]

Differences in temperament lay close beneath the surface, but to the casual eye Professor and Mrs. Canfield were a charming couple. James Hulme Canfield was active in the National Education Association, and in 1889, after serving competently for a number of years as its secretary, he was elected its president. That year the national convention was held in Nashville, Tennessee. Professor and Mrs. Canfield were, of course, in attendance, and in spare moments Mrs. Canfield wrote letters home. Flavia never hesitated to say what she thought, and the conditions she saw in the South stirred her Northern abolitionist convictions to lively expression. One of her letters almost caused a major disaster.

She was writing to her Kansas friend Mrs. Hudson, when she observed:

. . . The train this time had two cars, one for whites and the other for blacks. Several colored girls, well-dressed and quiet, got into the car we were in, while we were waiting for the time to start. The conductor told them they must go in the other car. They left the train with indignant faces, and did not go at all. I discussed this incident with a Southern woman who sat next to me in the car. "Those girls ought not to have been allowed to enter the car," she said. I asked her if the colored people often demanded equal rights of this sort. "Oh no," she said, "as a rule the negroes are right obedient." "They have to be," she added. So you see the color line is drawn sharply and is sometimes resented. We will see more of this no doubt as the meetings go on. The race question is the question of our time, I believe. The blacks are increasing faster than the whites. It is only a question of time when they will outnumber the whites two to one. They are strong and sturdy, they are being educated and have the ballot. What is to hinder them from having the power in their own hands some day? May I then be in some convenient corner in the sky to look down on the spectacle of black heels on white necks. "Cursed be Canaan," will do now, but it won't last forever.[2]

For a Northern woman of Vermont family, these sentiments were not at all unusual thirty years after the Civil War, and her Kansas friend would have concurred in her opinions fully. As a personal letter between friends the epistle would have caused no problems. However, Mrs. Hudson's husband happened to be the editor of the *Topeka* (Kansas) *Capitol.* Newsy letters from local travelers are always good copy, so he printed Flavia Canfield's letter to his wife as something that might interest other friends at home. The *Nashville American* copied the story, and newspapers throughout the South cried out their anger at the wife of the newly elected president of the NEA.

As a result President Canfield submitted his resignation to the convention, but it was not accepted. Flavia made public apologies, but most Southerners felt that they were neither full nor sincere enough. At home the controversial Professor Canfield (and his outspoken wife) were passed over for the vacant position of chancellor of the University of Kansas.

The University of Missouri had also been seeking a new president, but it, too, now turned away from the Canfields. The *Columbia* (Missouri) *Herald* commented: "Prof. James H. Canfield, of the University of Kansas, has been favorably mentioned by several Missouri papers . . . as just the man for the presidency of the University of Missouri. Perhaps he is. But what about his wife? . . . However well Professor Canfield might suit as president of the University, Mrs. Canfield would hardly be welcome in our midst."[3]

The next winter Flavia went to Paris to study art and took her daughter Dorothy with her. When they came back the whole family moved to Nebraska, where James Hulme Canfield had accepted the position of chancellor of the State University in Lincoln.

Before going to Nebraska, Professor Canfield had written to his father:

I have your letter — full of loving solicitude. I am doing no more than I am really obliged to do. I am not doing half I am constantly asked to do. Large numbers of very good people think me unkind and selfish because I do not do more, at their request. It is worry, and not work, that breaks men down — and I have stopped worrying! The future, like the past, is in other hands. I am only trying to do well the task of the hour and day. I have not laid out work for myself for years — it is all laid out for me. Much of the time it is not what I would choose, largely because I would naturally and characteristically choose indolence. But I am with busy stirring, people — and must do my share or be trodden under.

Do you honestly think the outcome of my life would be wiser and better if I gave up all this, and dropped forever out of sight, say at Williamstown? Answer this question frankly and soon — for that place is still open to me.[4]

James's father must have agreed with Jonas Wilder that the only way to live was to accept opportunities and challenges. In any case, Professor Canfield turned his back on the easy berth "back east" and went forth to a great missionary effort for public education in the new, raw West.

Not all of the ten years Dorothy lived in Kansas were as turbulent as the last one. For the most part, she spent her winters going to the public schools of Lawrence, her summers visiting Canfield relatives at the "Brick House" in Arlington, Vermont. It was, she recalled later,

full of old folks — my grandfather, my great-uncle (especially loved by me), my great-aunt, my aunt, an occasionally visiting other great-uncle. They were all great talkers, great tellers of stories of old times in Vermont. Uncle Zed *said* he could remember seeing red-coated British soldiers, taken prisoners in the war of 1812, resting near the Brick farmhouse (two miles north of the village) in the North District of Arlington which was always one of the family houses for the Canfields.[5]

One summer Dorothy's uncle gave her a little part-Morgan horse, and on it she spent many happy, solitary hours, roaming the countryside about Arlington.

The year in Paris was a challenging one for the little Kansas-and-Vermont schoolgirl. While Flavia Canfield reveled in her association with art and artists, Dorothy was placed in a French school, a sink-or-swim experience in learning French. Fortunately, she had a natural gift for languages and was soon her mother's interpreter in the foreign culture. This was the first of a number of Paris experiences, for Flavia was caught by the magic of the famous city. She never learned French or any other foreign language, and so Dorothy was an essential companion in her travels. "I was with her in Paris, off and on," Dorothy recalled, "all through my childhood and youth, getting an education — if it could be called that — very oddly divided between Paris studio life, art galleries, and the classrooms of a school kept by Roman Catholic sisters, and later, when I was older, in the Sorbonne and the École des Hautes Études."[6] As a schoolgirl in France she formed a close friendship with a French schoolmate, Céline Sibut, a friendship that lasted for more than fifty years and is recorded in letters exchanged throughout this period. The experience with French schools was not altogether a happy one, however, and when her own children were growing up Dorothy wrote to a friend: "Some time we ought to take the children back for another year of French life to fix their French in their memories, but oh how I hate French schools."[7]

When Flavia and Dorothy returned from France in 1891, they joined Chancellor Canfield in Lincoln, Nebraska. The university was then only twenty-two years old, and the position of chancellor offered a challenge that Professor Canfield welcomed with joy and vigor.

"To the Canfield family," Dorothy and her brother recalled later in a jointly authored article, "Nebraska is not a geographical spot — It is a state of mind, bright with youth and vigor and hope; for the four years our father spent there were, we think, the happiest years of his life."[8] He was in his prime, and he rejoiced in the new challenges, the opportunities to make new converts to the cause of public education. He traveled throughout the new state wherever people would listen to him and preached the truth as he saw it.

His credo was simple with the candid simplicity of a major truth — what he never tired of saying, with all his heart in his words, was that education, trained minds, intellectual honesty and power are democracy's only hope, and are also the supreme good for each individual life. . . . He said that people whose brains were in good working order were worth more to themselves and to the world than people with uninformed untrained brains who had happened to make money out of a sudden rise in the value of real estate, out of a speculation in stocks, or by any other chance result of mere luck. He said — we know with what fervor for we heard him say it every day, in and out of our home, and always with as fresh and ringing an enthusiastic conviction as if it were the first time — he cried out that the door to intellectual *growth* (though not necessarily to notable achievement) was never shut to any human being of character, and that anyone who had helped to push it open so that the younger generation could go through, had done something to make his life worthwhile, no matter how shabby his clothes, how flat his purse, how withered his hopes for material prosperity. . . . He often spoke of the state system of education as a ladder reaching from the first grade of every primary school straight to the open gate of the University. In the smaller country towns and cities, poor and fighting for their very lives against economic difficulties, the rungs of the ladder most often missing were the four years of high school training. So on his speaking trips the Chancellor of the University campaigned for more and better high schools with all the fervor of his generous and imaginative nature.[9]

After a talk along these lines to some group of farmers gathered in a bare schoolhouse, he would take the night train home and then be "up the next morning early to tramp briskly along S Street to what he saw as The Golden Door, The Way to the Future, The Great Opportunity, and what was probably, in literal fact (at least so the old photographs show it) a few ugly buildings put up as cheaply as possible, scattered around on a rough and unfinished prairie campus."[10]

While James Canfield was carrying on the fight to make the University of Nebraska a real part of every citizen's life in the state at large, within the university he was trying to see that education was really reaching those for whom it was intended. "What a steady struggle he carried on," his children remembered, "inside the University against the letter of intellectual life that killeth, and against the equally fatal error of cheap low standards of scholarship."[11]

In a memorial address shortly after his death, his friend Nicholas Murray Butler recalled a story from this period:

> Toward the close of the college year a young tutor of mathematics who was completing his first year of service came into the Chancellor's office and asked whether he was to be reappointed for another year. The Chancellor said, "Well, what do you yourself think of your work? What have you done that you are proud of?" The young tutor answered, "Mr. Chancellor, I have just held such a stiff examination in my course that I have flunked sixty members of the freshman class." The Chancellor looked at him kindly and said, "Young man, suppose I gave you a herd of one hundred cattle to drive to Kansas City, or Omaha, and you came in to tell me that you had driven them so fast, and so hard, and had made such good time that 60 per cent of them had died on the way. Do you think that I should want you to drive any more cattle to the Missouri River?" "No, sir," said the tutor. "Well, I do not think we will let you drive any more freshmen."[12]

The chancellor's personal interest in his students was genuine and translated into action, as were all his convictions. He spoke with them as he crossed the campus, and he opened his house and heart to them. A letter he wrote at this time tells of taking a student into his own home to recover from an injury suffered in a football game.[13]

Dorothy was twelve when her father became chancellor of the University of Nebraska. After a year of public school, she entered the university preparatory school near her home, a school her father had just established "to help Nebraska country students to get proper preparation for the University."[14] In this school she had a class under John Pershing, the man who was to command American forces in World War I. She said later,

> A few other youngsters from our part of the city attended the preparatory school instead of the high school, but all the rest of the students were serious minded young men, desperately anxious to make up for deficiencies which might hamper them in their University work. Pershing taught a first year geometry course in which I was a student along with a formidable number of formidably tall, very earnest young men intending to be engineers.[15]

It was in these growing years that Dorothy had her first experience of the peculiar power of literature. She described this awakening in an article entitled "My Most Unforgettable Book."[16] Her unlikely choice for that honor was Thackeray's *Vanity Fair,* because it was here that she first found a revelation of what lay beneath the surface of human actions and speech. She was still emotionally a child, but she was a precocious reader and "opened the book just because it lay on a table."[17] Within the covers she found "the excitement of understanding what was going on under the surface of grown-up life, as I never had in real life. Thackeray's author's explanations captivated me as much as they pained later English-language novelists, trying to be austerely objective, like Flaubert. At twelve, or maybe it was thirteen, it seemed too good to be true to be listening to living grown-ups talk, and once in a while to see what they meant."[18] Her reading of the novel was a milestone in her life; after passing it, the usual occupations of childhood no longer seemed so important to her.

> From the time "Vanity Fair" opened my eyes to the excitements of watching human beings live, move, love, hate and die, mere bodily speed, beating someone in a game, mere sensory impressions, have taken a back seat — as pastimes, no more . . . for the first time I was reading a story not to find out what happened next, but to understand why it happened . . . at intervals I caught a glimpse of the depths within our human hearts, for good and for bad. . . . An idea stood off there, in the distance, waiting for me to grow up to it — the idea that as men and women live, they cannot remain unchanged, they are shaped by what happens to them."[19]

As Dorothy read, the future author began to awake in her, an author who was to be primarily concerned with why people are the way they are, with what forces shape them, and how that shaping or misshaping takes place.

Dorothy's brother Jim was a university student during the Nebraska years, and through him Dorothy came to know the undergraduate world. An important result was the beginning of a lasting friendship with one of Jim's classmates, the author Willa Cather. Throughout their long and productive lives, Dorothy and Willa exchanged frequent letters, warmly reflecting a community of background and interests, and actively encouraging each other in writing. For Willa, the child of pioneering parents and the spokesperson for the immigrant in America, the state university had proved to be just such a Golden Door as Chancellor Canfield had envisioned it, and one for which she was always warmly grateful.

In the winter of 1893–94 the high school student Dorothy and college student Willa collaborated on a fantastic ghost story. Dorothy gave this account of the way it was written:

> At a football game where we happened to be on the same grandstand, I gave her the idea of a football story—of all things! A fancy that had just occurred to me. She wrote the story, and very generously, I thought, put my name with hers as if I had helped write her story although I would have been perfectly incapable of that at that age. The story got a prize, $10.00—all of that! She gave me half of it. I thought it was generosity itself and still do."[20]

The result of their collaboration, "The Fear That Walks by Noonday," was published in the 1894 university yearbook, *The Sombrero*.[21] In 1931 the story returned to haunt Dorothy again. Willa Cather had resisted all attempts to have her early stories published in book form. Finally, Ralph Allan persuaded her to have a limited edition made of one early story, "The Fear That Walks by Noonday." Dorothy was asked to give her permission for publication, and the tale was published in a limited edition of thirty numbered copies by the Phoenix Book Shop in New York.[22]

Dorothy was in her last year of preparation for college when a new challenge came for her vigorous and controversial father in the form of a call to the presidency of Ohio State University. The years in Nebraska had been good ones—the university had come through a difficult growing period, emerging to a stronger and more useful place in the life of the new state and its people. The Canfield family was growing up, too. Dorothy's brother Jim graduated from the University of Nebraska in 1895, and Dorothy was that year ready to enter college.

When the invitation to Ohio first came, Chancellor Canfield hesitated. Did the new position really offer a greater opportunity? In 1894 he wrote:

> I should wish to know a great deal more about the University than I do at present before I could answer with definiteness. I have never chosen my own field of work. It has always been chosen for me. I think I am honest

in saying that I desire only the field which gives the largest opportunity for efficient public service. By this I mean in this particular connection, that if Ohio promised this larger field there is nothing that keeps me in Nebraska. Personal considerations are of a secondary nature.[23]

The authorities at Ohio State University, who had been watching Chancellor Canfield's vigorous and effective leadership in the frontier setting of Lincoln, and his transformation of shapeless raw material into a fine university, tried to persuade him that they could offer him a wider field of challenge. When the position was first definitely offered, however, he declined, and when asked to reconsider his decision he answered with a series of questions, including these:

Do you wish the University to become the leader of the common, public-school system? . . . Do the people of Ohio really believe in the *public* schools as the great resolvent of American life? Do they recognize them as necessary to the perpetuation of real democracy? . . . Do you really wish the boy in the lowest social rank to have this ladder of promotion, this shining pathway, to usefulness and good repute? . . . Are you an institution thoroughly and heartily committed to co-education in the broadest and truest sense of the word? . . . And do the people of the State favor this, sincerely and without cant on the one side or doubt and hesitation on the other?[24]

The misgivings that James Canfield had about going to Ohio proved to be only too well based. Nebraska was pioneer country and had a clear-eyed attention to essentials born of desperate necessity combined with the optimism of every beginning. Chancellor Canfield's honesty, vigor, and glowing faith in the power of education for the common person found a grateful echo in the hearts of the plain farmers who had come to conquer the prairie. Many of them were immigrants, whose own flame of hope had been dimmed by years of struggle and poverty. With his faith in their children, James Canfield kindled hope in them anew.

Ohio, on the other hand, had left its pioneer days far enough behind to be just a little ashamed of them. Its people were trying to forget that they had ever been overalled farmers, and especially in university circles they were looking to the old established universities of the East for their models. James Canfield was a graduate of Williams College, one of the most distinguished schools of the East. The Ohio State University trustees forgot that he had spent thirty years in the raw West, and they could hardly have known how brightly the educating, democratic, crusading spirit of his Vermont grandmother lived on in him.

Dorothy was always very close to her controversial father. She had been proud and apprehensive during his campaign for free trade in Kansas, she had rejoiced with him in his success in Nebraska, and now she was to suffer the most acute and painful embarrassment during his presidency of the Ohio State University.

After President Canfield arrived on the Ohio campus, one of his first concerns was to see that the citizens of the state were aware of the existence of their state university and the opportunities it offered. A chronicler of the university reports:

He invited the public to a series of concerts on the campus and advertised them by posters on street cars. The concerts were well attended and . . . "during them the buildings were brilliantly lighted, and the President himself was conspicuous at one of the prominent windows of his office, engaged in running a typewriter, at which he was an adept." But there were those who felt that such practices were out of harmony with the best college traditions.[25]

The vigorous campaign by President Canfield to popularize and strengthen the university had tangible results during his four-year administration in the increase in enrollment from 754 to 1,178 and in the administrative reorganization of the university into six colleges, with the addition of new departments, such as domestic science and physical training. For his daughter, however, one of the most significant aspects of her father's presidency was his active espousal of the cause of coeducation for women. In his second annual report President Canfield observed:

Neither the world nor the Universities have as yet quite determined just what they will do for the education of women. . . . So it happens that even in Ohio there seems to be still some doubt as to the wisdom and propriety of co-education; and so it happens that the State University is almost the only institution of high standing in the state that offers co-education in the broadest and truest sense of the word. No educator of high standing . . . longer questions the fundamental propositions that women desire, deserve, appreciate and are strengthened by higher education; that it is unquestionably to the advantage of the whole race and to their half of it that women have the best education attainable; . . . that this inter-training and equal training takes the simper out of the young woman and roughness out of the young men.[26]

President Canfield's daughter Dorothy later analyzed the reasons that lay back of her father's views:

My father always stood firm against special favors for men students as against women, for white students as against Negroes. What burned in his mind was not the injustice to the excluded, but the danger to the nation, which needed every single one of its brainy straight-fibred citizens or there would just not be enough superior people to go around. "No superior class, only superior individuals," was his slogan, and he could never see that it did not apply to the world of scholarly learning as much as to any other milieu.[27]

In a letter to Pearl Buck, Dorothy recalled that her father's recognition of distinction, regardless of race, sometimes had widespread repercussions. "My father, when he was President of Ohio State University, set all half southern states by the ears . . . by inviting Booker Washington (as the President of another institution of learning and hence a colleague) to lunch with us in our home.[28]

While President Canfield was pressing on with a vigor that was called by his opponents "high-handed" for the growth of the Ohio State University as an institution belonging to all the people, not just the intellectual elite, Mrs. Canfield was building organizations for women, to bring cultural interest into their starved lives; James was becoming established in business; and Dorothy was absorbing from her college and home environments all the impressions they could make on a sensitive and receptive personality.

On the surface, Dorothy was an intensely alive and successful young woman, brilliant in her schoolwork, musical, athletic, and popular. She kept far below the surface those conflicts she was later to pour out in her literary work. Two undated poems from these student years suggest, however, that she was already beginning to wrestle with herself and the problems of communication. The first is her very personal answer to stoicism.

To Marcus Aurelius and His Followers

All wise ones of the earth conspire to hearten me
Dreading the swift-advancing unknown years.
Serene and steady-eyed they stand, steadfast and free,
Telling me how there is no need for tears.

"Fear not at all!" they say, "A pure and upright mind
Will turn to gold all happenings of life,
Griefs bravely borne, ennobling are. No chain can bind
One freed by mastery of self from strife."

How alien and remote their comfort sounds to me,

From their stronghold of peace, shut out, apart!
It is not grief I fear, nor pain, nor poverty,
Failure or loneliness—but my own heart![29]

Dorothy grew up with a New England tradition of reticence in the expression of emotion. In the second poem from her college years, she takes issue with this heritage.

Unspoken Words

Words spoken are like birds who strong of flight
Wing swift their straight irrevocable way
Upon the heart where kind, harsh, sad or gay,
They do their various tasks with blind sure might.
Words thought but never said, though not in sight
Have their lives too. Cruel unkind ones may
Like fettered vultures strain to wound their prey
But ever fail lost in kind silence' night,
And words of wisdom dumb unspoken cry
Voiceless advice which if but heard, might show
To straying feet the path to safety's fold—
But saddest are the words who silent fly
In piteous sorrow longing to bestow
Their sweet but fruitless store of love untold.[30]

This early comment on the tragedy of the unspoken word is noteworthy, for it is prophetic of Dorothy's later literary work, where the failure to communicate the heart's contents at the right time forms the basis of tragedy in most of her novels.

Another prophecy of the future can be found in Dorothy's graduating thesis, *Émile Augier, Playwright—Moralist—Poet, A Study*.[31] In summing up the work of the French writer, who lived from 1820 to 1889, Dorothy writes:

I have one more word to say about what seems to be his most characteristic quality and the most valuable one: that is, his power of treating at the same time and satisfactorily problems and characters. He slights neither and holds his balance even. He cuts to the quick, in depicting problems, leaving for less acute and less deep-thinking minds the accidents and incidents which transpire, amusing and instructive enough, but not of deep significance, on the surface. He takes one down with him to still depths lucent with a tranquil light, and there shows, unconfused by non-essentials, men's real selves.

His dialogue is always singularly significant, and at his crises, by its perfection of preparation and quiet art, he suddenly presents to you *real life*. His realism is no longer artistic counterfeiting. One does not think of the theatre, of his talent, of the force of the situation. It is life itself, taking place before your eyes, without effort, and as completely devoid of the straining for effect as are the actions of actual people in the crisis of their lives. It is the *soul* of a problem, of a society, of an epoch, which reveals itself.[32]

What Dorothy saw in Augier's work, others later saw in hers, so that reading a novel of hers was for the reader "experience."[33]

Of Augier's realism, which she found particularly in his later prose, Dorothy wrote that he showed "clear-sighted observation and faithful and powerful portrayal of the everyday people around him,[34]" a comment that has also been made about her own work.[35] She went on to define Augier's particular kind of "realism" carefully:

Even when he takes a somewhat familiar subject, as in "Le Mariage d'Olympe," he treats it in a most refreshing and realistic way. I do not like to use the term realistic because it is liable to be misunderstood. With Augier, realism means realism in the actual sense of the word, and not in the technical meaning which has recently become attached to it. Augier is realistic not because he presents with disgusting accuracy of detail, scenes from irregular life, or because he deals in irrelevant touches — always disagreeable — of random characterization, but because of his true grasp of the real underlying motives, no matter how subtle, of psychological phenomena. He is realistic because the false does not impose on him in any direction.[36]

It is interesting that this thesis, written long before Dorothy had any idea of becoming a writer of fiction herself, describes so accurately the kind of fiction she would later write.

Dorothy's graduation from college coincided with her father's resignation from the presidency of the university. When President Canfield left Ohio State University, many at the institution were not altogether sorry to see him go. By temperament a vigorous initiator rather than a calm administrator, he was reluctant to let power fall out of his hands into those of others. Even the restrained phrases of the university chronicler reflect the stresses of the Canfield administration:

The University he left was a far different place from what it was when he began his presidency. . . . He was in such strong contrast to any of his predecessors that some of his methods were bound to provoke criticism and resistance. But on the whole the standing of the University was improved, its outreach was strengthened, its standards were raised and the public was far more aware of it and of its role in the life of the state than it was when he came on the scene. Relatively brief though it was, his regime speeded the emergence of the real University which the next twenty-five years were to bring under a different kind of leader and different conditions.[37]

Because of conflicts within the academic community, which received publicity in the press, there was considerable university pressure put on President Canfield to resign. When his resignation was finally submitted and accepted, however, letters poured in from dismayed well-wishers in the surrounding area. As evidence of the value of his work in Ohio, James Canfield had a number of these letters bound into a volume for his family.

The scores of letters are a touching and convincing tribute to a man who truly loved and was loved by his fellow human beings. They come from people in all walks of life, streetcar conductors, corporation executives, shopkeepers, and leaders of fraternal organizations. All express their appreciation for his devotion to the people, gratitude for acts of simple friendliness, and regret at his departure. A letter from a Union Station employee recalls: "And you have seemed to think that we were human beings, and entitled to be treated so, and you don't forget us but speak to us as you come and go, and even tell us a story occasionally."[38] From a business leader, Major Harry Ward of the Champlain Printing Company:

I wish you could hear as I do, the warm words of the businessmen of Columbus. It is not only a public loss but a private one. We all feel it. You have helped so many of us with your counsel, and with your appreciation, and with yourself. We felt that we could talk to you, and get right near you. The next fellow elected will probably be someone who will strut round and put on airs because he is President of the University, and who would not wipe his old shoes on us fellows. But you have been very near us, and it has been really a great thing for us to know you, and — Oh. . .it! you are not only a President but you are a *man*! I wish there was something that the citizens of Columbus could do to keep you here.[39]

Dorothy always thought of her father as the civic-minded, responsible one of her parents and saw her mother as temperamental and irresponsible. It was true that her mother detested routine and tradition and believed that she had put all the old-fashioned Vermont values out of her life. Traditions are not, however, so easily dismissed. In the early years of her marriage in Kansas, Flavia began to carry her share of community responsibility in a characteristic way. While her husband was crusading for free education and free trade, she was busy trying to bring more color and interest into the lives of the women of the community around her. She said later of this time: "When I joined my first woman's club in Kansas, I could see right away what such organizations could mean to women in small towns and country districts. Didn't I know that ache to do things, see things and meet people? It's hard in this day of magazines, movies and automobiles to imagine what the average woman's life was like in those days. Before she was rescued by the club her life was bounded by the cook-stove, the chicken-coop and the crib."[40] Her early interest in women's clubs continued; in 1898 she organized the women's clubs of Ohio into a federation and was elected its first president.

In the fall of 1899, when Dorothy's father embarked on his new job as librarian of Columbia University, her mother was in Paris studying art, and Dorothy was with her there, studying at the Sorbonne and the École des Hautes Études. Traveling with her mother was always a rather harrowing and unpredictable experience for Dorothy because Flavia pursued art with the true devotion of a fanatic. Dorothy remained necessary to her as an interpreter, because her mother always remained "detached from the stupid, wasteful Tower-of-Babel multiplicity of languages, never bothered to learn a word of anything but her native Vermontese."[41] This particular winter, her mother was seized by the enthusiasm for Velásquez, which was at that time sweeping the Paris art world, and decided to set out immediately for Madrid. Dorothy, of course, had to accompany her, leaving her studies at the Sorbonne behind. The trip in winter through the Pyrenees was a nightmare of jolting discomfort and penetrating cold, and when they arrived in Madrid Flavia was very sick indeed. Dorothy recalled:

> The people at the hotel looked at her, groaning, racked with pain, ashy-faced, bowed together weakly as she hung on my arm. Evidently they thought she was likely to die and felt a superstitious fear against letting her into the house. But we pushed our way in and upstairs, behind a reluctant chambermaid, to a tile-floored room, as cold as the train we had left.
>
> There was a fireplace in it. It was a black, empty, yawning, dust-filled cavity. But a fireplace. I hurried my mother into bed with a hot brick or two beside her. My considerable acquaintance with unheated European hotels had made me hope there would be soapstones or bricks on the back of the cookstove in the big kitchen, and I ran down and snatched them.
>
> Then I began to argue with the hotel people about firewood. Nobody at the hotel spoke a word of French or English, it being a meager little inn,

all that we could afford. But, as my mother predicted, I did learn Spanish, with as scared a speed as a chased cat climbs a tree. One of the first sentences I understood was that there was no firewood. I pointed out to the proprietors that if a fireplace had been built there must have been something to burn in it. No, the season had gone by for heat in bedrooms. Winter was over — or would be soon. No firewood in the fuel-merchants' shops. But how about sick people, new babies, very old people, I insisted, in what rags and scraps of Spanish I had, raising my voice belligerently to match their attempt to drown me out by vociferations. Finally to get rid of me, they admitted that sometimes one could buy a sack of dug-up dried tree roots, said to be combustible. Leaving my poor mother huddled in bed, looking and feeling deathly sick, I raced away to find a merchant who would sell tree roots.[42]

Mrs. Canfield had been warned against letting Dorothy go out on the street alone in Spain, that is was "simply not *safe* for a respectable girl to leave the house by herself."[43] Dorothy had her own way of dealing with this situation.

Having for years scurried along Paris streets without a companion, I had already discovered that pleasure-seeking men are repelled (as a dog by a pail of cold water) by a swift ejaculation of obviously sincere exasperation, the equivalent of "Oh! For goodness' sakes! I've got something else on my mind! Go along and find someone else." Hastily learning enough Spanish phrases for an approximation of these sentiments, I rushed here and there, up and down all kinds of Madrid streets and alley ways, by day and night; to the pharmacist's; to the doctor's; to the fuel merchant's; to the markets, trying to find something that could be made fit for an invalid to eat; to the householdware shops hunting for utensils in which I could cook that food over an open fire. It turned out, as I expected, that my mother had been accurate in her estimate of the perils of the late nineteenth century equivalent of wolf-calls. I had some disagreeable but no alarming experiences, in my headlong, hurried errands.[44]

As soon as her mother had recovered enough to stand on her own feet again, she had Dorothy take her to the Prado. There, while her mother worshiped at the altar of art, Dorothy had a significant experience of another sort. Her mother's way of studying a painting was to make a careful copy of it, so while her mother was engaged in this painstaking work, Dorothy spent many hours in the Prado. Sometimes she studied for her courses at the Sorbonne, sometimes talked to the guards, sometimes stood before a picture until she "sank deep into that rare, trancelike, timeless gaze, which penetrates by divination to the inner meaning which perhaps, in spite of the theories of the professional technicians, is the core of every great artist's intention."[45]

Years later she wrote:

It was with this mesmerized gaze that I looked long at one of the Velásquez court dwarfs. There are several of these strange figures in the Prado. From one of them, a lack-witted, simpering moron, I turned away with a shudder. But another — was he called Sebastian de Morra? — that name sticks in my mind when I remember him — was not young. Above his dwarfed body, there looked out a full-grown man's face, terrible in its quiet sadness. I could not pass along that wall without stopping to meet his darkly shadowed eyes. It was as if he had a wordless message for me, a compelling one. In the end even the hard, adolescent crust over my shallow undeveloped young heart was pierced with an involuntary, persistent compassion for human ills, which has been for me, as for everybody who admits that skeleton into his inner closet, a disquieting cause for heavy-heartedness.[46]

Dorothy's mother was "lifted out of herself by the ethereal radiance of light-suffused air, presented on nobly painted canvases."[47] What Dorothy saw was very different, however:

The sad-faced dwarf, bearing with patience the ignominy of his misshapen body, was a victim of man's inability in the 17th century to cure glandular lacks which now our modern medical skill easily sets straight. The tragedy of the dwarf man, the dignity of that helplessly suffering face . . . they had opened my heart to share the sorrow of the victims of modern man's ignorant inability to mend flaws in the social structure and standards, which cause just as much misery as glandular lacks ever did centuries ago.[48]

The trip to Spain resulted not only in new maturity of outlook for Dorothy but also in her first publicly published piece of writing, "Holy Week in Spain," in the *New York Times,* March 23, 1902. In a note about the article Dorothy said:

This was, I think, the first writing of mine to be published — and it was not intended, when written, for publication. I was studying at Columbia for my Ph.D. without the slightest idea that I might ever be an author. Some one in the editorial office of The Times had, by chance, seen some family letters written from Spain three years before this date, when I was there with my mother, who was studying and copying the Velásquez at the Prado. He (the editor) suggested that they might be published if I ran two or three of the letters together. I did this and was astonished to the limit and beyond, when they were printed and I was paid for this casual, nineteen-year-old home letter.[49]

The article describes the colorful Palm Sunday service in the royal chapel and the elaborate religious processions in Toledo. The future author had already learned how to bring a picture to life before a reader's eyes and to make the reader see a foreign scene with her through the evocative power of her words.

3
Transitions

Back in New York Dorothy's father continued to set the dominant tone in her life. The battlefield had changed, but James Hulme Canfield still "burned with zeal about advancing the cause of democracy." When, in 1952, Dorothy wrote a biographical sketch of her father for a Columbia publication, she recalled how he would have answered the question: "But what's a man doing as Librarian in an institution of learning, if what he wants is to advance the cause of democracy? . . .

Squaring his powerful shoulders, his brilliant black eyes shining, he carried the war with flame and sword into the enemy's territory, about like this: — "The implication in your question is that there is an innate contradiction between scholarly learning and democracy. Never, never, never! That idea — that scholarly learning can exist only or exist better where there are upper and lower classes — it came from the Dark Ages, crossed the Atlantic as a stowaway and never should have been allowed to land. "A *gentleman* and a scholar!" Nonsense! The gentry make very poor scholars. They're brought up to ease. Other people do their work for them. You can't be a scholar without the ability to work hard and long. Scholars are needed in a democracy, and they need a democracy to live in. A library, particularly, perhaps, a great University library, is a front-line post in the battle to preserve and give value to the democratic way of life. Only if that way of life survives, will true scholars have a life worth an honest man's bothering with. Why do we have institutions of learning anyhow? It is a horror to think — let the thought be ever so secret and unavowed — that they exist to help a part of the younger generation get into a class which thinks itself socially superior." Flames of scorn leaped sulphurously out from the word "socially" when my father pronounced it in speaking its vulgar presumption in pushing its way into the world of the intellect.[1]

Enthusiasm like James Hulme Canfield's was contagious. He saw his task as the "responsibility . . . to further intellectual development as far as that could be done by means of books. . . . He carried the staff with him in ardor for this responsibility. Luckily ardor is as infectious a quality as apathy and cynicism, although rather more rare."[2]

As strong and controversial a person as Dorothy's father naturally aroused opposition, too. "He was quite aware that he was disliked and looked down on by those scholars who preferred the society of incunabula and costly first-editions to that of flesh-and-blood students. Well, that was all right. It was only fair. He disliked and looked down on such 'mediaeval personalities' as he heartily called them."[3]

There are echoes of Grandmother Almera's "multiplying-glass" in Librarian Canfield's dealings with the students. "He longed to make book-using the tyrannical, not-to-be-resisted reflex-habit of every student."[4] He made it his custom to leave his comfortable, isolated, well-appointed office from time to time to roam through the library.

> Did a student doze, inconspicuously, over a Columbia Library book? My father, up in arms to nurture the life of the intellect, wanted to know why? Was the Library too hot? Was the book the wrong one for that student or for the phase of intellectual growth attained by him? Or perhaps it was just that the student had too little money to eat properly. Or he might be a non-intellectual who should not be in college at all. Possibly, on the other hand, he might be a potential scholar of value, but obliged to stoke a furnace, or wait on table to earn his food and lodging, so that when he sat down with a book, he could not give it the absolute concentration of attention it deserved. My father considered it part of his job to use his tact and charm and resourcefulness (and he had a great deal of those qualities when he wanted) to look into such situations, and try with humane, discreet, good manners and good intentions to "do something."[5]

"On the principle of Martin Luther's objection to letting the devil have all the good tunes, he welcomed everything that would make the life of the intelligence more stirring to the imagination, more quickening to the heart of man."[6]

There was also a whimsical, puckish streak in James Hulme Canfield. He and Nicholas Murray Butler, the president of Columbia University, were close friends and could often be seen walking across the campus together. Harry Norris, after he retired from serving as superintendent of buildings and grounds at the university, told Dorothy how

> one afternoon he saw President Butler and the Librarian together, as they often were, walking slowly down the steps of the library, deep in talk. A

sight-seeing bus lumbered around the corner of 116th Street and stopped. The guide stood up, put his megaphone to his lips and began to yell hoarsely into it, that they were now before Columbia University, and that "Down the steps is coming Nich-o-las Murray But-ler, the Pres-i-dent of the —"

Mr. Norris told me with laughter as fresh as though he had seen it only yesterday, that my father instantly swept off his hat and with a grandly theatrical gesture bowed low to the people in the bus, while Dr. Butler, enchanted by the absurdity, collapsed in laughter against the statue of Alma Mater.[7]

In a memorial address President Butler recalled, "I used to say to him, partly in jest but more in earnest than he knew, that while I had known Christian women, he was the only Christian man I had ever met. His religion, his faith, his devotion, his service, his sacrifice, were genuine, and real, and boundless, and unending."[8] Summing up the quality of James Canfield's life, he said, "His was a life of singular beauty and usefulness. What others preached, he lived. What burdens others bore, he bore. With a soul naturally attuned to the voice of humanity in its broadest sense, his life was one of constant widening of view and constant deepening of sympathies, a life lived for God in that it was devoted to the best interests of his fellows."[9]

During the Columbia years Dorothy threw herself wholeheartedly into her studies for a doctorate in French, and into all the happy experiences that are peripheral to graduate work. The Canfield home in New York was again a gathering place for students, among them many youthful admirers of Dorothy. Alfred Harcourt, the publisher, recalled in his memoirs, "My roommate, John Fisher, took me to tea at the Canfield home. Dorothy was very lovely — so lovely that we callow youths vied for her favor, entirely unconscious of her extraordinary ability."[10]

One of her admirers, a young surgeon named William Noyes, wrote the following verses to her in 1903:

Gladys and Her Gowns

Oh Gladys clad in white and pink!
    As much at home, and quite as free
    In ball room whirl and gaiety,
    As bird in any forest tree!
And all young men who catch your glance
Cry "Gladys, join us in the dance!
We dare not speak the thoughts we think!"
    And I apart cry sulkily,

"Oh Gladys, dance alone with me!"

Oh Gladys clad in serious blue!
You gather children to your heart,
Not one resists your magic art,
Cupid himself forgets his dart!
And all your flock cry joyously,
"How like the fairy godmother she must be!
Oh Mistress Gladys let us learn of you!"
    And I alone cry sulkily,
    "Oh why will Gladys not teach me?"

Oh Gladys clad in apron clean!
    No labor seems to cause you fear;
    Is there not any mirror near,
    To prove how fair you now appear!
When you take part in any household toil,
And even your dainty fingers deign to soil,
How like a witch or fair magician you seem!
    And I with hunger cry out sulkily,
    "Oh dainty Gladys labor once for me!"

Oh Gladys clad in gown of red!
    What mystic circles homes contain!
    Your evening lamp is lit again,
    Once more begins some evening game:
Lights of a home are like the lights divine,
That burn before the altar of a shrine,
The very games you play are sacred rites, 'tis said,
    And I apart cry sulkily,
    "Oh Gladys shares no evening light with me!"

Oh Gladys clad with modest brown!
    When you walk out upon the street,
    And crowds of little children meet,
    And swarming round your very feet,
They cry, "Oh Gladys, come and join our play
Oh stay awhile! Don't go away!"
    And I in haste cry sulkily,
    "Oh Gladys, hurry on with me!"

Oh Gladys clad in pious black!
    Her very features seem devout!

> Thoughts of the world are all cast out!
> Banished every sin and doubt!
> And all who see her think of some pure saint,
> The old time masters used to paint.
> Faces like hers can never worship lack!
> And I without cry sulkily,
> "Oh saintly Gladys, pray for me!"
>
> Oh Gladys clad in spotless white!
> If heaven there be, I do not know!
> Me thinks 'tis heaven here below,
> With you nearby in garments white as snow!
> Yet you like some pure saint before me rise,
> You seem to dwell remote in Paradise!
> Singing sweet hymns in pure celestial light!
> And I lost soul cry sulkily,
> "Oh holy Gladys sings no song with me!"[11]

It was a good life, full of friends, free of burdens, yet not without challenges. Dorothy continued her studies at Columbia, at home she was surrounded with warmth and affection, and her free time was taken up by hiking parties along the Palisades, dances, and the other lighthearted pastimes of youth. She enjoyed her academic work and found the long hours spent in the libraries of Paris and London, as well as those at home, happy and satisfying.

In 1904 Dorothy Canfield received the Ph.D. degree in French from Columbia University. Her thesis, which was published the next year, was entitled *Corneille and Racine in England: A Study of the English Translations of the Two Corneilles and Racine, with Especial Reference to Their Presentation on the English Stage.*[12] One of the real challenges to the completion of the degree had been Professor Cohn, her adviser, a firm antifeminist. Afterward she wrote with mischievous delight to her friend Céline Sibut: "He told me that he was perversely proud of me in spite of his profound disapproval of women who study, . . . he called me 'his nice little intellectual daughter.' At this last phrase I could hardly contain myself, it seemed so funny to me to have for an 'intellectual father' this curious and hardly agreeable scholar. . . . Goodness! how glad I am that I no longer have to take his courses!"[13]

The doctorate is the end of one academic road and normally the beginning of another. The year before Dorothy received her Ph.D. the other path opened with an offer of the position of assistant professor in French and German at Western Reserve University in Cleveland, Ohio. At first Dorothy was elated, but the evident distress of her father and mother at the thought of having her go so far away from them alone to a strange city made her quickly close the door on that opportunity. She wrote bravely to Céline:

> It was a perfect surprise for everybody and one that had very different effects! While I jumped with joy at the thought that I had been found learned enough for a place in a university, father and mother looked at me shocked and asked severely — "And you can think of going so far from us to spend all winter?" I said, "Oh no, no. I would not leave New York because of that, but think of the honor!"[14]

Instead, she accepted a position at the experimental Horace Mann School in New York. Her title was "Secretary," but her duties included arranging social affairs, conducting tours for foreign visitors, and helping out wherever she could. She enjoyed the work and the financial independence it provided, and the summer following her second year there she went by herself to Norway and then to Paris.

During the winter of 1904–5 she had spent spare moments writing and had sold a number of stories to current magazines. In May she wrote to her friend Céline: "I write all the time — stories: funny, sad, short, long; articles serious and light; and I'm on the way to writing another book."[15]

A poem published at this time reflects her work experience near children:

Kindergarten in an Office-Building

The city-stained, dishonored, grimy skies
    Heavy across the tall roofs weigh.
The horses strain in slipping struggles where
    The snow lies piled in heaps of gray.

Inside are gloom and dirt and weary haste,
    And men too tired to know they're sad;
A thousand prison-rooms where dingy life
    No time or strength finds to be glad.

Sudden from out a partly opened door
    There comes a sound, oh, sweet and dear,
And dauntless with unconscious courage bright —
    Incredible it should be here!

Peal after peal of children's happy mirth
    Rings joyously through that sad space,
A fearless challenge to the unbelief
    In beauty of the ugly place.

A cheerful Credo—"We believe, we *know,*
   That life is innocent and gay,
That joy is real!" A moment touched and thrilled,
   Those doubting hearts an "Amen" say.[16]

The picture of the city in these verses, a dirty prison in which men live harried, joyless lives, foreshadows Dorothy's move to the country and echoes through a number of her later prose works.

A second poem, written on the back of a sheet of Horace Mann School stationery but unpublished, gives an indication that the young writer sensed the impermanence of her present situation and that an anxious and troubled heart often beat under her calm and cheerful appearance.

Exultant in my youth and present joy
I lingered on a richly shadowed road
Where proud full-throated summer bore her load
Of beauty in a bliss without alloy.
There was no timorous charm, doubtful and coy
Like that of spring: but life that could not bode
Of change, or dream that time can strength corrode, —
Youth knowing not all that the years destroy.
Sudden a red flash, ominous of fears,
Gleamed from the thick green woods. A slender tree
Burning in anguish cried prophetical
"Soon on this joy of life shall ruin fall."
The hills smiled gay. I only seemed to see
Cassandra of the woods calling deaf ears.[17]

After a summer spent in Norway, Dorothy stopped in Paris to visit her friend Céline. It was 1905, Dorothy was twenty-six years old, and in answer to the usual questions about suitors she told Céline about several of the young men she knew, whom she described as "suitors perhaps, but certainly friends."[18] Of these Céline immediately expressed a preference for John Fisher: "That's the one I like best, and the one who would be the best for you."[19]

John Fisher had been a frequent visitor at the Canfield home and a member of the parties that hiked and picnicked along the cliffs by the Hudson River. Dorothy herself dated her first real interest in him from May 1904, when he sent her hepaticas.[20]

Hepaticas are not a usual florist's flower. They are small, delicate, and fragrant and grow in the northern woods in early spring. To Dorothy they signified Vermont, with all its warm memories, combined with the heady awakening of the world in spring, nowhere so startling and intoxicating as in the frozen mountains of northern New England. Dorothy had found in John Fisher someone who could see through the bright urbane facade of her social personality to the real person within.

When Dorothy returned from Europe in September 1905 to take up her duties at the Horace Mann School again, she found chaos at home. Her mother was ill and in need of constant care. The New England morality allowed no choice: Dorothy resigned from her job and stayed home to take care of her ailing mother. It was a second blow from home to a promising professional future. Dorothy wrote to Céline:

> Mother is not at all well. I don't know exactly what is wrong with her. It seems to be a kind of nervous weakness. Father says that he believes that it is a result of worrying about my brother all summer. She is not precisely sick, but she eats almost nothing, does not sleep well, and seems so tired, so broken, so sad all the time that I am desolate. She says that the fact is that she has become old all of a sudden and needs her daughter at home. And, my dear, I am forced to consider seriously the question if it isn't my duty to leave the school and all regular work to be able to be home more.[21]

At first she was restless. Early in 1906 she wrote to Céline that she was an egotist who wanted for herself "everything, the free life and the ordered life."[22] Gradually, however, she began to use her new freedom from scheduled living for increased literary work, and before the winter was over she was sure that she could earn her living by her pen, and even a better living than that provided by the position she had left. This was not the deciding factor, however. She found that she loved writing. "Céline, I am a convert – a real woman of letters. I adore my new profession, and there is no greater pleasure on earth than that which my stories give me."[23]

Dorothy wrote incessantly during that winter at home, and large numbers of her stories were accepted for publication by the leading magazines of the time, *Harper's, American, Everybody's,* and *Munsey's.* In the last of these, so many of Dorothy's stories were published that the editors assigned her a pseudonym, and a few of her stories appeared authored by a fictitious "Stanley Crenshawe." Years later, Dorothy recalled: "I didn't see any harm in it, but after a few times I asked them to stop because I got tired of explaining to fan-letters writing to Stanley Crenshawe, who I was. I remember I had a letter from Reynolds . . . saying he had been struck with some story or other appearing under that name and would like to be Stanley Crenshawe's agent. So I called them off and haven't thought of it since."[24]

Her reply to Paul Reynolds's letter was a polite but rather curt refusal. She wrote, "I am very glad you liked 'The Platonic Friends,' and feel flattered by

your wishing to handle my stories but under my own name 'Dorothy Canfield.' . . . For the present I feel that I do not need a literary agent — the importance of my work hardly warranting it, but I shall be glad to avail myself
of your offer in the future if conditions change."[25] Reynolds persisted, assur-
ing her that he could sell her stories for considerably higher fees than she was
then receiving. Finally, in 1912, she agreed to let him try. He proved to be as
good as his word; she was completely satisfied with him and came to rely on
his judgment. He sold her stories, articles, and the serialized versions of her
novels from then on. After Reynolds sold one story, "What Really Happened!", for $400 in 1916, Dorothy wrote to him, "Although I blush to take as
much as that for any story of mine, (I never can believe they are worth so
much!) I overcome my blushings with great ease!"[26]

Dorothy would often consult Paul Reynolds about some story she was
writing or planned to write. After a visit to New York in 1919, she reported,

> It's funny, I come down to the city from the country for a day or so — or
> come back from France after a long stay — and in a day see a perfect pro-
> cession of different personalities, every-man-Jack of them putting out his
> energy to make me see things his way, do what he wants me to do, feel that
> he is forceful and clever and deep. And at the end of the day I always have
> the same impression — that among them all, Mr. Reynolds' personality
> stands out as the one which has most weight with me, — he's more and
> more the person whose judgment I really, in the old-fashioned sense of
> the word, *respect*."[27]

The early stories deal with the worlds Dorothy knew, and the characters
are representatives of the various environments in which the author had lived
herself: the world of Americans in Europe ("Romance Is Dead," "A Philanthropic Honeymoon," "The Rejected Suitor"), the midwestern town with its
combination of frontier necessity and class snobbery ("The Story of Ralph
Miller," "The Pants-Button"), and New England with its characteristic people and customs ("The Bedquilt," "A Man of Ideas," "A Dweller in the
Wilderness").[28] The chief characteristic of these tales, many of them
"storiettes" rather than stories, is the use of contrast. Sometimes it is a difference between two points of view, urban and rural, old and young, male
and female. However, it is even more frequently the contrast between what
appears on the surface and the inner reality beneath. They are embryonic
results of Dorothy's perception that human life is complex, and in them people achieve a knowledge of themselves as often as they come to understand
others.

Dorothy's early literary people do not fit into standard stereotypes. The
apparently philistine traveling American businessman in "Romance Is Dead"

turns out to have more essentially romantic traits than the sentimental young lady who at first misunderstands him. The genuinely academic young woman in "The Awakening"[29] gradually comes to know herself. The characters are lonely, and only rarely do they find a sense of understanding in another human being that relieves their isolation. The human spirit, however, emerges already in these earliest stories as able to conquer and endure even that worst and hardest of all pieces of knowledge, the realization of weakness in oneself and in loved ones. "The Last of the Garrison,"[30] the story of an old soldier who inspires all the elderly people of his village with pride and courage, is the literary embodiment of one of Dorothy's favorite quotations, a line from Burke: "Never despair; but if you do, work on in despair." In 1946 she wrote, "I hung that over my desk in the darkest days of the last war, when none of us were sure that the fascist forces might not, by their innate aptitude for waging war, overcome the western democracies."[31] And she went on to call it "a big boulder against which I can set my back, when things look too black to be borne."[32] Many of her stories — for example, "The Piano," "The Story of Ralph Miller," and "A Pyrrhic Victory"[33] — would be pessimistic in their realism, if they did not contain this quality of the dogged persistence of the indestructible human spirit in the face of destruction of hopes and illusions.

Dorothy's own favorite among her early stories was "A Good Fight and the Faith Kept," the tale of a man's successful struggle against inherited melancholia. When she first showed this story to Paul Reynolds, he suggested a change in the ending, which she adopted. Later, she wrote about this incident to Mrs. Reynolds, "He helped me write, you know, the best short story I have ever done (or it is my favorite, at least) A Good Fight and the Faith Kept. I took lunch with Mr. Reynolds while that story was still in the fluid state, and what he said induced me very considerably to alter it, greatly to its benefit!"[34]

To the period of these early stories belongs also a poem that describes the coming of a summer storm and creates a tense mood of quiet desperation.

Summer Rain

All day the clouds had heavy hung and low,
All day the world had frowned in sluggish pain,
Had suffered the dull pangs that yet remain
When strength to feel the anguish of the blow
Of grief has died in weariness of woe.
The gray mists straining hung, as they were fain
To break th' embittering restraint and rain
Down healing tears upon Earth's desperate brow.

Then in the deathlike hush of unknown fears
The wind wakes to fresh stirring life each leaf,
A few hot drops fall in the thirsty glen,
Sudden the trees flash in the longed-for tears
Of Nature, washing her heart clean from grief
So that to-morrow she may smile on me.[35]

The choice of scene may have reflected Dorothy's current mood, but it is significant that in these lines the young poet has tried to transmit nature's mood, to achieve empathy rather than expression of self. In this the poem foreshadows the later novelist, who throughout her writing career tried to explain human beings to themselves, rather than to tell the world of the sufferings of her own heart and soul.

During the winter of 1905-6, partly because of his mother's ill health, Dorothy's brother Jim moved east from Columbus, Ohio, to New York, where he became the president of a wholesale paper company. In the spring Dorothy went to Vermont for a visit with the old Canfield family. Her sister-in-law and two small nephews joined her, but, unprepared for the bitter weather that often interrupts the arrival of spring in Vermont valleys, one of the little boys fell seriously ill, and for a while his life was in danger. It was an anxious winter and spring, and by its end Dorothy found herself emotionally drained. She wrote to Céline that perhaps she had been attacked so violently by one emotion that it had destroyed her defenses against another. In any case, several of her old friends suddenly turned "like magicians" into suitors.[36]

Letters, telegrams, and unexpected visits broke the quiet of her Vermont existence. "The little village has been electrified several times," she wrote to Céline, "by a gentleman from New York who asked the road to the Canfield house; and I have come out of my room at the little farm to find a man, serious, enraged, resolute, or tender, as the case might be, until it seemed almost comical to me how tense my nerves were."[37]

Among those who came was John Fisher, and to his suit Dorothy finally said yes. It was not a completely unequivocal yes, however, and shortly afterward she could write to Céline that she probably would not have given in if she had not been weakened by all the preceding emotional stress: "You know how I always have control of myself, how proud I am of my self-control? Well, it took all this emotion to break down the walls and to show me how I love with all my heart this John Fisher."[38] In the same letter she confesses to "a kind of horror when I think of marriage," and she is glad that John does not press for an early wedding. She reports that he says that he has worked for two years to get her used to the idea of becoming engaged, and now he is going to change base and start to work to get her used to the idea of marriage. "John says again and again, with his endless patience, 'But see here, what is the trouble with you? You are not merely going to get married, which in itself would be moving, but you are going to marry me, which is the most natural thing in the world.' "[39] For her part, she reports, "It is more than probable that I shall be engaged a long time — a very long time! Which pleases me enormously."[40]

John had been the captain of the Columbia football team — a college hero. As Dorothy herself admitted, at first glance they would hardly seem to be made for each other. Yet he was also "the most intelligent man I know when it comes to literature, the most sensitive about art, and the best in character — good the way my brother is good."[41] John had a position with a literary bureau, later worked for the Simplified Spelling Board, and encouraged Dorothy in her writing, which he wanted her to continue after their marriage.

The wedding took place a year later in May 1907, and John and Dorothy moved to Vermont, to a small house on one of the Canfield farms in the North District of Arlington. Their withdrawal from the sophisticated intellectual world of New York drew a horrified reaction from most of their friends, who could not understand how two talented young people could stand such isolation from all the current streams of thought. The unique home that these two young people developed would have troubled their friends still more.

Part 2

The Early Works

"As men and women live, they cannot remain unchanged, they are shaped by what happens to them."

My Most Unforgettable Book

4
Serious Writing

In December 1908, a year and a half after Dorothy and John Fisher had moved to Arlington, Vermont, a little sketch of village life appeared in *Scribner's Magazine.*[1] Here, under the fictitious name Hillsboro, Dorothy portrayed her own village of Arlington and explained publicly why she chose it as a place to live.

Her thesis is that it is only in the small town that people really get to know one another. She contrasts Hillsboro with the "great cities, where people seem to be doing everything that was ever done or thought of except just living. City dwellers make money, make reputations (good and bad), make museums and subways, make charitable institutions, make with a hysteric rapidity, like excited spiders, more and yet more complications in the mazy labyrinths of their lives, but they never make each other's acquaintances . . . and that is all that is worth doing in the world."[2]

She feels sorry for the city dwellers, "so inexorably shut away from the bracing, tonic shock of knowing men utterly diverse"[3] from themselves. She suggests that it may be a craving for experience of other human beings and their lives that leads city dwellers to read novels and go to the theater.

In Hillsboro we explain to ourselves the enormous amount of novel-reading and play-going in the great cities as due to a perverted form of this natural hunger for human life. If people are so situated they can't get it fresh, they will take it canned, which is undoubtedly good for those in the canning business; but we feel that we who have better food ought not to be expected to treat their boughten canned goods very seriously. We can't help smiling at the life-and-death discussions of literary people about their preference in style and plot and treatment . . . their favorite brand on the can, so to speak.

To tell the truth, all novels seem to us badly written, they are so faint and faded in comparison to the brilliant colors of the life which palpitates up and down our village street, called by strangers, "so quaint and sleepy-looking." What does the author of a novel do for you, after all, even the best author? He presents to you people not nearly so interesting as your next-door neighbors, makes them do things not nearly so exciting as what happened to your grandfather, and doles out to you in meager paragraphs snatches of that comprehending and consolatory philosophy of life, which long ago you should have learned to manufacture for yourself out of every incident in your daily routine. Of course, if you don't know your next-door neighbors, and have never had time to listen to what happened to your grandfather, and are too busy catching trains to philosophize on those subjects if you did know them, no more remains to be said. By all means patronize the next shop you see which displays in its show windows canned romances, adventures, tragedies, farces, and the like line of goods. Live vicariously, if you can't at first hand; but don't be annoyed at our pity for your method of passing blindfold through life.[4]

These comments, particularly interesting from a writer of fiction who later became one of the leading novelists of her day, are followed by a concrete example, in which she becomes even more an iconoclast, contrasting "the feeble plots of Ibsen and the tame inventions of Bernard Shaw" with the "really exciting, perplexing, and stimulating events" in the life of village people.[5] Such preposterous claims must be supported, and she does so in the following passage:

In "Ghosts," Ibsen preaches a terrible sermon on the responsibility of one generation for the next, but not all his relentless logic can move you to the sharp throb of horrified sympathy you feel as you see Nelse Pettingrew's poor mother run down the street, her shawl flung hastily over her head, framing a face of despairing resolve, such as can never look at you out of the pages of a book. Somebody has told her that Nelse has been drinking again and "is beginning to get ugly." For Hillsboro is no model village, but the world entire, with hateful forces of evil lying in wait for weakness. Who will not lay down "Ghosts" to watch, with a painfully beating heart, the progress of this living "Mrs. Alving" past the house, leading, persuading, coaxing the burly weakling, who will be saved from a week's debauch if she can only get him safely home now, and keep him quiet till "the fit goes by."

At the sight everybody in Hillsboro realizes that Nelse "got it from his father," with a penetrating sense of the tragedy of heredity, quite as stimulating to self-control in the future as Ibsen is able to make us feel in "Ghosts." But we know something better than Ibsen, for Mrs. Pettingrew is no "Mrs. Alving." She is a plain, hard-featured woman who takes in sewing for a living, and she is quite unlettered, but she is a general in the army of spiritual forces. She does not despair, she does not give up like the half-hearted mother in "Ghosts," she does not waste her strength in concealments; she stands up to her enemy and fights. She fought the wild beast in Nelse's father, hand to hand, all his life, and he died a better man than when she married him. Undaunted, she fought it in Nelse as a boy, and now as a man; and in the flowering of his physical forces when the wind of his youth blows most wildly through the hateful thicket of inherited weaknesses she generally wins the battle.

And this she has done with none of the hard, consistent strength and intelligence of your make-believe heroine in a book, so disheartening an example to our faltering impulses for good. She has been infinitely human and pathetically fallible; she has cried out and hesitated and complained and done the wrong thing and wept and failed and still fought on, till to think of her is, for the weakest of us, like a bugle call to high endeavor. Nelse is now a better man than his father, and we shut up "Ghosts" with impatience that Ibsen should have selected that story to tell out of all the tales there must have been in the village where *he* lived.[6]

Dorothy moved away from the metropolis to be nearer to people and to know them better, but it was a particular way of knowing them that led her to serious writing. In later years she dated the urge to write back to the awareness of human suffering that penetrated her consciousness as she looked at the Velásquez painting of a court dwarf in the Prado.

"The subject of one of the first stories I wrote," she recalled,

was as helplessly starved as the Spanish dwarf of what all human beings need for growth—was as humbled before her fellow-men through no fault of hers . . . as defenselessly given over to the careless mockery of those luckier than she. This by no glandular lack—by the social code of her time which decreed that plain women without money, who did not have husbands, who had never been admired by men, were only outcasts from the normal group—grotesque deformities, so that to look at them was to laugh at them!

I had never known, had never before thought, what had been the impulse which in my youth had inexplicably detached me from the study of phonetic changes in Old French, to which I had been set as a part of the training to earn my living; the impulse which had lifted me away from my textbooks to gaze, deeply sorrowing with her, into the patient remembered eyes of an insignificant old maid whom I had known in my careless childhood; the impulse which had forced me into facing the enormous difficulties of story telling, often enough too great for my powers to cope with.

Well, now I had a clue to that impulse. A message received from the marvelously painted, dark, tragic eyes of Sebastian de Morra had forced me to look deep into the faded blue eyes of Aunt Mehetabel. With that look the walls which keep a scholar's room windless and still, had fallen, leaving me in the heartsick turmoil of a compulsion to imagine and desperately to try to portray a human being not as what she seemed, but what she was — to convince people who in life hardly even noticed her existence that she shared in the human dignity of the instinct to create.[7]

In a talk at Yale University in 1928, Dorothy spoke of the genesis of this early story, "The Bedquilt," and her remarks were later recalled by Professor Frederick A. Pottle in an article entitled "Catharsis."[8] Here he suggests that the author is freed from a troubling experience by incorporating it in a fictional situation and thus enables the reader to experience the same kind of release. "A purging which operated in the mind of an artist as she transmuted the stuff of personal pity and fear into a fiction," he wrote, "is the same sort of thing as the purging which operates in the mind of a reader when someone, by a fiction, rouses up his personal pity and fear and then allays it."[9]

Aunt Mehetabel had her origin, Mrs. Fisher told us, in an elderly relative of her own, whom she would refer to as "Cousin Margaret." Cousin Margaret was an old woman, but her mind had never developed. . . . Her relatives took care of her by turns, . . . but sometimes she arrived at what seemed to be the most inopportune moments. On one occasion, when Mrs. Fisher was still a little girl, her parents unexpectedly received word that Cousin Margaret was on her way to visit them. . . . The Canfields were that day giving a dinner party, in the very middle of which Cousin Margaret's train was due to arrive. Mrs. Canfield . . . arranged for a cab to meet Cousin Margaret at the station, and got Dorothy to meet her at the door and conduct her up the back stairs to her room. . . .

Cousin Margaret was not beautiful. She was old, and she couldn't dress herself properly, and her face was tired and streaked with dirt. She had expected a relative to meet her at the station, and was still somewhat confused and upset. "Hello, Cousin Margaret," said Dorothy. "Mother and Father are busy, but they asked me to meet you and take you up to your room." Cousin Margaret sat still and looked at her. At the time the look made no particular impression on the child at all.

Years afterward, Mrs. Fisher was in Norway, spending the summer with a Norwegian family. In this family there were two daughters. The younger was pretty, was married, and had a fine baby; the older was lame and ugly and would never be married. Like Aunt Mehetabel in the story, she did most of the hard work about the house, wore plain clothes while her sister wore pretty ones, and was never noticed by anybody. Mrs. Fisher went out to pick currants in the garden. . . . Kneeling there between the rows of currant bushes, she could watch unobserved the older sister, who besides doing the housework that morning had also been taking care of her sister's baby. She had soothed him when he was fretful, had bathed and fed him, and now, having dressed him in a clean dress, had sat down with him a moment on the grass. Almost at once the younger sister, cool and pretty and unfatigued by housework or caring for her child, came, caught up the baby, and bore him off to be admired. Over the older sister's face came a look of profound sadness. She did not cry out, nor did she shed tears; it was a feeling so common with her that she did not think of rebelling against it. It was the dumb, patient, but deeply hurt look of a human creature who knew that she was merely taken for granted.

In a flash there came back to the unseen observer that look on Cousin Margaret's face years back. The recollection cut her like a knife, so that she began to cry with the sharpness of the pain. How could they have been so cruel? . . . Cousin Margaret was long since in her grave. . . . What could they have done? It makes people happy to be admired. Perhaps they could have paid more attention to some activity of Cousin Margaret's. Had she been in the habit of doing something they might have praised? She had not been at all clever, but Mrs. Fisher could remember that she used to crochet. Her mind played with that and a remarkable thing happened. Gradually, without noticing the transition, she moved away from the historically limited matter of Cousin Margaret and began to compose a fiction. Not elaborated yet, but clear enough, the plot of *The Bedquilt* came into her mind. "And from that moment," said Mrs. Fisher, "I stopped crying, because the thought of Cousin Margaret stopped hurting me."[10]

Dorothy took issue with the idea that she wrote to relieve herself of pain. She had experienced relief, she said, not because she had expressed her feelings but because she had understood them. "I think the pain had gone out of the recollection because a new understanding of the facts had come into my mind. This kind of understanding of what has happened to you in the past comes into everybody's mind as he gets older. It is one of the benedictions of increasing years. For the inability to understand is the real unbearable tragedy of human existence."[11]

She went on to say that she wrote not so much for the relief of her own feelings as for the illumination of others' understanding, and she spoke of "the distinction between two kinds of fiction writing — the kind of story writing which offers the reader an escape from human life, and the kind which is an invitation to him to reflect more deeply than he has upon the significance of human life."[12] It was the challenge to writing of the second kind which was able to draw her away from a successful academic career.

Dorothy explained the writer's (that is, her own) relationship to human understanding thus:

> Our position, I mean the position of the human race, in regard to understanding its own behavior and the forces of its behavior, is in ignorance, I think very much like the ignorance of the cave man in regard to the physical phenomena of the world. He knew nothing whatever about the sources of the physical phenomena — nothing about the law of gravity, the succession of the seasons, had only the dimmest ideas of what sunlight did for the world. My impression is that as far as knowledge of human nature is concerned we are still wandering in that kind of foggy and dim guessing. So that any moment of vision which brings even a little crumb of understanding of any human phenomenon is a priceless event.
>
> The non-writing person accepts that new understanding and incorporates it with his own personal life. The impulse of the writing person is to share this new understanding with the rest of humanity. He feels its importance as a help to understand what takes place around us, and can hardly wait until he has put it in some form in which, he hopes, others may see the significance of events in human life which they have been taking perhaps callously, perhaps just with dull or slow lack of understanding.[13]

Dorothy was often asked just how she went about writing a story, and in 1920, with a good many misgivings, she consented to write an essay on the subject for a school anthology. She expressed her doubts about this assignment in a letter to Alfred Harcourt. "I have decided forty times different ways," she wrote, "whether it would or wouldn't be a good thing to have it printed, and finally think I can manage so it won't sound like a 'sure rule' for writing a story. My experience in didactic writing and speaking has made me all-fired wary about trying to tell folks how things are done, because the average run of folks are just crazy to get a rule of thumb and will grab one out of the most carefully constructed general consideration of any problem."[14]

In the essay on her own creative process, "How 'Flint and Fire' Started and Grew," she begins with qualifying remarks:

> I feel very dubious about the wisdom or usefulness of publishing the following statement of how one of my stories came into existence. This is not on account of the obvious danger of seeming to have illusions about

the value of my work, as though I imagined one of my stories was inherently worth in itself a careful public analysis of its growth; the chance, remote as it might be, of usefulness to students, would outweigh this personal consideration. What is more important is the danger that some student may take the explanation as a recipe or rule for the construction of other stories, and I totally disbelieve in such rules or recipes.

As a rule, when a story is finished, and certainly always by the time it is published, I have no recollection of the various phases of its development. In the case of "Flint and Fire," an old friend chanced to ask me, shortly after the tale was completed, to write out for his English classes, the stages of the construction of a short story. I set them down, hastily, formlessly, but just as they happened, and this gives me a record which I could not reproduce for any other story I ever wrote. These notes are here published on the chance that such a truthful record of the growth of one short story may have some general suggestiveness for students.[15]

She goes on to say that all of her stories start with

a generally intensified emotional sensibility, such as every human being experiences with more or less frequency. Everybody knows such occasional hours or days of freshened emotional responses when events that usually pass almost unnoticed, suddenly move you deeply, when a sunset lifts you to exaltation, when a squeaking door throws you into a fit of exasperation, when a clear look of trust in a child's eyes moves you to tears, or an injustice reported in the newspapers to flaming indignation, a good action to a sunny warm love of human nature, a discovered meanness in yourself or another, to despair.

I have no idea whence this tide comes, or where it goes, but when it begins to rise in my heart, I know that a story is hovering in the offing. It does not always come safely to port. The daily routine of ordinary life kills off many a vagrant emotion. Or if daily humdrum occupation does not stifle it, perhaps this saturated solution of feeling does not happen to crystallize about any concrete fact, episode, word or phrase. In my own case, it is far more likely to seize on some slight trifle, the shade of expression on somebody's face, or the tone of somebody's voice, than to accept a more complete, ready-made episode. . . .

The beginning of a story is then for me in more than usual sensitiveness to emotion. If this encounters the right focus (and heaven only knows why it is the "right" one) I get simultaneously a strong thrill of intense feeling, and an intense desire to pass it on to other people. This emotion may be any one of the infinitely varied ones which life affords, laughter, sorrow, indignation, gayety, admiration, scorn, pleasure. I recognize it for the "right" one when it brings with it an irresistible impulse to try to make other people feel it. And I know that when it comes, the story is begun. At this point, the story begins to be more or less under my conscious control, and it is here that the work of construction begins.

"Flint and Fire" thus hovered vaguely in a shimmer of general emotional tensity, and thus abruptly crystallized itself about a chance phrase and the cadence of the voice which pronounced it. For several days I had been almost painfully alive to the beauty of an especially lovely spring, always so lovely after the long winter in the mountains. One evening, going on a very prosaic errand to a farm-house of our region, I walked along a narrow path through dark pines, beside a brook swollen with melting snow, and found the old man I came to see, sitting silent and alone before his blackened small old house. I did my errand, and then not to offend against our country standards of sociability, sat for half an hour beside him.

The old man had been for some years desperately unhappy about a tragic and permanent element in his life. I had known this, every one knew it. But that evening, played upon as I had been by the stars, the darkness of the pines and the shouting voice of the brook, I suddenly stopped merely knowing it, and felt it. It seemed to me that his misery emanated from him like a soundless wail of anguish. We talked very little, odds and ends of neighborhood gossip, until the old man, shifting his position, drew a long breath and said, "Seems to me I never heard the brook sound so loud as it has this spring." There came instantly to my mind the recollection that his grandfather had drowned himself in that brook, and I sat silent, shaken by that thought and by the sound of his voice. I have no words to attempt to reproduce his voice, or to try to make you feel as I did, hot and cold with the awe of that glimpse into a naked human heart. I felt my own heart contract dreadfully with helpless sympathy . . . and, I hope this is not as ugly as it sounds, I knew at the same instant that I would try to get the pang of emotion into a story and make other people feel it.

That is all. That particular phase of the construction of the story came and went between two heart-beats.

I came home by the same path through the same pines along the same brook, sinfully blind and deaf to the beauty that had so moved me an hour ago. I was too busy now to notice anything outside the rapid activity going on inside my head. My mind was working with a swiftness and a coolness which I am somewhat ashamed to mention, and my emotions were calmed, relaxed, let down from the tension of the last few days and the last few moments. They had found their way out to an attempt at self-expression and were at rest. I realize that this is not at all estimable. The old man was just as unhappy as he had been when I had felt my heart breaking with sympathy for him, but now he seemed very far away.

I was snatching up one possibility after another, considering it for a moment, casting it away and pouncing on another. First of all, the story must be made as remote as possible from resembling the old man or his trouble, lest he or any one in the world might think he was intended, and be wounded.

What is the opposite pole from an old man's tragedy? A lover's tragedy, of course. Yes, it must be separated lovers, young and passionate and beautiful, because they would fit in with the back-ground of spring, and swollen shouting starlit brooks, and the yearly resurrection which was so closely connected with that ache of emotion that they were a part of it.

Should the separation come from the weakness or faithlessness of one of the lovers? No, ah no, I wanted it without ugliness, pure beautiful sorrow, to fit that dark shadow of the pines . . . the lovers must be separated by outside forces.

What outside forces? Lack of money? Family opposition? Both, perhaps. I knew plenty of cases of both in the life of our valley.

By this time I had come again to our own house and was swallowed in the usual thousand home-activities. But underneath all that, quite steadily my mind continued to work on the story as a wasp in a barn keeps on silently plastering up the cells of his nest in the midst of the noisy activities of farm-life.[16]

Dorothy goes on to relate how the details of the story were developed around the interruptions of a busy household, until she could say:

Now the materials were ready, the characters fully alive in my mind and entirely visualized. . . . The story was now ready to write.

I drew a long breath of mingled anticipation and apprehension, somewhat as you do when you stand, breathing quickly, balanced on your skis, at the top of a long white slope you are not sure you are clever enough to manage. Sitting down at my desk one morning, I "pushed off" and with a tingle of not altogether pleasurable excitement and alarm, felt myself "going." I "went" almost as precipitately as skis go down a long white slope, scribbling as rapidly as my pencil could go, indicating whole words with a dash and a jiggle, filling page after page with scrawls — it seemed to me that I had been at work perhaps half an hour, when someone was calling me impatiently to lunch. I had been writing four hours without stopping. My cheeks were flaming, my feet were cold, my lips parched. It was high time someone called me to lunch.

The next morning, back at the desk, I looked over what I had written, conquered the usual sick qualms of discouragement at finding it so infinitely flat and insipid compared to what I had wished to make it, and with a very clear idea of what remained to be done, plodded ahead doggedly, and finished the first draught before noon. It was almost twice too long.

After this came a period of steady desk work, every morning, of re-writing, compression, more compression, and the more or less mechanical work of technical revision, what a member of my family calls "cutting out the 'whiches'." The first thing to do each morning was to read a part of it over aloud, sentence by sentence, to try to catch clumsy, ungraceful phrases, overweights at one end or the other, "ringing" them as you ring a dubious coin, clipping off too-trailing relative clauses, "listening" hard. This work depends on what is known in music as "ear," and in my case it cannot be kept up long at a time, because I find my attention flagging. When I begin to suspect that my ear is dulling, I turn to other varieties of revision, of which there are plenty to keep anybody busy. . . . Now the story was what one calls "finished," and I made a clear copy, picking my way with difficulty among the alterations, the scratched-out passages, and the cued-in paragraphs, the inserted pages, the re-arranged phrases. As I typed, the interest and pleasure in the story lasted just through that process. It still seemed pretty good to me. . . .

But on taking up the legible typed copy and beginning to glance rapidly over it, I felt fall over me the black shadow of that intolerable reaction which is enough to make any author abjure his calling for ever. By the time I had reached the end, the full misery was there, the heart-sick, helpless consciousness of failure. What! I had had the presumption to try to translate into words, and make others feel a thrill of sacred living human feeling, that should not be touched save by worthy hands. And what had I produced? A trivial, paltry, complicated tale, with certain cheaply ingenious devices in it. I heard again the incommunicable note of profound emotion in the old man's voice, suffered again with his sufferings; and those little black marks on white paper lay dead, dead in my hands. What horrible people second-rate authors were! They ought to be prohibited by law from sending out their caricatures of life. I would never write again. All that effort, enough to have achieved a master-piece it seemed at the time—and this, *this,* for result!

From the subconscious depths of long experience came up the cynical, slightly contemptuous consolation, "You know this never lasts. You always throw this same fit, and get over it."

So, suffering from really acute humiliation and unhappiness, I went out hastily to weed a flower-bed.

And sure enough, the next morning, after a long night's sleep, I felt quite rested, calm, and blessedly matter-of-fact. "Flint and Fire" seemed already very far away and vague, and the question of whether it was good or bad, not very important or interesting, like the chart of your temperature in a fever now gone by.[17]

Dorothy always tried to protect the persons who had inspired her stories by disguising them from recognition. The extent to which she hid them, even in this essay about writing a story, is shown in a conflicting report of how "Flint and Fire" was written, which John Fisher gave after her death. "It happened this way," he wrote.

Visiting a neighbor who we guessed was broken down by an unhappy marriage, her words "Seems as if I never heard the Mill Brook so loud as it is this Spring." caught Dorothy's ear like the key-words spoken by an actress on the stage. In real life nothing happened so far as we know. The wife died some years later from natural causes. The callous husband didn't mourn for long, married again—another unhappy wife.

But those words kept ringing in Dorothy's ears. So she invented the young girl crossed in love, the attempted suicide which solves the family feud by shocking the elderly sisters into seeing that their pride must not wreck the lives of the young lovers, and called her story Flint and Fire.[18]

Dorothy was from the very first a highly successful short-story writer. She longed, however, to try her talents on a longer narrative, and during her summer trip in 1905 she began *Gunhild*.

5

Gunhild

From Norway Dorothy wrote home on July 30, 1905:

I haven't written much — (one story "The Poet and the Scullery Maid" which is sad but somewhere near what I meant to say) but I've thought a lot more about my Norwegian story. If I could write that as I now conceive it, it would be something I'd not be ashamed of. But of course I can't. I expect a fearful set-back when I begin work on it — the method will have to be so different from my written-at-one-spurt short stories. I have it pretty well planned — fourteen chapters, scenes here and in Christiansand but oh, my hero is so frightfully complicated a person. It wears me out to follow him in and out of the labyrinth of motives he gets himself tied up in. The old aunt is Aunt Phebe with a sense of humor added. She's the only one from life — every scrap of the rest is pure make-up. I'm afraid I've set myself too hard a task in managing so many people. . . . Did I tell you I had a long letter from Mr. Sedgwick (Leslie's Editor you know) very warm and friendly and unexpectedly serious. He says that my "talent, heaven be praised, lies outside the ordinary channels of magazine literature. Don't try to make it run in those shallow ways. You can write stories with big ideas and true ones back of them. *Do* it! Don't be willing to be amusing when you can do more" etc. etc. . . . I said "big ideas as he put it weren't exactly in my line but I did mean to try honestly to have the ideas I was trying to express true ones, and to try and move people to more than a passing interest in a certain verbal dexterity."[1]

Gunhild, Dorothy's first novel, is set in Norway and subtitled "A Norwegian-American Episode." The plot and the main characters are indeed complex, and the reader is sometimes inclined to agree with the young author that she has set herself "too hard a task."

A group of American travelers are stranded in an isolated Norwegian community by Aunt Nancy's sudden and severe attack of sciatica. The group consists of the elderly New England spinster, Aunt Nancy, her nephew Harry Fox who has been brought up in Europe by a culture-seeking mother after the death of his rancher father, and two sisters, Caroline and Pollie Norton, who are traveling in Aunt Nancy's care. Caroline is cosmopolitan, selfish, and spoiled; Pollie, young, candid, and full of energy.

Into their isolation comes a Norwegian beauty Gunhild Larsen as interpreter. Born in Kansas, where her father worked on the railroad, she has had to give up plans for an American education and return to Norway with her stepmother and half brothers and half sisters because of her homesick father's dying wish. In Norway Gunhild has worked at menial tasks until the recent remarriage of her stepmother, who has taken all the children except a deformed and demented brother Ingolf. Just as her father longed for the cool fjords of Norway, so Gunhild is now homesick for the bright Kansas sun and delighted to see people from "home." Her American speech, however, alternately amuses and shocks the cultured travelers, for it is the uneducated, often crude language of the laboring immigrant.

Against this framework of situation and background, the diverse group of characters gradually get into a thoroughly miserable state. The working out of the novel might be called a study in various kinds of social and personal martyrdom. We learn that Aunt Nancy has left her comfortable home in New England to travel with the two spoiled young ladies, not out of a love of travel or even from a Puritan sense of duty but in the hope that by doing so she "may perhaps earn an absent smile of approval"[2] from their father, for whom she has long cherished a secret affection. She would even sacrifice her nephew's future by making a match between him and the spoiled Caroline to win the approval of Caroline's father. Aunt Nancy's plans seem to be going well until Gunhild appears. Her arrival marks the end of Harry's attraction to Caroline, with whom he would have continued his empty life of sophisticated rootlessness. Gunhild loves the wide western plains Harry remembers nostalgically from his childhood, and she shows him an example of true nobility of character, but her superficial crudities of speech and occupation offend his finely trained sensibilities, and he postpones asking her to marry him while he struggles with his own scruples. It never occurs to him that she might not wait for his proposal or might not be delighted to accept him, and he is completely crushed by her refusal. In his misery the only comfort his aunt can offer is: "Stand up straight, and bear your burden. It will be the making of you—as it has been of me."[3] Caroline is left equally miserable, for she wanted to marry Harry. Pollie in her youthful candor is in constant disgrace, while she serves as a catalyst by repeatedly making remarks that are socially disastrous but psychologically informative. All the characters leave the stage more mature but unsatisfied, not one having achieved his or her goal. Even the apparently contented Gunhild, who is engaged to a Norwegian officer, has to remind herself of her grandfather's courage, symbolized by a military medal, as she turns her back forever on the sunny Kansas plains.

The novel is a study of different motivating forces behind human behavior, and also of the incomprehensibility of one person's motives to another. The author brings to the story her familiarity with Norway, Paris, London, Kansas, New York, and New England. The language barrier between the stranded Americans and their Norwegian environment is used and played upon in two languages, and lessons in Norwegian serve to bring Harry and Gunhild together. Harry vainly questions the innkeeper in English, and his exasperated cry, "Why any dog in New York could understand as much as that," is echoed in the answering comment of Kaptejn Rivedal in Norwegian, "How can anyone be so dense as not to understand so simple a thing. Why, my very horses could take that in."[4] In fact, the misunderstanding based on difference in language could serve as a symbol for the whole work, for in a deeper sense the plot develops from the fact that no two persons in the novel speak the same language.

Harry's reading of an old Norse saga leads him to see Gunhild as a sleeping Norse princess who needs only the magic kiss of the timely lover to free her from the enchantment that ties her to the frozen North. In naive romanticizing he casts himself in the role of hero and expects the "princess" to remain asleep until he wakes her. On the other hand, Gunhild sees any American as a figure from her pioneering railroad-building childhood. It does not occur to her that the phrases of railroading slang, in which she takes such delight, could be offensive to the ear of any fellow American.

The novel is also a study in courage without hope, but the only character who lives in this state throughout the book is Aunt Nancy. The others maintain hope during the course of the novel, and the reader expectantly awaits a happy solution with them, only to be brought at the end to the irrevocable loss of the dreams for which they have all been living. The author asks the question, How can a human being go on living when the only thing that gave life meaning has been taken away? The answer she gives is a grim and not wholly satisfying one, when she has Aunt Nancy tell Harry to "Right dress" — that is, to look down the long line of other human marchers who keep going even as he must, without a goal.[5] Dropping the story at this point — where most of the characters have met defeat but have not yet converted it into productive compromise — is depressing.

Contemporary reviewers noted this mood of resignation as the weak point of the book, although they commended the young author for great skill in writing. One reviewer reported, "It is an interesting book, though readers will likely differ as to whether the author has given the episode the best or most satisfactory solution."[6] Another remarked that "on the whole, the book is a model of its particular style of fiction,"[7] but a third complained that "it is so well written as to leave one distinctly depressed."[8]

The author claimed to have drawn only Aunt Nancy directly from life. Her real counterpart was Dorothy's Aunt Phebe, a relative of her mother's, whom Dorothy admired for her qualities of selfless devotion and hard unappreciated work for others.[9] The other characters, however, show her wide acquaintance with different sorts of human beings and her accurate observation of them.

Dorothy once asserted: "Personally, although I never used as material any events in my own intimate life. . . . I can write nothing at all about places, people or phases of life which I do not intimately know, down to the last detail. If my life depended on it, it does not seem to me I could possibly write a story about Siberian hunters or East-side factory hands without having lived long among them."[10]

Harry is the American who has "gone European" and has acquired urbane mannerisms and a scorn of manual labor, while at the same time retaining a sentimental glorification of rugged Americanism that makes him despise his own distaste for rough and illiterate people. Caroline is the epitome of spoiled American womanhood, giving the impression to an obtuse English visitor of vigor and capability but totally lacking in inner resources to draw on in the boredom of isolation from outside entertainment. Gunhild is the child of Scandinavian American immigrants, many of whom attended the western universities that Dorothy knew in her childhood. Aunt Nancy, with her capacity for wry humor, her stiff upper lip, and her sparing speech, is the crusty New Englander. Pollie is the least successful of the characters, lacking consistency and appearing sometimes too old, sometimes too young. The grotesque dwarf Ingolf is also hard to accept and plays too often the role of a deus ex machina in furthering the plot.

Bringing all these different characters together in one place to act and interact was almost too great a task for the inexperienced novelist. She is, however, very successful in evoking the physical atmosphere and mood of the remote Norwegian setting she has chosen. This she does not so much by direct description of landscape as by showing the emotional reactions of different personalities to it. Thus we see some characters who thrive on the mystery of the native legends, some who find the isolation of the wild headlands intolerable, and others who are caught and bound by local superstitions.

Gunhild is the only novel Dorothy Canfield wrote before her marriage, and it is interesting to note that no marriage is portrayed within it. The group of American travelers is a group of single persons. Marriage is a goal, but one that is attained only by Gunhild, and that after the conclusion of the story.

Gunhild was with the publisher when Dorothy and John Fisher were married in 1907. It was not a successful book from the standpoint of sales. In the optimistic years at the beginning of the twentieth century, its stoic gloom could hardly have found wide reception. In detail the novel is brilliantly written, but its many threads are not always convincingly interwoven into a satisfying fabric. The short-story writer had not yet fully mastered the novelist's craft.

6
The Squirrel-Cage

Between 1907, when *Gunhild* appeared, and 1910, when Dorothy began work on her second novel, *The Squirrel-Cage,* a number of changes took place in her own personal life. The original plan had been for both Dorothy and John to write for a living, but Dorothy's work was more successful commercially, and the family schedule was gradually arranged to give her writing priority and to place John in a supportive role.

Dorothy described her writing day as beginning in reality the night before:

> I would go to bed thinking about whatever book I was writing. As you often do, you know, your mind having been active in sleep, I would wake up all ready to start in. Got up and made myself a cup of coffee, and whirled in. Then worked until noon, or lunch. Then I was tired, couldn't go on. I've never been able to work more than half a day, on my own writing — except revision, of course: that you can do anytime. You have to do that twenty-four hours a day when you really get at it.[1]

Dorothy's short stories continued to be very popular, and by 1909 she had sold enough to pay for a trip to Europe. She was traveling in France when the news reached her in March that her father had died suddenly of an apoplectic stroke. For Dorothy, who had always felt close to her vigorous, controversial, crusading father, this was an irreplaceable loss. Eleven years after his death she was able to write to her friend Blanche Sibut, "I have come, little by little to feel about my father's loss . . . that I have not *lost* him . . . that the innumerable vivid memories of him which constantly fill my heart are an inheritance from him that nobody can take away."[2] But a year later she wrote to Sarah Cleghorn, "The loss of my father has never been much softened to me by the passage of years. I miss him still with the unendurable stab."[3]

When her son was born in December 1913, Dorothy named him James Canfield Fisher for her father. Two years later she sent a picture of the little boy to her father's old friend Henry Holt with the plea, "Do say he looks like my father. I hope so much he will!"[4] And in 1929, when Dorothy was awarded an honorary doctorate by Columbia University, she wrote to Alfred Harcourt of her pleasure in hearing her father mentioned at the ceremony: "Dr. Butler in conferring my degree made an affectionate reference to Father which pleased me very much. I'm always so glad when I get some evidence that he is not forgotten yet. Why should I, I wonder, care more about that than about my not being forgotten myself? That never gives me a pang. Perhaps because I'm still alive?"[5]

In 1909 Dorothy was very much alive, for only a few months after her father's sudden death her first child Sally arrived on July 30. At the age of thirty Dorothy had lost the parent to whom she could turn for support and had taken on the challenging role of parenthood herself. Here was a new world to be understood, and new insights to be put into fictional form.

The home into which the new life came was a harmonious but unconventional one. It was set in a small Vermont community, where individual patterns of living were accepted almost without question. Dorothy was the chief breadwinner, and John assumed an editorial, consultative relationship to her work. Dorothy thus played the major role in the outside world; at home, however, her respect and affection for her husband were constant, and she sought his judgment on matters practical and literary and submitted to his direction in the details of everyday life.[6]

The unconventional arrangement of the Fisher home was one that grew naturally from needs and circumstances, but Dorothy did not have to look far to find very different life patterns. Her brother Jim, as president of a paper company with offices in New York City, was living in suburban Pleasantville and fighting the battles of the industrial world. Dorothy often stayed with Jim and Stella when she went to New York, and she viewed her brother's life with mixed admiration and horror. After one such visit she wrote to her mother:

Poor Jim is under a terrible nervous strain. His business is in a critical position — businesses always seem to be! — and while he is making a lot of money, he is making it out of his very life-blood, in the way of care and anxiety and desperate plannings and contrivings, and such physical fatigue as makes my heart ache to see! . . . There's a quiet sort of heroism about that sort of a life, don't you think, though it has none of the usual dramatic marks of heroism. He is making an effort with all his strength not to get one-sided, not to fail here because he's under an almost superhuman strain in the city! . . . I said, "Jim, however do you stand it!" He answered, with his patient smile, "Well, I do get pretty tired! I can hardly remember going to bed when I wasn't so tired that it seemed as though I'd like never to wake up!" It seems to me business is all wrong when it takes it out of human beings in that way![7]

Back in Vermont, at about this time, a local tragedy made a sharp impact on Dorothy's sensitive nature and focused her search for understanding on a particular set of questions. Among the neighbors in the narrow mountain valley were a young couple, a local country boy and a girl with a flair for fashion and social life. At the young wife's urging they moved away from their native area to be nearer the centers of town activity, and in an effort to make more money the young husband turned dishonest, was discovered, and finally, in deep depression and homesickness, took his own life. The tragedy shocked Dorothy, and the circumstances surrounding it haunted her. To her mother she wrote, "and of course they all, everyone who knew the circumstances, blame . . . [the] poor silly wife . . . who kept 'egging him on to make more money every minute.' "[8] Echoes of the strains of the business world in tragic combination with shallow feminine ambition are found in Dorothy's second novel.

The *Squirrel-Cage* was published in 1912. If the hero of *Gunhild* had been too complicated a character for the young author, she went to the other extreme in the central character of her next book. Lydia is simple and passive, the battleground for two opposing groups of dominant personalities, each of them determined to see her shaped to its own ideas.

The 370 pages of the novel are divided into four "books": "The Fairy Princess," "In the Locomotive Cab," "A Suitable Marriage," "But It Is Not Too Late for Ariadne." The Fairy Princess of Book I is the heroine, Lydia Emery, nineteen years old and just returned from a year in Europe to the little Ohio town of Endbury, where her father is a judge and her mother a very anxious social climber. There is an older daughter, Marietta, who has experienced her mother's attempts to keep up with the "best" people in town as more of a painful than a challenging experience. Two older sons have left Endbury: one has left for a brilliant city career; the other, a rebel, has turned his back on his mother's standards, married a grocer's daughter, and gone west to live happily and unfashionably on a ranch. Lydia has seen none of the struggle, only the rewards, and is the petted and spoiled youngest, a symbol of the success her mother has striven for and achieved. She is lovely and shallow, following every suggestion without resistance, and only occasionally exhibiting the disturbing traits of an honest and inquiring mind. Mrs. Emery is determined that this daughter shall have the coming-out party she could not afford for her older sister.

The title of Book II, "The Locomotive Cab," refers to the courting of Lydia by Paul Hollister, Endbury's most eligible bachelor. Lydia is the debutante of the season, much sought after for all social occasions, and escorted everywhere by Paul. She describes her whirlwind courtship as giving her the feeling of riding in the cab of a fast-moving train. The only discordant notes in Lydia's success come from her godfather, a crochety old bachelor doctor, and from his eccentric friend Daniel Rankin, a man who has given up a promising position in the insurance business to become a cabinetmaker. In defense of this move Rankin says:

> I did not like the insurance business as I saw it from the inside, and the more I saw of it, the less I liked it. I couldn't see how I could earn my living at it and arrive at the age of forty with an honest scruple left. . . . I like the cabinetmaker's trade, and I couldn't see that practicing it would interfere with my growing all the honest scruples that were in me. . . . At any rate, it looked as though there were a chance for me to lead the life I wanted, and I had an idea that if I started myself in square and straight, maybe after a little while I could see clearer about how to help other people to occupations that would let them live a little as well as make money, and let them grow a few scruples into the bargain.[9]

Book III, "A Suitable Marriage," describes the reality of Lydia's life as Mrs. Paul Hollister. Her spoiled childhood has ill prepared her to deal with the problems of running a household for a rising young executive. One domestic disaster follows another. Paul, driving himself relentlessly to achieve success in the business world, is appalled by the domestic chaos that greets him on his brief visits home. Lydia feels trapped in a labyrinth from which she does not know how to escape. She names her first child Ariadne, the name borne by the mythical chracter who found her way out of the classical labyrinth inhabited by the monster Minotaur. Motherhood gives Lydia a concern for the future, and her father's death from overwork makes her reflect on the past, with consequent deepening and maturing of her personality, but her attempts to share her insights with Paul or to get him to share his business interests with her meet consistently with failure. She is pregnant with her second child, a son, when Paul is killed in an industrial accident. In the first shock of loss she blurts out, "We never knew each other. . . . We were never married. . . I could have loved him!"[10] and faints away.

Book IV, "But It Is Not Too Late for Ariadne," deals with the time from the death of Paul to the birth of Lydia's son. Dr. Melton fears for her mind, which seems to be completely deranged, as she asserts, "The Minotaur! He got Paul—I must hide the children from him!"[11]

Daniel Rankin is the one who provides the solution, emerging from his carpenter shop in the woods to calm Lydia and eventually adopt the children, to the dismay of Paul's and Lydia's relatives. The novel closes with the implication that Lydia will recover and become the wife of Rankin, who is in Lydia's world "the only one who is really trying" to break the economic law and live with "the real things."[12]

Primarily an indictment of modern society, *The Squirrel-Cage* attacks materialism, social indifference, and the condemnation of women to aimless lives. It was regarded in its own time as a "shocker" because it held generally accepted American circumstances and ideals up to question. Yet, whereas *The Squirrel-Cage* comes closer to offering a solution to the problems it raises than does *Gunhild,* the answer it gives lies in the absence of evil rather than in the presence of positive good, and the hope offered at the end of the novel is in a very minor key.

There are no real heroes in this book. Environment is stronger than any of the characters, and it is a negative force. As Lydia's older sister says: "Oh, it's a hateful, horrid sort of world we're all so eager to push her into. It's like a can full of angleworms, everlastingly squirming and wriggling to get to the top."[13] Even the most positive character, Daniel Rankin, admits that he has merely avoided, not corrected the ills of society, and that his solution is a personal, not a general, one, when he says, "I have to try to find some firm ground where I can make a path of my own, up which I can plod in my own way."[14]

The pessimism of *The Squirrel-Cage* did not escape reviewers. While one critic noted its "sanity, restraint, and quiet power,"[15] another observed, "Under this charming surface, however, the story is one of human sacrifice,"[16] and a third, stressing its social message, remarked that it was "full of the most acute and damning observation."[17] Although in 1912 *The Squirrel-Cage* could be seen as an "acute and damning" criticism of society, in 1931, in the depth of the depression, a critic labeled the book out-of-date.[18]

The two major emotional crises in the novel, the death of Lydia's father and the death of Paul Hollister, stem from two tragic flaws in the accepted social role of American women. Paul's death reveals the emptiness of his relationship with Lydia, one based on only the most superficial sharing. This is the same message in a different setting as that of Ibsen's play *The Doll's House,* which had shocked Western audiences not long before. The death of Lydia's father is tragic for her because it brings the realization that she has never known her father, that she has lost what she never possessed. For Lydia's mother, however, the death of her husband causes a complete breakdown, for she knows that it was her demands on her husband for the symbols of social success that caused his overwork and death. The answer to the problem thus posed is that women ought to be given a share in earning as well as spending. "It's the most precious possession we have," Daniel Rankin says of work. "We ought to share it more evenly."[19]

Structurally, the book is closely organized, with the basic problems of the morality of materialistic America clearly and consistently focused in the main character Lydia. The author was writing about people and situations she knew, and her insights ring true. Her main character is a woman in transition from girlhood to maturity, the years that Dorothy herself had been living. When she began writing the novel, she was already the mother of a little daughter. The year after the novel appeared in book form, she became the mother of a son.

Dorothy was eager to improve her skill as a novelist. When she returned the signed contracts for *The Squirrel-Cage,* she asked to

see the report of my friend, Professor Trent on this manuscript, or to have your permission to write him myself asking for a criticism on it? If I were in the city I should probably go to see him personally, as I did (at his request and Mr. Holt's suggestion) after he had read "Gunhild". . . . His criticisms and suggestions have been very helpful to me, and if it is possible, I should profit, I feel sure, by his remarks on "The Squirrel-Cage." There are so few constructive critics to whom a novel-writer, eager to improve in the practise of his art, can apply! And one has such need of outside criticism![20]

7
The Bent Twig and *Understood Betsy*

In 1911 *The Squirrel-Cage* was accepted for serial publication by *Everybody's Magazine*. The $2,000 paid for the manuscript provided ample funds for a trip to Rome, where Dorothy visited the famous school of Maria Montessori. The "Montessori Method" of education was the subject of lively discussion across America at that time, and Dorothy found herself besieged by questions on her return. She reported:

> I observed that my family and circle of friends were in a very different state of mind from that usually found by the homecoming traveller. I was not depressed by the usual conscientious effort to appear interested in what I had seen; not once did I encounter the wavering eye and flagging attention which are such invariable accompaniments to anecdotes of European travel, nor the usual elated rebound into topics of local interest after a tribute to the miles I had travelled, in some such generalizing phrase of finality as, "Well, I suppose you enjoyed Europe as much as ever?" . . . I found myself set upon and required to give an account of what I had seen, not only by my family and friends, but by callers, by acquaintances in the street, by friends of acquaintances, by letters from people I knew and many from those whose names were unfamiliar. . . . How many evenings have I talked from the appearance of the coffee-cups till a very late bedtime, in answer to the demand, "Now, you've been to Rome; you've seen the Montessori schools. You saw a great deal of Dr. Montessori herself, and were in close personal relations with her. Tell us all about it. Is it really so wonderful? Or is it just a fad? Is it true that the children are allowed to do exactly as they please? I should think it would spoil them beyond endurance. Do they really learn to read and write so young? And isn't it very bad for them to stimulate them so unnaturally? And . . ."—this was a never-failing cry—"What is there in it for our children, situated as we are?[1]

The results of Dorothy's experience with Montessori ideas formed the basis for two novels, *The Bent Twig* (1915) and *Understood Betsy* (1917). In *The Bent Twig* Dorothy gives a serious fictional treatment of the problems of growing up and proclaims the feasibility of training for real independence. Her heroine is given the necessary practical skills to earn her own living and provide for her physical needs. Her marketable skill is her ability to give piano lessons, and she can also clean and cook and sew. Yet she is further taught by her free-thinking parents to be socially, morally, and spiritually self-reliant. After this training for independence is complete, she is subjected to a series of tests, which are not only personal trials but also proofs of the training she has received. In the novel as in the outside world of 1915, the Victorian tradition of feminine helplessness was still a reality to American women, and the main character has to struggle against traditional expectations of dependency to emerge a mature, self-reliant individual.

The home in which Sylvia Marshall grows up is a Montessori home. Everyone takes part in the work, and the children learn by being included in adult activities. Sylvia also has a very different kind of mother from Lydia Emery (of *The Squirrel-Cage*). Mrs. Emery was shallow in her human perceptions, had great social ambition, and used her daughter as an instrument to achieve some of her social goals. Mrs. Marshall, on the other hand, large both physically and in spirit, controls her family and influences her daughter's development toward the sensible rather than the fashionable.

Dorothy Canfield's academic background is visible in her first three novels, in each of which a literary or classical theme furnishes the pattern for plot development. *Gunhild* takes its direction from a Norse legend, which leads Harry Fox to identify unrealistically with the hero Sigurd and to expect Gunhild to assume the role of the sleeping Brunhilda. In *The Squirrel-Cage* the social system becomes a minotaur in a labyrinth demanding the sacrifice of human victims, and the tragedy of those who fail is that they find no path of escape but waste their lives because, in Mrs. Emery's anguished words, "There was nothing else to do!"[2]

The titles of the four "books" into which *The Bent Twig* is divided suggest a different classical themology: "In Arcadia," "A False Start to Athens," "In Capua at Last," and "The Strait Path."

"Arcadia" is Sylvia's childhood home in La Chance, where her father is a professor of economics at the state university. The Marshall family lives somewhat outside the mainstream of faculty social life. Its home is an old farmhouse, and its large garden is tended by Mrs. Marshall, whose Vermont background has given her a steady, practical outlook on life. The family is a Montessori ideal, where each child takes a responsible part in activities, a part suited to age and capability. Sylvia conforms outwardly to her home environment but feels an almost constant rebellion against the sense of being different from the surrounding community. "Every detail of the Marshalls' life was in contradiction not only to the standards and ideals of the exclusive 'town set,' but to those of their own colleagues. They did not live in the right part of town. They did not live in the right sort of a house. They did not live in the right sort of a way. And consequently, although no family had more visitors, they were not the right sort of visitors."[3]

The differences from the rest of the intellectual community are described in detail: "Instead of living in a small rented house on a closely built-up street near the campus in the section of the city occupied by the other faculty families, they lived in a rambling, large-roomed old farmhouse with five acres of land around it, on the edge of the West Side,"[4] "with a family routine which included housework for every one of them . . . part of the family fun,"[5] and an "extraordinary assortment of visitors at the Marshall house . . . every sort of person in the world, from spiritualists to atheists — everybody except swells."[6] A musical group led by an old German violinist, who is frequently drunk, meets regularly at the Marshalls' house, and this music is an important part of the development of the sensitive child Sylvia. Intellectual argument is also a constant feature of her environment, within the family and with the groups of students and friends who wander continually in and out.

Sylvia is not sent to the local high school but is prepared for the university at home, where

> although during those years she was almost literally rooted to the Marshall soil, watered by Marshall convictions, and fed by Marshall information, the usual miracle of irresistibly individual growth went silently and unconsciously forward in her. She was growing up to be herself, and not her mother or her father, little as any one in her world suspected the presence of this unceasingly recurrent phenomenon of growth. She was alive to all the impressions reflected so insistently upon her, but she transmuted them into products which would immensely have surprised her parents, they being under the usual parental delusion that they knew every corner of her heart. Her budding aversions, convictions, ambitions were not in the least the aversions, convictions, and ambitions so loudly voiced about her; and a good deal of her energy was taken up in a more or less conscious reaction from the family catchwords, with especial emphasis laid on an objection to the family habit of taking their convictions with great seriousness.[7]

The conviction to which Sylvia reacts most consciously and violently is expressed in her father's favorite quotation from Emerson: "What will you have, quoth God. Take it and pay for it."[8]

The tests of this early education take several forms, personified by as many different characters. The "False Start to Athens" is a whirlwind courtship by Jerry Fiske, the son of a prominent but unscrupulous politician. Sylvia accepts his proposal of marriage but then flees from the passionate sensuality that he subsequently displays. Jerry is a coarser version of Paul Hollister (of *The Squirrel-Cage*), involved in politics rather than business, attracted by the beauty and charm of the heroine but with no comprehension of, or interest in, any deeper nature she might possess. Sylvia's early training, physical and moral, gives her the strength to escape from the temptations of material prosperity and social prominence; she returns to the university and buries herself in her studies and her music.

The second test of her early education comes with an invitation to spend the summer months in Lydford, Vermont, with her Aunt Victoria. Aunt Victoria is the only sister of Sylvia's father, a wealthy widow who takes pride in the distance she can maintain from the sordid details of life. She surrounds herself with beautiful objects and sophisticated people and spends her time between the family summer mansion in Vermont and an apartment in Paris. One of the members of her circle is an art critic, Felix Morrison. Others are wealthy Mr. Somerville, his granddaughter Molly, and Aunt Victoria's stepson Arnold Smith.

Sylvia feels that she is a Carthaginian arrived in Capua, the land of elegance. Here her temptation is to become part of the unreal world of aesthetic luxury, where existence is far removed from the physical basis on which it rests. Sylvia feels at first that she has reached "real earth in the real world"[9] after being transplanted from the "moral hot-house"[10] of her early home. She is drawn magnetically to Felix Morrison, and she is rescued from an engagement to him only by his sudden and economically more advantageous marriage to the heiress Molly. The appearance on the scene of a millionaire with a social conscience, Austin Page, confuses Sylvia. She escapes from Lydford by traveling with her aunt to Europe but is called home from Italy by her mother's sudden death.

Dropped again precipitately into the world from which she came, and shocked by her personal encounter with tragedy, Sylvia recovers old values and chooses "The Strait Path" with Austin. Austin Page is a more fully developed example of the social rebel Daniel Rankin (of *The Squirrel-Cage*). He not only gives up more for the sake of his socialist ideas because he is wealthier and has more to give up, but he also puts his energies into a more socially productive form. He turns over his Colorado coal mines, on which his wealth rests, to an enlightened management in which the miners themselves have a voice, and he devotes his own energies to a long-range program of forest improvement on his farm in Vermont.

In *The Bent Twig* Dorothy has left the rather limited and austere structure of *The Squirrel-Cage* behind and has returned to the diversity of complicated personalities that crowded the pages of *Gunhild*. In this third novel, however, it is clear that the earlier immature novelist who had difficulty keeping all the threads of her narrative fabric in hand has grown into a master artist. *The Bent Twig* is a magnificent tapestry of lights and shadows, of colorful scenes and people, where, as in masterpieces of the medieval weaver's art, all peripheral material contributes to the clearer understanding of the central figure.

Although the focus of attention never slips from Sylvia, some of the secondary characters are drawn with a sure artistry that deserves special attention. Aunt Victoria's artificiality is suggested in her first visit to La Chance early in the novel, is touched on from time to time in the narration, and is boldly satirized in scenes like the one in Paris, where we see her "seated on a little yellow-painted iron chair, the fifteen-centime kind, at the top of the great flight of steps leading to the wide expanse of the Tapis Vert . . . alternately reading Huysmans' highly imaginative ideas on Gothic cathedrals, and letting her eyes stray up and down the long facade of the great Louis. Her powers of aesthetic assimilation seemed to be proof against this extraordinary mixture of impressions."[11] The author's sharply critical intent in this scene is underlined by a comment in a letter to a cousin that Huysmans is "one who always makes my bristles rise."[12]

The sacrifice of women of ability to social convention, which was a major theme of *The Squirrel-Cage*, receives poignant treatment in the tragic minor plot thread of Molly, the pretty heiress. A forest-fire emergency shows Molly at her best, as she springs into effective action, organizing and directing all those around her. In the words of her cousin, Austin Page, "The incident shows what I've always maintained about Molly: that she is, like 'most everybody, lamentably miscast. Molly's spirit oughtn't to have taken up its abiding place in that highly ornamental blond shell, condemned after a fashionable girl's education to pendulum swings between Paris and New York and Lydford. It doesn't fit for a cent. It ought to have for habitation a big, gaunt, powerful man's body, and for occupation the running of a big factory."[13] A few months after Molly's capacities are thrown away in a fashionable marriage, her crushed body is found under the wreck of her fast car, an evident suicide.

There are echoes of Dorothy's abolitionist parents and grandparents in the painful racial incident of Sylvia's grammar school days, where Sylvia's sister Judith appears as a fictional incarnation of the fiery spirit of Almera Hawley Canfield. In a fit of righteous wrath, Judith throws picnic supplies gathered by the fifth-grade girls into the river because they will not allow a

Negro girl to join their expedition and then justifies her actions by saying: "If she couldn't have a good time—and no fault of hers—I wasn't going to let *them* have a good time either."[14]

The two vivid portraits of Professor Marshall are a background for Sylvia's own development from childhood to maturity. At first he is seen as a laughing young professor, romping with his children, playing baseball with his students, the one who understands his sensitive little daughter and who insists on her acceptance of his free-thinking philosophical approach to life. After the death of Sylvia's mother, he "no longer seemed her father, created to protect and cherish her."[15] In the extremity of his grief, described with stark realism, he is like a weak lost child whom Sylvia must protect. He now welcomes crazy Cousin Parnelia and her practices of spiritualism, which he earlier despised, a change that seems to Sylvia a final indication of dissolution and helplessness.

A meeting of past with present can be seen in the use of images from one of Dorothy's early unpublished poems (cf. p. 38 above) in the scene by a Vermont roadside, where Sylvia deliberately makes clever conversation about the contrast between the flaming scarlet of a sumac tree and the blackness of the pines. "There's Cassandra," she says. "She's trying to warn the pines." Austin replies, "She's using some very fine language for her warning, but like some other fine language it's a trifle misapplied. She forgets that no doom hangs over the pines. *She's* the fated one. They're safe enough."[16] The conversation continues, and, in Austin's gently ironic answers to Sylvia's whimsical flights of fancy, one can see the author in her realistic maturity looking back with tolerant amusement at the melodramatic fancies of her own youth.

In *The Bent Twig*, as in Dorothy's other fictional works, the character types and the physical settings are those with which she was well acquainted. Paris, Vermont, and the midwest college town were all home to her, and she understood the people of the world of art, of academia, and of rural America with the familiarity of long association.

When the novel was about to appear, Dorothy suffered her usual anxiety. She wrote to Paul Reynolds, "The Bent Twig comes out in two or three days now, and I'm beginning to feel the usual qualm of apprehension. *Do* you suppose everybody will think it awfully long-winded? It is, you know, outrageously long. And old Mr. Holt found it too everlastingly full of domestic details: shopping, tomato-canning, dish-washing etc. But I didn't take 'em out to please him. Life *is* full of such details. Why can't I be smart enough to make them vital. I will yet, see if I don't!"[17]

When Dorothy sent the manuscript to Henry Holt, he read the first fifth and then wrote to her, "Oughtn't a story to take shape earlier than the close of its first fifth? Yours does not, and there is a good deal in that first fifth that cannot by any possibility that I can conceive be a part of the integral structure."[18]

She replied:

I'm greatly interested in your comments on the first fifth; but not as much alarmed by them as I would be if you'd read more. For I think by this time . . . that you see how from my standpoint the "story" does begin at the very beginning. I mean, you see how there isn't any "story" except my Sylvia, and that what I'm trying to do is to tell what sort of clay she was made of, and into what sort of a vessel she was finally shaped by the moulding of circumstance.

Of course in that sort of a book, the "plot" in the Victorian sense isn't the important thing; and the thread of the story does not run through a sequence of events but connects one phase of inner development with another.[19]

After completing his reading of the manuscript, Holt felt that it was "encrusted with rather more superfluous matter than equally good books often are," and he suggested that beauty could be "defined as freedom from superfluity."[20] He asserted further that "the book would greatly gain by filing and sandpapering off from, perhaps, a fifth to a quarter."[21] Among the parts he would cut are descriptions of domestic activities, for, he said, "There is also a good deal of a good housekeeper's interest in domestic affairs that will not interest a good many of your readers, especially those who are going to form public opinion; for the majority of them, being men, are presumably not interested in such affairs."[22]

Dorothy replied to the demand for cutting, "If you think there is a great deal in this book and a great many characters, too much of everything — you just ought to see the mass of what was left out, the crowds of characters clamoring to be put in that never had a chance to show their poor noses!"[23]

The only part of the "story" to which Holt objected was the courtship of Sylvia by Austin Page, which takes place partly through letters. In fact, the whole character of Page irritated him. Holt wrote:

I consider that whole letter business between Page and Sylvia impossible. Perhaps a man who was crank enough to put those mines in other hands instead of running them himself the best he knew how, would be crank enough to leave all that matter for a letter, without talking it over with Sylvia before he left her; but his leaving it for a letter is no more admirable than it is probable; and yet yu [sic] intend him of course to be a hero. I don't think, anyhow, that men worth their salt do much of their lovemaking by letter, where they have a chance to do it any other way. But as I said, I'm romantic, and perhaps I'm particularly sore on this point, because a rather good friend of mine lost his girl by it, as I think he deserved to."[24]

Dorothy's answer to Holt's criticism is a postscript: "Austin Page is *not* a crank! Just wait till I see you!"[25]

Holt also objected to Dorothy's punctuation, especially to her use of commas. To this criticism Dorothy replied:

> The subject of the punctuation of the book is one for laughter and tears! Those aren't *my* commas! I won't *have* them wished on to me! They're Holt and Co. commas! When Mr. Brace and Mr. Harcourt came up here in the summer, they insisted that they had read with ease the interlined, cued-in and cut-to-pieces Mss. I then had, and that it would need no retyping for the printers. I protested that John had typed part of it, and I part, and that the punctuation had had little attention and certainly wouldn't be consistent, because John punctuates prayerfully and well, and I carelessly and ill. They said, "Oh we'll send directions out to Rahway to have it punctuated consistently according to their usual formulae, the way they do all our books." Yessir! That's the way it was.[26]

A letter from John Fisher to Alfred Harcourt reports:

> H. H. writes that he would as soon let the printing house settle his style as his punctuation. I wouldn't. I think there is some chance of the style being appreciated by the intelligent reader, and I don't think the punctuation is noticed by one per cent of even the better class of readers, — that is if it isn't eccentric. H. H. also says that letting the printing house decide on punctuation is like letting Rodgers Peet & Co. decide on the style of one's clothes. Exactly I think, the two are of the same sort, bad only when pronounced and unusual. So as a matter of course I do always let R. P. & Co., or some other large firm decide the style of my clothes for me. All this merely points out that we differ from H. H. on several points of view towards things in general.[27]

John also admitted, "I lean a good deal toward fine points of punctuation and diction myself, but I am coming to think less of them. Art as the specialists of such things understand it tends so to be dry and limited. I'm getting to think that the main thing is creation, and that criticism has rights only when it doesn't drain the blood out of the creation."[28]

As for the detailed criticisms, which Henry Holt had written in the margins of the manuscript, Dorothy called them "illuminating, full, precise and accurate as a surgeon's scalpel"[29] and was grateful to him for taking pains with her work. About a technical correction, she remarked in mild fun over his simplified spelling, "You are right, English is a tuf language! There do be times when it seems to me it would be easier to do washings for one's living than to try to write it correctly. But on the other hand Flaubert and de Maupassant both went insane over writing French!"[30]

One of the novel's characters, the art critic Morrison, who was criticized by Holt, came in for Dorothy's special defense. She wrote:

> I meant him to be (like every merely aesthetic man I ever met) something of an intellectual prig and somewhat conscious of his own perfections. But I wanted him to seem so only to the mature and discerning reader, not at all to Sylvia who was, for all her ideas of her cleverness, really very unsophisticated; nor to Aunt Victoria who was looking for leisurely and intelligent and sophisticated men so diligently that she would overlook self-consciousness and aesthetic priggishness. But in my little Sally's phrase, it was as hard as the dickleums to walk that tight-rope, to make him not wholly a cad or an aesthete, to make him really enough of a man to take Sylvia in, with his fine phrases, and yet to make him sufficiently less of a man to throw Austin into relief. I don't pretend to know whether I've made the least beginning of a success in my attempt. I feared I'd finally made him too obviously a phrase-maker and too pontifical.[31]

One of Dorothy's good friends, who was married to an artist, said, however, that "she thought he was entirely fascinating, too much so for the good of the book, because she didn't see how Sylvia could want to marry anybody else! That surprised me vastly (Morrison being no admiration of mine!)," Dorothy reported, "but reassured me as to the impression he'd really make on such women as . . . my Sylvia."[32]

Holt had also questioned the use of Mrs. Marshall's death to resolve plot problems. Dorothy's comment was:

> Of course you must have known how many times I'd examined my conscience on the use of Mrs. Marshall's death. But though you gave me a turn, I still stick to my guns. I have a reasoned belief on the subject of accidents in fiction which I want to talk to you about, some day. I've thought myself gray-headed about it, and though my ideas aren't orthodox, I can't change them. Ich kann nicht anders, if I burn for it! I don't see why they haven't a place in fiction as in life! If a character is affected by an accident as he really would be in life. . . .[33]

While Dorothy was expressing gratitude for Holt's interest in her work and the time he had taken to make suggestions for improvements, John

Fisher was writing to Alfred Harcourt:

> Mr. Holt's bark was rather worse than his bite. When the first letter came
> I thought we were in for a rumpus . . . and it was a consolation to me to
> think that several other publishing firms had solicited Dorothy's work if
> she should have any falling out with H. H. & Co. However when his real
> suggestions got here I didn't think them anything to worry about. A few
> of them were of value. The majority seemed futile. . . . We may say, that
> though we don't agree with him, we think he has made his suggestions in a
> very gentlemanly way. Much, much better than his reputation.[34]

John's suggestion that they might take Dorothy's work elsewhere brought
this plea from Alfred Harcourt: "What you say about publishers comes very
close. I have more heart in publishing for Dorothy than for any one else, and
you know my work is much of my life. If ever, and this seemingly simple matter shows the possibilities, you folks have any doubts or questions about being here, please promise you won't commit yourselves elsewhere without having the situation out with me personally fully."[35]

In answer to Mr. Holt's concern that she might feel hurt by his criticism,
Dorothy replied:

> Of course I'm not "hurt" by what you say. How could I be! In the first
> place your comments seem very carefully and considerately phrased,
> compared to much of the criticism which I invite and get from frank-
> minded friends, who are used by this time to my great desire for other peo-
> ple's points of view. And then your criticism goes straight to the mark. It's
> a delight! What I'm trying to do is to write the best novel I can, and how, I
> ask you, could I be hurt by anything that helps me to? And lastly (a
> somewhat malicious consolation which sustains me even under the batter-
> ing assaults of my brother's and my husband's sharp remarks) the author
> criticised has a final advantage over her poor critics in that she doesn't in
> the least need to take advice which doesn't appeal to her.[36]

John's criticisms may have been sharp, but of the final product he wrote
to Alfred Harcourt, "As I read the book over I like it better than ever. A
number of things in it might easily be better, but they don't seem important.
The whole effect is of life and solidity. The detailed background is better than
in any work she has yet done, and I'm not sure that this isn't the most important part of a novel."[37]

The Bent Twig received excellent reviews. Critics praised its "brave out-
spokenness and . . . wise understanding"[38] and called it "realism in its best
application to American fiction,"[39] commenting on its ability to hold interest
by giving "the impression of . . . that unbroken continuity which is life

itself"[40] without depending "upon shocking the reader to secure attention."[41] The popularity of *The Bent Twig* in England received additional impetus from the approval of Viscount Grey of Fallodon, when he named Dorothy Canfield in a short list of outstanding American authors and cited her *Bent Twig* as "outstanding in American fiction."[42]

The early reviewers all centered their attention on the portrayal of Sylvia and her mother. It was years after the appearance of the book before Dorothy saw a review that finally caught the essence of *The Bent Twig* as she had intended it. She wrote to Alfred Harcourt:

> I'm enclosing a review of the Bent Twig from a *Delhi* newspaper or magazine which interested me; partly because of the quaint Indian mistake about LaChance being in Vermont, and mostly because the review is really very intelligent, and is the first one to pick out that saying of Emerson's as being the key-note of the story, the one which it is built around. I was greatly pleased to have, after—how long? seven years?—the point of the story recognized by a reviewer.[43]

Dorothy's friend Sarah Cleghorn wrote in 1935 about the continued popularity of the book: "It became at once the favorite it still is. The stream of letters about it has never run dry in all these twenty years; a typical one came as I was writing this. 'I am reading *The Bent Twig* for the twentieth time,' wrote this apparently middle-aged man in New Jersey. 'It's like "William Tell" . . . I can go back to it over and over again and know that I am in the presence of something true and significant.' "[44]

The Bent Twig was translated twice into German, with two quite different titles. As *Sylvia Marshalls Weg zum Ich* (Sylvia Marshall's Path to Identity), it appeared in Vienna in 1947, recognizing that one aspect of the narrative is Sylvia's search for her real self among the complex and conflicting patterns of life with which she is surrounded. The second German translation, *Die schwingende Saite* (The Vibrating String), appeared in Wiesbaden in 1948. The string that vibrates is, of course, Sylvia's finely tuned nature, which is stirred by the surroundings in which she is placed.

The basic message of the novel lies, however, in the homely proverb of which the American title is a part: "As the twig is bent, the tree will grow." The story of Sylvia Marshall is, in the final analysis, the story of the effectiveness of a Montessori education as a preparation for life.

The second fictional treatment of the Montessori method is a story for children, *Understood Betsy,* which appeared first in serial form in *St. Nicholas* in 1916. It was immediately popular, and Alfred Harcourt predicted that it might "in the long run outsell any of her other books."[45] However, although the heroine in the story is a little girl less than ten years old, and the narrative is related from the child's point of view, the substance of the work is directed at least as much at the adult world responsible for the education of children as at the recipients of that training. Dorothy called it "a real juvenile, but one which perhaps might interest grown-ups."[46]

In the first chapter we meet Elizabeth Ann, an orphan child adopted by Aunt Frances and Aunt Harriet, who live in a small midwestern town. Aunt Frances reads all the books on child raising she can find — "So you can see that by the time Elizabeth Ann was nine years old Aunt Frances must have known all that anybody can know about how to bring up children. And Elizabeth Ann got the benefit of it all."[47] Aunt Frances is determined to "understand" Elizabeth Ann. She questions her about her dreams and her school experiences and transmits to her in the process all her own fears and worries, so that at nine she was "very small for her age, with a rather pale face and big dark eyes which had in them a frightened, wistful expression."[48]

At this point Aunt Harriet develops a cough and must move south, and Elizabeth Ann is sent to live with cousins in Vermont, where her life is as different as possible from that with Aunt Frances — and very close to the Montessori ideal of training for self-reliant independence. Instead of the constant, smothering love and attention that she received from Aunt Frances, Elizabeth Ann is now directed in taking care of herself by a brusque New England spinster, Cousin Ann. This change in environment is reflected in a change of name, as the romantic Elizabeth Ann is replaced by the homely nickname Betsy.

Betsy's development from helplessness and dependency to independence and responsibility is traced step by step through the next nine chapters of adventures on the Vermont farm, in the course of which she learns to do her share of the work of the household and the school and to be responsible for those younger or less fortunate than she. In the final chapter Aunt Frances appears again, and Betsy, who has become strong and self-reliant, recognizes Aunt Frances for the weak and helpless person she really is. Aunt Frances departs to marry a man who is "big and strong" and "just loves to take care of people."[49] Betsy stays happily on the farm, where she has become capable and content.

There is a great deal of good storytelling in Betsy's encounters with the one-room school, her resourcefulness in rescuing little Molly from the wolf pit, her sewing project for poor 'Lias, and her adventures at the county fair. Almost any child would envy her the chance to make butter and to have a kitten of her very own. The deeper message of the story lies, however, in the sharp satire of the first chapter against the kind of education that puts an adult's need for emotional satisfaction ahead of a child's need to grow strong and free. The practical application of this message is found in the careful depiction of the steps by which strength and freedom can be developed in a young human being.

Part 3

The Mature Novels

"But fiction, that's more like falling in love, which can't be done by will-power or purpose, but concerns the whole personality."
Letter to Anna Pettit Broomell, 1944

8
World War I and Its Aftermath:
The Deepening Stream

The years 1915 and 1916 were filled with increasingly darkening storm clouds for the Fisher family. John and Dorothy had close friends in France, and they could not understand how America could stand idly by and watch the progress of the German war machine. In December 1915, Dorothy wrote to her French friend Céline:

> John and I have gone through a very intense emotional crisis. We were becoming so completely unhappy on the subject of our country's attitude toward the war that, one day, I proposed to John that we leave our home and take the children to Paris. He could certainly become useful as an ambulance driver or as a worker in a hospital—or something like that, and perhaps I, too, might find something to do. We considered this plan for three days and we were both on the point of doing it but finally—with many tears on my part—we gave it up because of the children and the dangers of the crossing.[1]

Three months later Dorothy and John were still debating the question of how to help and were moving closer to personal action. On March 8, 1916, Dorothy wrote to Céline:

> John and I have finally decided that we cannot put up with this inactivity any more. I do not claim to judge for my country and I do not want to condemn our President who has done, without doubt, the best he could. I don't even want to say that in his place I would have done otherwise. But, thank God I am not in his place; I am in my own which is difficult enough! I can no longer continue to do nothing personally in this great world crisis. It's *our* decision to do something personal as well as send money. We do not yet know what form "doing something personal" will take because that depends on you and on the American Committee of the American Ambulance Hospital, to whom John has written.[2]

The decision for John to participate was made, but the terrible choice remained to Dorothy whether to stay in America or go to France. She calls it "the serious question — shall I go with John, take the children and try to set up a home in France for the present? Or, shall I let John go alone, which would be almost impossible for me because I depend upon him so much, and stay here with the children?"[3] Dorothy's ignorance of conditions in a country at war is shown by her idyllic picture of the life she would have in France, as she asked:

> How are living conditions in France now, conditions which touch the life of small children? Is there some risk to their health? . . . Do you think that I could find some little place — probably not in Paris but nearby where John would be busy and where I could see him? Could I arrange some kind of a life which would give me leisure for writing, something I shall need to do in order to continue to earn money, since John would not be earning?[4]

John's and Dorothy's families were solidly opposed to taking children into a war zone, but Dorothy refused to give up her plans:

> You can imagine how horrified our two families and our friends have been when they hear that we hope to find something to do to help France. They have said to us a thousand times, "The first duty of parents is toward their children. Think of the Zeppelin raids! If John is killed like other Americans who have driven ambulances — " When I say that we believe in giving our children an ideal which is as important for them as a childhood completely free of danger, they think I am mad. I am not unaware of the dangers but I think that our families exaggerate them.[5]

There is more than a trace of wishful thinking, of unrealistic dreaming, in Dorothy's further questions:

> People are wrong, aren't they, when they say that France is in material distress — that there isn't enough milk or butter, that living is terribly expensive, that the Germans are a threat even in the region south of Paris, and even in Normandy? Send me quickly all the details you can since we must make up our minds this spring. I like to think of myself settled somewhere with the children, busy writing and earning money so as to continue giving what money we can to your soldiers, orphans, and so on. Do you think that we can live with the children, one servant, and a kind of governess for six hundred twenty-five francs a month, or for seven hundred fifty francs?[6]

Eleven days later another letter continues this theme: "It seems quite possible for me to arrange a healthful and calm life for them over there, but my family

and John's treat me as though I were mad to think about it!"[7]
Dorothy also wrote to Céline's sister Blanche:

John and I are all stirred up over the possibility of our going to France.
Our respective families don't approve, of course, because everybody in
this country has an exaggerated idea of the risk of such an expedition. It
all seems very simple and obvious to us. We want to do all that we can to
help on the cause of the Allies which seems to us both the cause of civilization. Here I can send money; but John's strength and devotion are not at
work; and he is eager to have them.[8]

The outer struggle with family and friends and the inner struggle with
conscience went on. Céline advised against the trip for Dorothy and the
children, writing, "You must realize the ever increasing difficulty of living
over here."[9] On April 2, Dorothy wrote: "*If we did not have the children*—we
always come back to this agonizing question of our responsibility toward the
children. Up to what point should we sacrifice our convictions for them?"[10]
When John sailed on April 22, Dorothy and the children remained
behind. "For the first time in my life," Dorothy wrote to Céline, "I have settled a serious question according to the opinions of others and not according
to my own judgment. May God grant that all the rest of you are right!"[11]
John was to serve with the Automobile Ambulance Service of the American
Ambulance Hospital in Neuilly. Dorothy decided to spend a while with
John's family in Swiftwater, Pennsylvania, and then go to Thetford, Vermont, where Sally could be in a girls' camp. She wrote, "I could not stand
Arlington without John. I shall wander about somewhere until I can join
him."[12]
The news of John's safe arrival in France filled Dorothy with joy mixed
with bitterness "at the thought that I might have made the trip with the
children."[13] In June, Dorothy heard with relief that John was in Paris still.
She reported to Alfred Harcourt, "He is working ten hours a day (and apparently more at times) repairing cars in the repair garage, and doesn't know
at all how long he may be there."[14] She said further, "It makes me perfectly
crazy to think of him settled so near Paris and me drifting around in this
tragic and absurd way. . . . I need him so much, and there is nothing really
gained, now that Mother is more like herself, by my undergoing this separation."[15] She wrote to Céline, "Mother seems less terrified at the thought of a
transatlantic trip and, although she is still definitely opposed to the idea of a
stay in France, she does not appear as nervous about it as she was. At last I am
beginning to be hopeful."[16]
Before the end of June, Dorothy was sure that she had to follow John.

She wrote to Paul Reynolds, "I'm going to France, after all, to join my husband. I can't stand this! Life's too short for husbands and wives to be apart unless it's ever so necessary."[17]

News came from Paris that John had been sent to the front, and Dorothy was "amazed, saddened, and . . . discouraged," saying that she "can't understand it."[18] Her family and friends told her, "Oh, you can wait now — he won't be there, what is the use of going now?"[19] Dorothy's mind was set, however, and she embarked for France with the children in August.

The months before their departure were hectic ones. At first, after John left in April, Dorothy found it hard to settle down. She wrote to Céline:

> I am proud to tell you that I let him leave without bursting into tears. Now I am trying to write. I have made a tremendous effort to be busy, but I must confess that up until now it just doesn't work! The upheaval has been too great for me to recover completely right off, but I am doing a little better every day. I shall succeed, I am sure, because I must do it! And as a beginning, I am going to stop writing to you today and settle down to my work![20]

As the time for sailing drew near, Dorothy rushed to complete projects in progress. She wrote to Céline:

> I keep thinking of settling in Paris and I believe that arranging our little home will be a real rest for me after these three months of incessant intellectual effort. I have never worked more hastily or feverishly. And I have done so much! I have only one chapter to add to the book for girls [*Understood Betsy*] and a few pages to the other [*Fellow Captains*] and then I shall be free to leave! I am not planning to do any writing at the beginning because I want to have a good long rest and a dose of domestic life. I am really very tired. I want to spend a few weeks arranging our little home, playing with the children, seeing you and feeling that I am near John. And since he will be so near, I shall be able to live again with my husband who is for me an element of life as essential as air itself![21]

Dorothy's life in France was far from the romantic idyll she had envisioned in her letters to Céline. John was at the front and only rarely able to be with her and the children. In Paris Dorothy became involved almost immediately in work for the war blind, and during the winter she organized the printing and distribution of books in Braille. In addition to this and other relief projects, she wrote incessantly, both stories and articles, trying to explain to the people back home what was really happening in France. To Paul Reynolds, who was marketing her stories in America, she wrote, "It's good to be too busy to think, when such news as that of the Belgian deportations comes in! That's simply intolerable! When you have friends in those towns, women — *isn't* it all like a hideous dream!"[22]

The war was still not being taken seriously in America. Dorothy wrote with the desperation of one who knows a need to those who are indifferent, and she poured the money that she earned from her writing into the support of projects in France. As she sent Paul Reynolds two war sketches, "The Little Soldier of France" and "In the Brussels Jail," she wrote that she wanted to be "perfectly and absolutely authentic" rather than sensational.

> My object in both of them was to try to get something to the American public which would sound *real* to them, would sound like what might happen to any one of us, in comfortable homes in suburbs — and as I remember the war stuff I used to read it didn't make that impression on me because of its very vociferous quality. There was so much 'punch' that subconsciously I thought of it as exciting fiction. Now of course my attempt to pitch war articles in a lower tone may fall on ears so deafened by atrocity tales that they can't even hear the sound of my voice.[23]

In December John was returned to Paris to train ambulance drivers there, and in the spring he was running a training camp for American ambulance drivers in the war zone at Crouy. In June Dorothy turned over the Braille press to her French friend Marguerite Fischbacher and joined John in Crouy, where she took charge of getting and preparing food for the camp. This meant that Dorothy had to "drive an auto forty miles a day and buy food for a hundred and fifty men and run the housekeeping for them."[24] In October the camp was closed, John went back to the front, and Dorothy and the children returned to Paris.

It had been a satisfying summer for Dorothy, together with her family and busy in productive activity, but it was followed by a winter nightmare. Shortly after the return to Paris, Sally contracted typhoid fever, and her bout with the disease was a long, frightening ordeal for the whole family. When serious illness gave way to slow convalescence, Dorothy took the children to the milder climate of Guethary in the Basque country. There Sally gradually regained her health, both children played on the hills and along the seashore, and while watching them Dorothy grew to love the Basque people, who reminded her of the independent Vermonters at home. In Guethary Dorothy was completely isolated from the cosmopolitanism of Paris, so much so that when Paul Reynolds asked for some reports about Americans in France, she replied, "The difficulty about my writing about Americans, as I think I have written you before, is that I don't see any! Somehow my work and life are always happening where I am the only American for miles and miles."[25]

Many French children were being sent to the Basque resort area from Paris at that time to escape the shelling of "Big Bertha," the German cannon. In addition to caring for her own children there, Dorothy worked to establish a home for refugee children. John worried about the way this active relief work was interfering with Dorothy's writing. In a letter to Alfred Harcourt she said, "He talked to me very seriously while he was here, about trying to write more and getting less absorbed in definite war-relief work. . . . It's a little, it seems to me, as though he thought I ought to say 'Yes, I know there is a starving child over there but I can't go and give her anything to eat because I have a story to write.' "[26]

Funds often ran low, so Dorothy did continue to write stories and articles for the American market. About the question of whether to send the money she earned to her in France or keep it in a bank in America, she wrote:

> John thinks we ought to have a fairly sizeable lump sum actually here — because conditions may change with lightning-like rapidity. Also life costs and costs and costs — especially as these earnings enable me to take in other people under our roof frequently and give them the hearty diet which most people here are going without. To fill up again and again the plates of hungry children is about as good a comfort as any these war-times hold for me![27]

A confusion of spirit pervades Dorothy's fictional writing about the war and filled her letters home as well. Sarah Cleghorn received a letter from Dorothy in her second year in France that read:

> I wonder if you realize how faint-hearted and sick I am most of the time, even with the feeling not wavering that there was nothing for the French and Belgians to do but to defend their countries? . . . I have the feeling that our generation is pretty well done for, stunned and stupefied with the bludgeon of the war, and that it is only from the children that the future will draw enough vitality to stagger along. . . . Last night, as I sat at my desk writing, Emilie came in to call. She said, "Oh, don't let me interrupt you — go on writing."
>
> I said, "What do you suppose I am writing? I am setting down for my own benefit the reasons why I am not a thorough-going non-resistant pacifist."[28]

Sarah Cleghorn tells further how Dorothy's letter "went on to describe a perpetual recoil from what she was seeing, the actualities of war, yet how she was held back all the time by a sense that in spite of everything war was a means of righting present wrongs, and preserving humanity's faith in justice and in the future."[29]

About the same time, Dorothy wrote to Sarah about the effect of passivity on brute force.

I know you won't remember a sketch I wrote, years ago,[30] about a young wife who found that her new husband had fits of inexplicable bad temper—when no matter how gentle and ingenious tender she was, everything she did only irritated him the more. After a conversation with his old nurse who described him as a child, she takes another course, flies into a pretended rage herself, scolds and threatens and cries. He is astonished and a little bit daunted, finally (her rage acting as a sort of lightning rod to carry off his bad temper) quite changed in humor, pets her and persuades her out of her "pet," and ends by carrying her off to the theatre and a supper afterwards. It all sounded like light comedy but I felt so deeply the sadness of it I couldn't let it go like that and made an unexpected turn at the ending, where the young wife has a moment of tragic gaze into the future as she sees what manner of man she has united her life to. It was crudely enough done, but it expresses an observation of human nature which fifteen years longer watching of life has not changed. I have observed, or I think I have, that there are certain natures, whom non-resistance acts upon like a sort of irresistible excitant, like a poison, like a powerful drug which they can't resist. It excites them to deeds of brutality which if they had been kept in normal condition by a conviction of the impossibility of their immunity, they would never have thought of doing. I have always labeled them to myself undeveloped characters, people who have stayed an aeon or two behind the rest of humanity. . . . I suppose there are remnants of that stone-age savagery in the best humans, but there are more of them in some than in others—that at least is what my observation has shown me. Now it has been my feeling that the Prussian military party is, among nations what that sort of a man is among people—that they just lose their heads altogether when such a chance is put in their hands as Trotsky put, and *can't* be decent, any more than a man with an irresistible temptation to drink can resist a whisky bottle. The thing to do, for such people and such nations, it seems to me, is to introduce prohibition and introduce it by force if necessary. . . . I don't think moral suasion can work with such people nor appeals to their honor. I think there aren't many of them left in comparison with the great majority, so few that rules and laws oughtn't to be made solely with regard to them as we still so much continue to do. But I do think there are some of them. And I think we have been horribly clumsy and wrong in many many ways we have conducted this attempt to set right things—it seems to me I am always clumsy and wrong in the way I try to do things — but I can't do anything but go on trying to do.[31]

That same spring in Guethary, Dorothy was wrestling with her conscience on problems of religion. To Sarah she wrote in April:

I have often thought that I never was a Pacifist, really; just as I often think that I never was nor can be a "literal" Christian. I am in the midst of a very Catholic circle here, as at Crouy, with priests and sisters of Charity and devout people of all sorts. I go a great deal to Mass, partly because it would hurt their feelings if I didn't, and partly because I do like all churches, all religions — I wonder if this means I am really an irreligious person. . . . I am even more startlingly convinced than ever how impossible the smallest degree of *real* religious conformity would be for me. If these dear people could see into my heart they would think me a "Monster of the Sin Pride of the Intellect" for it is literally inconceivable to me, resigning my judgment in any degree to any authority whatever. It seems to me that that would be the last sin, the worst crime against my better nature, the final abyss of cowardice and moral laziness — *to take somebody's else word for what is right.*[32]

She regretted, she wrote a month later, her "small-minded helpless dependence on 'sense' "[33] (by which she clearly meant powers of the intellect). She envied her good friends their faith in benevolent supernatural powers.

Now what I mean when I say you and Zephine and Marguerite Fischbacher are different from me in that is that you don't depend on sense, you have seen how in the past it has often been another name for cowardice or dulled perceptions or uninventiveness, and you demand, burningly demand actions based on something higher. I'm very thankful to have you demand it — I'm a little like a deaf person who is glad to *see* other people getting inspiration out of music, inaudible to him. But it would be getting me into water where I couldn't swim, if I tried to follow you — there you are, you see. *You* three would just push off anyhow whether you could swim or not — and most likely you would find you could.[34]

Dorothy missed her congenial friend Sarah terribly during her time in France and felt poignantly the limitations of letters. "I wish, oh tremendously wish," she wrote,

that I could *talk* with you for just half an hour — but we would fall to talking about the children and who Jimmy looked like and how much white there is in my hair and how Sally and Dalton compared in size — we have so many *many* dear and common interests together as well as the great ones. I must stop — it isn't right to give myself the luxury of writing you at such length, but it has done me good to do it. I have such a solitary sort of life, with all my busy many-colored occupation much-peopled days. Nobody *really* to talk to, at all, although I am always talking to somebody.[35]

Dorothy's own experience of the war years found full fictional expression only ten years later in *The Deepening Stream*. Before then the postwar years brought new problems into Dorothy's personal life. Before the war John and Dorothy had become accustomed to a domestic arrangement in which her earnings provided the financial basis for living, while together they shared home and family responsibilities and took part in community affairs. Their war work interrupted this rural idyll and changed their roles. Although Dorothy continued her combined activities of mother, writer, and neighbor in France, active service to the community now claimed first place in her life, and her writing served primarily as a means of supporting it.

The changes wrought by the war were much greater for John. He went to France as a volunteer ambulance driver, was soon training other drivers, and rose to the position of supervisor of the training camp for American ambulance drivers at Crouy. In this setting Dorothy was his subordinate, in charge of the purchase and preparation of food for the men in the camp.

Dorothy received a letter from Alfred Harcourt while she and John were in France, in which Alfred remarked prophetically, "We shall almost be different folks when we all get together again. I am anxious for a long visit with John to see what the war has done to him. I have had some notion of what this experience has done to you from your letters."[36]

When the Fishers returned to Arlington after the war, Dorothy took up her former life joyfully and was soon plunged into the absorbing and satisfying writing of another novel. Her war experiences had left painful scars, but they had also deepened her perceptions of life in ways valuable for a novelist. New vistas, wide and inviting, opened up before her.

For John, return to Vermont meant a shrinking of responsibilities and horizons. From supervisor responsible for hundreds of men, from active usefulness and courageous facing of open danger in the service of humanity, he came back to the quiet of a narrow Vermont valley and the rather anomalous position of editor and assistant to his successful author wife.

Dorothy's star was in its ascendancy. The doors to a world wider than any she had known were swinging open before her. Her new novel, *The Brimming Cup*, became an immediate best-seller. She was constantly called on to speak to audiences across the country, and although she turned down many invitations, she felt that she must accept many more. Her letters from the early 1920s indicate trips to Boston and Chicago, to New York and Detroit. She always returned exhausted and determined not to let herself be lured into another such trip, and always eventually set off again, to speak, to receive honorary degrees, to be wined and dined as a distinguished author.

Shortly after their return from Europe, John built a bungalow near their house in Vermont so that his old roommate Alfred Harcourt could come with his wife and son for extended visits during the summer months. The Harcourts and the Fishers were close friends, and when Alfred left the firm of Henry Holt and Company to start a publishing business of his own, John and Dorothy watched with mingled admiration and alarm. In June 1920, Dorothy wrote to Alfred, quoting words of encouragement from her businessman brother, who said, "Everybody has to take a chance at least once in his life, on an all or nothing possibility—it's fun, and with everybody in good health, not the slightest tragic quality even if you don't succeed—just turn in and start over!"[37]

Alfred did, however, succeed, as the lively correspondence between him and the Fishers in these years indicates. His new firm of Harcourt, Brace and Company published the two best-sellers of 1920 and 1921, Sinclair Lewis's *Main Street* and Dorothy Canfield's *The Brimming Cup*, and Dorothy's later works contributed their share to the continuing success of the firm. In Alfred Dorothy found not only a successful publisher but also an understanding friend. They corresponded regularly, and Dorothy rarely went to New York without visiting Alfred and Sue at their home or Alfred at his office. Looking back in 1933, Alfred wrote to her, "The business and personal relations that have developed between us in all these years have meant probably more to me than anything else I have got out of publishing."[38]

John Fisher's life in these same postwar years went from one discouragement to another. In the winter of 1919–20 he developed a serious knee infection that kept him immobilized for some time. The first day out after his recovery, he was cutting furnace wood with a circular saw when he slipped and nearly severed his thumb. A long period of hospitalization in Troy, New York, was followed by a frustrating spring, when he had to watch helplessly as the proper time for planting gardens passed before the doctor would permit him to work in his. In the fall of 1920, John ran for the state legislature and was defeated, as Dorothy wrote to the Harcourts, "by an unholy coalition of stingy farmers, resentful of the prohibition laws. . . . It was intended and openly proclaimed as an attack on the project for the new school and now we are in for a lively defense of it at Town Meeting next March."[39]

Dorothy's life focus was in her work. Even the bitter disappointment of seeing John defeated by a less qualified man for town representative called forth from her the comment that, although they were angry at the result, "It's all highly interesting to a novelist."[40]

In spite of his own problems, John continued to back Dorothy up in her work. Lying in his hospital bed in Troy, he read omnivorously. Among other books, he reread *The Bent Twig*, which he had not looked at since going over proofs with Dorothy years before. She reported his reaction in a letter to the Harcourts.

> He was surprised, so he said, and you'd better believe *I* was surprised, when he found it so much better than he remembered it. He sat up all one night to finish it — think of it! — and informed me in the morning that it was as good a novel as he's read at all, and a lot better than most! He was evidently surprised by this, said he could hardly believe it as he read along, and he has really vastly encouraged me for the new one by the unexpected praise![41]

Later, while Dorothy was on a speaking trip to Columbus, Ohio, John read the first part of her unfinished novel *The Brimming Cup*, and again his praise, never lightly given, encouraged her. "John read the first part of it while I was gone," she wrote to Alfred, "and greeted me by saying 'I think it's great!' which reduced me (groggy with lack of sleep as I was) almost to tears of thankfulness."[42]

Alfred tried to involve his old friend in literary work and sought his opinion on current books. A letter from John to Alfred in August 1920 shows independent and perceptive evaluations. About Parker's industrial essays, John wrote, "One thing that gave me a great deal of pleasure was the way that Parker accepted much of Freud's doctrine of suppressed desires without accepting sex as the master motive. This is surely a step towards sanity. Sex is of course more of a motive than the Victorian school imagined, but Freud is surely dotty in the emphasis he puts on it, and the doubles and twists he takes in making every other natural impulse somehow get its start in sex."[43] In the same letter John comments on the structure and form of a new novel, *Open the Door,* saying, "But, perhaps I'm old fashioned, I like a little more composition in a novel than one often finds in the life he is able to observe. People do inexplicable things, but an author ought to be a little god to his characters and have some idea about their motives."[44]

The community in Arlington claimed a good deal of Dorothy's and John's joint attention. Other persons of artistic and literary note were moving to the valley. In 1919 the illustrator Norman Rockwell and his family arrived, and in the same year the Robert Frost family, in dire economic circumstances, moved in nearby. Dorothy wrote to Alfred Harcourt, "The Frosts are on their farm now and the Lord he only knows whether they will make a go of it. John and I stand ready to do anything we can, from cookstoves to plumbing, if they only keep well."[45]

In 1921 Dorothy became the first woman to serve on the Vermont State Board of Education. She did so reluctantly and wrote to Sarah Cleghorn:

> I *wish* I didn't feel I ought to do this Board of Education work. It's a very heavy burden on my mind, and heart and time, and I know it interferes very much with my writing well. But I know I'm doing *some*thing there, (and I'm not by any means sure of that with my writing) and since a long talk with Governor Hartness up at Burlington I feel less than ever that I can indulge myself by getting out. But when I go to France, a year from now, automatically that will release me.[46]

The following January Dorothy came into such violent conflict with the state powers that she resigned from the board. She wrote to Paul Reynolds:

> The Vermont Legislature has busted loose with economy ideas and there are attacks on, against everything that keeps us from being absolutely medieval up here. Among them, an essential part of our public school system is concerned, and I feel so deeply the importance of that, that I am resolved to let that expense-cutting be done, only, so to speak, over my dead body. The hearing before the Legislative committee is in a few days now, and I can*not* take my mind off the preparation of material and planning of the campaign.[47]

Thirty-five years later, another Vermonter remembered how "the courageous little woman from Arlington at one time stood firmly on her feet and told the Vermont legislature to keep its political nose out of this state's education system. Her interests were the welfare of the children, and no legislator was going to push her aside and let it be otherwise!"[48]

Dorothy's friends reacted with mixed horror and amusement to her fight with the State of Vermont. In answer to Dorothy's heated report of the controversy, Sue Harcourt wrote her:

> Good for you, I'm glad you resigned. So is Alfred. It will be a mighty good thing for you all to get away to Europe if you're sure you won't become involved in even worse mix-ups. You seem fated to, you know. What's the matter with your Vermont lawmakers. They must be insane. No wonder you're rip-roaring *mad*. Do try to take it easy the rest of the winter. They may be ashamed of themselves before long and have a much-needed

change of heart.[49]

To the same letter Sue appended this postscript: "Alfred told me to tell you that it gave him such a curious sensation to hear about your big scrap—as though he were hearing you had a divorce from John and he didn't know why at all. These are his own words, which he asked me to tell you."

Sue Harcourt had been having serious nervous difficulties herself. In the summer of 1922 a letter from Dorothy to Alfred suggests that she be taken to "the very best nervous specialist there is," saying, "I think *constantly* of Sue, and with such a heavy heart wonder and wonder if there is the slightest thing I could do for her?"[50] A year later, Dorothy wrote to Céline Sibut, "Terrible news from our circle in America. Mrs. Harcourt, the wife of my publisher, has committed suicide. I shall tell you about it when I see you—a true drama."[51] Alfred soon married again, and the Fishers continued on friendly terms with him and his second wife, Ellen.

It was not until 1930 that Dorothy's memories of the war and its aftermath, which had lain hidden beneath the surface of her active life for more than a decade, were finally ready to emerge, in her most autobiographical novel, *The Deepening Stream.* By then she was able to see the intense pain of the war years and the troubled postwar period—together with the earlier conflicts of her childhood home—as parts of a larger life experience and to give this new understanding fictional form.

The Deepening Stream is the life current of Penelope (nicknamed "Matey") Gilbert. Matey grows up in college towns, where her father is a professor of French and her mother becomes involved in a variety of artistic projects. It seems to the community that she has "a perfectly lovely home, and she was a mighty lucky little girl to have such a fascinating father, such a wonderfully young-for-her-age mother—such wonderful parents both of them!—and such a perfectly wonderfully interesting family life!"[52] In reality a deep shadow hangs over her childhood in the relationship between her professor father and her talented mother, who compete bitterly for the limelight. Their superficial behavior is charming, but it conceals below-the-surface warfare, where every apparently harmless remark may contain a lethal weapon. In this environment Matey's brother Francis grows up morally weak and opportunistic, her sister Priscilla learns to hide her emotions with an impenetrable shell, and Matey is saved from permanent psychological deformity only by her honest mind and a number of chance experiences.

One of Matey's early memories is of a visit to her parents' old home in Rustdorf on the Hudson River in upstate New York. Dorothy's own familiarity with this area came from two winters (1926, 1927) she spent in

Poughkeepsie while her son Jimmy was a student at the Oakwood School there. Matey visits elderly Aunt Connie and is startled by the sudden appearance of bright-colored tulips growing out of unpromising materials: "What struck the small Matey was not so much that they were beautiful as that they were there at all so quickly! How had they ever done it? Dirt and stones and manure-stained straw lying at their feet. That was all they had to make themselves out of!"[53]

The tulips, which reappear later in the story, are a symbol for Matey herself. When two college students wrote to Dorothy to ask about this symbolism, she replied:

> The significance of the tulips is connected with the theme of growth and development which is of course the central idea of "The Deepening Stream." One of Matey's very first impressions you see was of the tulips suddenly being there in full beauty and glory, although only a short time ago there had been nothing but some clods of earth with strawy manure scattered over it. The theme is struck there: — of growth of beauty and strength out of very unpromising material. Matey's unhappy childhood and her arrested emotional development turn out in the end to have been the prelude to a full rich normal development.[54]

Other significant early experiences take place in France, where she stays with a musical family, the Vinets. There she is plunged into "a life of taut, driving activity, compared to which Matey's existence till then seemed like a sprawling dawdling vacation."[55] Matey gains a new idea of what it means to be grown up: "not only work and earning their living, but new vivid interests and pleasures that children knew nothing of, compared to which hide-and-seek were as silly as playing with a baby's rattle or rubber dog."[56] The place of the French adults in the growth process is in helping the children up to where they can take part in adult pleasures, and their comments to the children are "like outstretched hands of strong climbers to those below them on the path, as if they called, 'Come along up where the view is better.' "[57]

Matey stays with the Vinets whenever her father's studies call him to France. Finally, after a year at the Sorbonne, she returns to America and takes "a position in the French department at Western Reserve University."[57] This is the very position which Dorothy herself had reluctantly turned down twenty-five years before writing Matey's story.

Part 1 of *The Deepening Stream* ends on another autobiographical note, when Matey's father dies and she suddenly sees that there was a closer bond between her father and mother than she had ever realized, that their apparent strife had covered "a belonging together that outlived all else."[59] Dorothy's growing years had been troubled by the conflict of temperament between her parents. Among her unpublished papers, however, is this poem written by her mother after her father's death:

Widowed

I cannot put in words the aching of my heart,
God only knows my loneliness, my woe.
Yet still there's comfort in my nightly dreams,
The waking hope, my soul will soon meet his.[60]

Part 2 opens in a new place and with a new phase of Matey's life. She comes to Rustdorf to collect an inheritance inexplicably left her by Aunt Connie. Here she discovers for the first time what it is to have "family," for almost everyone in the sleepy old Dutch community is related. They all knew her parents, and they know all about her.

In Rustdorf Matey meets and eventually marries in 1907 (the year of Dorothy's marriage) Adrian Fort, a young man recently returned from studying art in Paris. Adrian's decision to return to work with his father in the little local bank has been a difficult one, based as it is on the realization that he lacks sufficient talent to be a great artist and that he can be more useful in the limited sphere of the family bank at home. The Forts are Quakers (as were the Fishers), and Adrian's widowed father is a loving portrait of Dorothy's own father-in-law. Dr. Fisher died in 1926, and on the following Easter Sunday Dorothy wrote to Alfred Harcourt, "I'll miss Dr. Fisher more than I can say. He has been a father to me, as tenderly, as wisely as it is possible to conceive, ever since I lost my own father. Few people have had two such fathers! I ought to be content with a memory which will always stand in the way of any mean conception of human beings."[61]

Two children are born to Matey and Adrian, a girl and a boy, born in 1909 and 1913 (the same years as Dorothy's own daughter and son). The children are still very young when news comes of the German invasion of France. Matey and Adrian both have close friends in France and feel a neighborly need to help in the emergency. Because of his Quaker pacifism, Adrian does not volunteer for military service but enlists in the Ambulance Corps (as John Fisher did). Matey sails with Adrian (as Dorothy wanted to) to help out in France in any way she can (as Dorothy did).

Part 3 shows Matey's personal and social maturation against the background of the war. The big question for Matey and Adrian (as it was for Dorothy and John Fisher) is what to do about the children. The fictional characters (like the real ones) face "the crowd of protesting prudent people who had ordinary good sense."[62] Matey and Adrian have, however, an unexpected ally in Adrian's father. When Matey's sister Priscilla objects to their taking the children with them, he answers, "Perhaps when they grow up, to know that they did not stand in the way of a generous-hearted action of their parents' but shared it will be no disadvantage."[63]

Only a small part of Dorothy's own war experience finds its way into this book, for Matey remains throughout the war with Mme. Vinet and shares with her the life of a typical French family in wartime. It is an effective literary device, however, to focus the effect of the war on a small group of people the reader has come to know in peacetime as childhood companions of the heroine, and one that makes the war experience more credible and powerful.

Part 4 takes place after the end of the war, as the persons of the story try to find their way back into peacetime living. The war-torn fragments of the French family struggle to piece together a life fabric again, and the Forts return to America. The war has disturbed the very roots of Adrian's existence, and he can hardly reconcile himself to a world that was able to make war. His father says of him, "Adrian thinks the war is an indictment of the universe. Instead of a mistake men make."[64]

Matey's French experiences have had a quite different effect on her. The dependence of others on her has uncovered hidden depths of character and strength. She is able to find in the bewildering and discouraging multitude of experiences a "certainty of wholeness,"[65] a joyful affirmation of life. When she first came to Rustdorf she needed the support of Adrian's personality. Now their relationship has changed. "It's the other way around with us from the way it used to be," she says. "I seem to have more capacity now for joy than he."[66] Matey decides to work in the bank with Adrian because "if we share life wholly, if we work together, why, whatever's in my life will be in his."[67] Again the novel strikes an autobiographical note, for Dorothy's prewar letters are full of anguished cries of her need for and dependence on John, and in the postwar period it was his need of her that kept them together through a troubled time.[68]

The unity of the long novel lies in its probing of the experiences underlying the development of maturity. The tulips in their full magnificence against the dirt and decay of their origin are Matey in her maturity, strong and beautiful in character against the unharmonious home and the terrible war in which she has developed her full personality. It is necessary to understand each of the vital human elements that she has drawn from her various surroundings, just as a plant draws essential chemical elements from the decaying animal and vegetable matter at its roots, in order to comprehend her development. Along the way are significant milestones, where the reader might think that the story is finished, but these only mark stages of growth. So the tragic understanding of her parents' relationship that signals the end of her childhood, or the achievement of a deep, personal, love relationship with Adrian, might be endings for the novel, if the goal of her life had been finding understanding or love. However, because the goal is the achievement of full maturity, these are not enough, and she must drink the cup of war suffering to its dregs. Then her statement of "capacity for joy" rests on a solid foundation, and the reader can believe that she can never be shaken from it.

As Dorothy worked on this novel, she worried about its length. In August 1927 she wrote to Alfred Harcourt that she was "working on the novel, deep in Dutchess County background now, and liking that part of it very much. As usual I've got millions too much to get in any one book. And it's heaving and boiling pretty fast and hard."[69] Later she wrote again:

> This novel I'm working on comes bailing out of my mind in alarming abundance. It must be, in the nature of things, long, because it takes in pretty nearly a whole life — and one part of it with the Great War as a "background." But how long *can* it be, without losing its readers just by its weight? How long are other full-length novels you're publishing now? How long do you think it's safe? I ask this because I think I'm getting a nervous misery over its length — hate to see the end of a page coming, — lose some of the necessary heat and vitality in considering and worrying about this. . . . I want it in three dimensions, roomy, with air enough for all the many people in it to breathe. What's about the limit: — How long was Arrowsmith? Do send me some reassurance. I've got the fidgits.[70]

As the novel neared completion Dorothy wrote again, this time exultantly: "Say — first thing you know you're going to have the manuscript of this new novel to read! It's getting itself finished! And so am I! But we'll probably come out together the book and I."[71] A subsequent comment shows how much the book meant to its author: "When I send it to you, don't you dare try to read it thru in your office with interruptions, and telephone calls. I've given a plumb year of heart's blood to it. You take it home and read it some evening when you can settle down to it!"[72]

After his first reading of the manuscript Alfred wrote to Dorothy, "It is all very powerful and moving. Of course, I can't read it as an outsider who doesn't know what a slice of your own life and your family life has gone into it, but I do know that I have had a profound and moving experience."[73] When the final manuscript came in the following year, another note from her publisher reaffirmed his earlier enthusiasm: "I've spent an hour over it before letting it go toward manufacture,and I'm all stirred and glowing from it again. What a moving rich book it is! I am *very* proud to be printing it for you."[74]

The reviewers of *The Deepening Stream* report almost unanimously that it is a very different book from most of those which are crossing their desks. It is different in its treatment of the war, in its portrayal of human relations, and in the style of its presentation. There may be a touch of bad conscience in their comments that less idealistic views of the war—for example, those of Matey's brother Francis—do not receive fair treatment. Critics are suspicious of "whitewashing" in the portrayal of a "good" marriage in an era of cynicism. The broadly epic style that creates life in all its manifold details is out of keeping with the almost telegraphic narrative style in vogue at the time. Yet, on the whole, reviewers lauded the book, and it was among the best-selling fiction books of its time.

After the publication of *The Deepening Stream,* Dorothy wrote to Alfred Harcourt, "My mail, you may be interested to know, is just full of letters from readers—more than I ever had. It's a snow-ball affair, I imagine, as many of them write as though they were old friends of mine, through other books. Lots from the West, this time, overbalancing the usual slew from New England. Massachusetts has always been a special home to readers of mine, and while I appreciate that, I like to get them from Idaho and the Dakotas."[75]

Dorothy's fears about the length of her book found a reassuring answer in a long letter from Harry Scherman. She had sent him the completed manuscript for criticism and suggestions before submitting it to the publisher. Harry wrote of "the immense and continuous enjoyment the book gave me" and went on to say that he didn't "see how anyone can think the book too long. For me there's not a word too much in it. In fact, I wanted to know more, and still more, about Matey, and Adrian, and their children, and the Vinets, and all the rest of your people."[76] Then, in justifying this feeling, he first observes that this is a different kind of book from the closely structured shorter narrative.

> After all, this is not the type of book—do you think?—that should be hammered away at and finished off like an *objet d'art.* It has its own form, of course, but the pleasure one gets from it, its special value, is so much richer than what one gets from the contemplation of something fashioned and cut and polished—which is always a joy, of course, but such a minor one, after all, compared with that so much finer thing in books—true, authentic human experience.[77]

In a comment that seems an echo of Dorothy's student thesis on Émile

Augier, Harry Scherman went on to elaborate on this view, saying:

> That is what, primarily, your book is to me—it carries a cargo of true human experience, such honest experience, and such shrewd meditation upon it—altogether a type of book requiring an entirely different form from a strictly objective bit of fiction. And so, I don't see how you can possibly cut it, without maiming it, nor why in the world you should. In fact, thinking over this point, — for this type of novel, covering as it does a good part of a lifetime, it seems to me you've done a simply remarkable job of condensation and selection, as it is.[78]

Harry Scherman spoke for many of Dorothy's readers when he reported that her novel restores a sense of the possibilities of fiction that he had lost in reading other contemporary writers. "It isn't so that we read books for an escape, to get vicarious experience," he says.

> Not the best kind of reading. We read really only to find out about people, out of a perfectly valid curiosity, because we are all so inarticulate and we all hide ourselves so much from others. So we read, really, hoping to learn something about new people whom we cannot hope to meet personally, and new *things* about the kind of people we do know. And I realize now that I was aware all through your book, most pleasantly aware, that this *was* a deepening stream, not only for Matey, but for me—and it is bound to be for every reader—that it was authentic, true and (to me) *new* experience. I hardly need to tell you, of all persons, how rare that is to find in a book nowadays. Will you believe this—I had come to feel that fiction was, after all, a rather pallid and not the most worth-while form of writing. But now again I am convinced, as I used to feel, that it is (as Broun once said and probably many others) the most searching of all truth, after all.[79]

9

The Brimming Cup and *Rough-Hewn*

When Dorothy came back home from France in 1919, she was exhausted. A year before her return she had written to Paul Reynolds of her "thorough war-weariness to the saturation point" and had exclaimed, "I often wonder if I shall *ever* write a novel again!"[1]

In February 1920, however, she wrote to Blanche Sibut, Céline's sister,

I have a piece of news for you, a piece of real author's news. I am really thinking of beginning on another novel! You know I felt so horribly tired and morally depressed when I came back from France that I thought I never would be able to do any creative fiction-writing again, and for all these months I have done nothing but some articles on education and such general topics. But I begin to feel much better and stronger, physically, I have gained much weight (I weigh a hundred and three pounds now!) and I have been much solicited by editors for another novel. And I really think I will begin on it soon . . . this means months and months and months of the most arduous work for me, and ups and downs of hopes and doubts (such as I dread to look forward to!) and such slow painful labor of converting a conception into reality. I dread it, but I look forward to it with interest, such as I had thought I would not feel again . . . and this is good news, which I send to you and Céline because I know you will be interested in it, and feel some sympathy with me in the mingled feeling of apprehension and anticipation with which I face it.[2]

Dorothy found it difficult to take a practical attitude toward her novel writing. She had told Sarah Cleghorn in 1917, "Alfred Harcourt always laughs at my naive surprise that books bring in money. It always *really* seems to me that we authors ought to pay for the privilege of being allowed to express our thoughts as we choose, instead of being paid for doing what we enjoy more than anything else!"[3]

When Paul Reynolds wanted to obtain a contract for serial publication of Dorothy's next novel even before it was written, and so asked for a summary to show to editors, her first reaction was negative. After considering his suggestion further, however, she wrote:

> I have thought a great deal about what you say of trying to sell that novel before it is written, and . . . quite to my own surprise, I have come to agree entirely with you, and will try to make it possible for you to have something to offer. . . . I will try to write you out an outline, or summary of the story, which will be more in the nature of a description of the different people in it, than an outline of action. It has come to be more and more vivid in my mind, and I begin to have the excited feeling which comes when you are really on the point of starting in on a big piece of work, as you walk out towards the end of the spring-board and feel it begin to teeter under your feet, and know that the water is very deep — for the water I want to get into is deep all right. . . . And such is my sceptical pessimistic view of editors, I own that I'll have the most agreeable surprise of my life, if you actually do get some editor to take it for a big price. It'll make a lot of difference to this family if you do — and I have come to feel the story so strong in my head that I don't believe the knowledge that it has been bought before-hand and that I've *got* to write it, will make a bit of difference to me, unsettle me in the least, once I get started on it.[4]

As she thinks about starting on the novel, Dorothy remarks on the inevitable and not so necessary interruptions in her work, which she can expect, saying, "Jimmy is having chicken-pox just now — there are bound to be a few interruptions like that, but I'm going to stop this foolish going-around-and-speaking, and being lunched and dined. It takes a lot of time and doesn't amount to a row of pins in one's work!"[5]

Dorothy looked forward to this new novel with a great deal more pleasure than she looked back on her very successful prewar books, and she said to Paul Reynolds, "I don't think I have told you that I *think* the next novel is going to be good — but what *I* think is good and what editors think, aren't always the same. I *think* it is going to be very human. I think I'm going to like it — but I'm not sure, of course. I never did like The Squirrel-Cage very much, and there are parts of The Bent Twig that make me sick to look at!"[6]

Reynolds thought that if Dorothy came to New York and had a personal interview with an editor, that might help the serial sale of her unwritten book, but Dorothy wrote back:

> As for personal impression, do you honestly think that seeing so very small and insignificant a person as me, would give an editor any higher idea of a possible novel! My notion is that it would *not*, for I observe whenever I go to make an address, the ladies of the reception committee

always have a moment of extreme surprise and disconcerted silence when I appear, and hardly ever fail to exclaim, "Oh, we thought we would see a much *larger* person!"[7]

In spite of Dorothy's skepticism, however, Reynolds did sell the book before she had started writing it. She was immensely surprised and wrote, "Your letter of the 6th is here with its remarkably good news of the sale for such a big price of that story before ever a word of it is written. I didn't think you could pull it off. And I take off my hat to you. Now I shudder and shiver in my boots at the idea that I've got to write it!"[8]

The serial version was to be somewhat shorter than the book, and Dorothy worried about the cutting that an editor might make. "If I can possibly help it," she wrote,

> I don't want Miss Beatty or anybody else to cut it. I hate other people's cuts. If she wants sixty-thousand words, I'll try to give her a version that has sixty-thousand words in it, and save the rest for book publication. This may complicate the writing of it, but I'm going to try. I haven't yet forgiven the way The Squirrel-Cage was cut for serial publication. Miss Beatty told me hopefully that she had just cut a story *one* third down, and that the author on seeing the proofs had said *she couldn't see where the cuts had been made,* and thought the story much improved. That sounded almost incredible to me, who notice when a word has been cut out, as though an exclamation point had been set into the paragraph, and I registered a vow then and there to try to manage to do my own cutting.[9]

By April 24, Dorothy could report that she had "about thirty-thousand words written, and every character introduced, except one."[10] She admitted, however, that her work had been interrupted by a major planting project. "I'm in the wild midst of spring planting just now, which is further complicated by just having made a trip to Ohio to make an address. We are planting five thousand baby pines, which must be got into the ground at once, or spoil."[11] She hesitates to let the editors, who are waiting for her work, know

> that this causes a temporary stoppage of literary labors—put it on "temperament," rather, which sounds more interesting and literary. But it is good for me, literarily too, to stop and work hard out-of-doors all day, because the novel was devouring me alive, and would make a nervous wreck of me if I kept up at that clip, steadily. And I never yet saw any *good* work, done under nervous strain. However, don't worry. Planting or no planting, it's still very much with me, the novel is, and I haven't the least doubt of being able to get it done pretty promptly. It's all "there."[12]

In August John wrote to Alfred Harcourt:

Our news is that we have managed to have a pretty tranquil summer and the draft of the novel is almost finished — one chapter to write and several to revise. It's been a big job ably carried through. By far the most important thing Dorothy has yet done. Of course when we get the serial off our minds, there will still be a lot of work to be done before the book is ready for you. I don't think anything material in the working out needs to be changed but there are any number of minor things: conversation to be vitalized, repetitions cut, all the sort of thing that a reader never guesses but which do add tremendously to the final effect."[13]

On November 10, Dorothy wrote to Alfred, "I'm just about done with The Brimming Cup, and John is just about starting in to type it."[14] A domestic footnote is added by another letter, a week later, which admits that John is working on house building and can type only nights, and Dorothy is typing the manuscript herself, "thus it doesn't go fast as it would if John could give all day to it."[15] The same letter ends with Dorothy's exasperated exclamation, "I must get back to that infernal typing, cuss it!"[16]

The Brimming Cup is the story of an American marriage, but primarily the wife's story. Marise, the sensitive, musical heroine, has grown up in France, where she has learned that "people who are clever and have their eyes wide open, people who really count . . . don't believe in humans, or goodness, or anything that's not base. They know life is mostly bad and cruel and dull and low, and above all that it's bound to fool you if you trust to it, or get off your guard a single minute."[17]

The second main character, Neale Crittendon, is a rather typical young American, a graduate of Columbia College, who is traveling about the world aimlessly seeking adventure, when he and Marise meet in Rome. He has just received word that his uncle has left him a lumber mill in a little town in the Vermont hills, coincidentally the same town where Marise has spent an occasional summer with her father's relatives. Marise finds in Neale's solid integrity a strength on which she can depend, and they return to America to make their home together in Vermont.

All this background material is related in a "Prelude," and the real story begins after Marise and Neale have been married for many years. Their youngest child is just setting out for his first day in school, and Marise is left to an empty house and the prospect of an empty life. Marise is a talented, sensitive woman in a dull, unstimulating environment, a New England counterpart to Gustave Flaubert's Madame Bovary or to the heroine of Sinclair Lewis's *Main Street*. For Marise, as for her literary sisters, temptation appears in her quiet surroundings in the form of an exciting, sophisticated, wealthy man, who tells her that she is much too alive and interesting to be buried in a small town and urges her to return with him to the excitement of the city. The answer she gives, however, sets her apart.

Marise is tempted by the opportunities for music and sophisticated living, but she decides to remain in her limited world. The reasons for this decision lie on two levels. The first is her realistic acceptance of life processes, including the process of aging, that will not let her delude herself into substituting the pleasures of youth for the rewards of middle age, when she is no longer young. The second reason lies in her use of sensitive powers of perception to share the real drama beneath the drab exterior of her neighbors' lives, and in the employment of her own talents to enrich their existence. She finds in the maturation of her own personality and in its extension into the small town the personal fulfillment that other restless, talented heroines of literature have sought outside themselves in the stimulations of new emotional attachments and livelier environments.

The technique of narration in *The Brimming Cup* is one in which the viewpoint constantly shifts, for the same set of people and circumstances are viewed through the eyes of one after another of the group of characters. We see the limited world of the Vermont hill town and its environs through the eyes of the heroine, through those of visitors from the outside world, through the eight-year-old daughter's view, and through Neale's. The diversely focused and largely introspective chapters are interspersed with chapters that bring together the different points of view and further the plot. This technique contributes to a comprehension of the situation as a whole, rather than limiting it to Marise's viewpoint. There is a tremendous wealth of environmental detail, and the balance between environment and personality is frequently a closely matched struggle. The final victory of the human spirit is not easily won, and it is a pretty grim victory. It involves at least as large a portion of resignation as of acceptance and offers as its final reward not the invitation to live "happily ever after" but to face whatever life may bring without fear. Marise's active and productive existence is a long step forward from Aunt Nancy's grim and unproductive stoicism in *Gunhild*, but there are underlying echoes of the older woman's self-abnegation even in Marise's positive affirmation of her life.

Marise's final acceptance of her life niche is precipitated by the death of Aunt Hetty, the ancient relative with whom she spent summers as a little girl. Aunt Hetty is modeled on Dorothy's own Aunt Mattie, her father's only sister, who died in December 1919, as Dorothy was planning the novel. In Aunt Hetty Dorothy created a fictional memorial to her own aunt, of whom she once wrote, "Useful, busy, untroubled, zestful, cheerful, she trotted indefatigably with that quick short step of hers, familiar to generations of Arlingtonians, from library to home, from home to Church, from Church to library, till death came for her, with a kind, merciful suddenness and total unexpectedness."[18]

There are two peripheral women characters in the novel whose presence serves to emphasize by contrast the personality of the heroine. Eugenia, the childhood friend who has become a self-centered fashionable woman, is a literary descendant of Aunt Victoria of *The Bent Twig*. She lives as far removed as possible from every contact with earthy reality, spending many hours trying to preserve her youth by artificial methods, an activity treated by the author with lively satire. Nelly Powers illustrates the opposite extreme. She is a very pretty woman who is completely satisfied in her domestic sphere, and who can think contentedly, "There wasn't anything that was better than giving people or animals what they liked to eat."[19] The end of Eugenia's life in emptiness and frustration, and of Nelly's in tragedy, is the author's fictional condemnation of their one-sided lives.

Marise is unlike the other literary women who are stifled by a prosaic husband and limited surroundings. Her problems lie primarily within her own nature, where she must reconcile the two inner selves that correspond to Eugenia and Nelly Powers. It is in the harmonizing of these two disparate parts of her personality that she achieves maturity and strength to direct the course of her life independently of those forces which would tempt her to deny one or the other aspect of her basic nature.

The Brimming Cup was hailed at its appearance in 1921 as an answer to Sinclair Lewis's more pessimistic treatment of the same theme in *Main Street,* which had appeared in 1920. This was evidently not the intention of Dorothy Canfield, for the first mention of *Main Street* in her correspondence comes in a letter to Alfred Harcourt just after she had finished writing *The Brimming Cup* in November 1920. It is clear that she has only just read Sinclair Lewis's book, and she comments:

Then I'll also tell you what I think about Sinclair Lewis's Main Street, which I read with the liveliest sympathy and interest and admiration, and certainty that Mr. Lewis takes a rather superficial view of human problems, but knows how to write a mighty good novel. The character of the husband, the country doctor, is I think by far the best thing in the book, absolutely "done," and finished and perfect, without a marring stroke in it, anywhere, an achievement that any writer in any age might be proud of and mighty few could have done. . . . You can imagine how violently I protest from much of his thesis, and how naive I find his idea that a geographical change could achieve anything — coelum non animam for ever, say I! Horace knew what he was talking about, as did old Pestalozzi when he insisted that "help comes from the bosom alone."[20]

The conviction that change must take place within the individual, that a change in outside circumstances does not make the real difference in human life, is perhaps the facet of Dorothy Canfield's work that distinguishes it most sharply from that of her contemporaries, and particularly from the comparable and contrasting *Main Street*. In her rejection of environment as the decisive determinant in human life, Dorothy shows herself alien to the contemporary school of naturalism and closer to the spirit of an earlier age.

William Lyon Phelps, writing in the *Literary Review* of March 19, 1921, observed, "Seldom have I read a novel written with such fierce conviction," and further, "The point of view is the opposite of that taken in 'Main Street' or in 'Madame Bovary.' There is not the faintest trace of irony or scorn. . . . The village is your novelist's laboratory."[21]

The laboratory approach to literature, significantly developed by the French author Émile Zola, gives the writer a chance to put hypothetical personalities in an experimental social environment to explore their reactions. The components of Dorothy's experiment are the European-ized, intelligent, sensitive, musical Marise immersed in the domestic tasks of the American family in an isolated Vermont village. A new and active element is introduced in the appearance of a sophisticated, urbane visitor, and the bond between Marise and her family is threatened. However, although the attraction to a new combination is strong, the older, deeper connections hold, and it is the new element that is thrown off and discarded.

William Allen White, in a review entitled "The Other Side of Main Street," observed that Dorothy had found "truth" in contrast to Sinclair Lewis's superficial "facts." He wrote: "Mr. Lewis seems to be dealing with facts; but he has only the facts about the east side of 'Main Street.' . . . So far as his facts go, they are irrefutable arguments for his thesis that the American country town, and the American city for that matter, are not worth while. But his facts fall short of the truth. Dorothy Canfield in 'The Brimming Cup' aims at the truth. She considers both sides of the street."[22] The review states further that "it is a question of whether one sees externals or internals in the facts or the truth."[23] Mr. White saw the two books arguing the case for the "old" way of life, as it can be found in isolated small towns, as opposed to the more sophisticated urban "new." In his analysis he defined the elements of the stories thus:

The husband of the lady in each novel — and these are good novels — incarnates and somewhat impersonates the country town. The heroine in each novel is more than a woman; she is the spirit of challenge. And the differences between "Main Street" and "The Brimming Cup" are the profound oppositions between the old and the new in American life and letters. "Main Street" presents admirably and with scientific consistency the case for the new; "The Brimming Cup" defends the old. The American country town stands in each book only as a symbol in two contending philosophies.[24]

That the American reading public shared the enthusiasm and interest of these erudite reviewers is shown by Alfred Harcourt's personal reminiscences of this time. In *Some Experiences,* published in 1951, he recalled that *Main Street* and *The Brimming Cup,* both published by his firm, "were number one and two on the best seller lists for months."[25]

Before *The Brimming Cup* was published in 1921, Dorothy was at work on another novel. Her first thought about the new work was that it should be something light and cheerful. To Paul Reynolds she wrote:

I *want* to write another novel when I can catch my breath from this, entirely different from this (I always want to do something entirely different from the last one!) something where folks don't take life with such fearful seriousness as in this last one, where there can be more fun and irony and liveliness. But I haven't it planned yet, and indeed the only subject that keeps sticking to me, is a terribly tragic one—such is the contrariness of the author's mind![26]

By October 1920 the novel was beginning to take shape, and she could outline her plans for it. "I am writing now to try tentatively on you," she wrote to Paul Reynolds,

an idea which has been slowly revolving in my head since I got the first draft of this novel done. I won't try today to make a real outline of it, but only set hastily down about what it would be, to see what you think of the possibilities of it.

It would be the opposite-of-a-sequel to this story (I don't know any other name to call it) that is, it would be the story of Marise's life and Neale's in their youth before they met each other, then their meeting, and betrothal. The end would be the same as the beginning of this, literally the same, the very same chapter.

The main idea would be a more "romantic" one than I usually treat, and it would be a sort of happy-ending story, in that you would see from the beginning two children growing up on opposite sides of the globe who needed each other to complete themselves, but who had not the slightest possible chance, in all ordinary probability, of ever ever laying eyes on each other's faces.

I don't know that this has been done before, the tracing out of the tiny incalculable causes which led, years and years before, to a decision which led to another, which led to another, all leading apparently to the meeting with the person who is the real mate. Marise's childhood is passed a good deal of it (you may happen to remember) in the old walled city of Bayonne in southern France, which I know very well, and which is picturesque and "different" with its part Basque color, to the last degree. Marise's father is an ordinary business man translated to France as the agent of an American machine, a typewriter, or reaper. Her mother would be a very interesting type to me, the sort of last-generation American woman, like Mrs. Wharton, who (so it seems to me) takes Europeans with a funny, prayerful certainty of their innate superiority. This American woman would consider that it was the opportunity of her life to become "cultured" and would do her pathetic, silly best to be like what she considers European women to be, even to the extent of trying to have a liaison with a young Frenchman, whom she drives to suicide, in the bay of Guethary. This is a real episode (this last) which I knew about, there, and it is the tragic story which I wrote you some months ago was continually haunting me. I think it is in its proper place now, as a part of a larger story.

The story of Neale is all in America of course, and I think could be extremely interesting, a young American of the very best sort, who doesn't know what path to take in the dark wood of this our life, and finds it with total unexpectedness in Rome, when he meets Marise and hears of the bequest of his old uncle to him of the small wood-working industry in Vermont.[27]

In a move very unusual for her works of fiction, Dorothy gave John part of the book to write, telling Paul Reynolds, "Mr. Fisher is going to take a certain number of the chapters of the man's life, especially the football and college."[28] John said later of this contribution, "My part in the work was to dig up from school and college memories a number of life-like incidents in keeping with Neale's character as we conceived it."[29]

Neale's life is closely tied to the earth and to material things. He grows up among the influences of fiercely competitive street play, which gives way to football in his college years and then to success in the competitive world of business. The shock of a broken engagement finally shows him the importance of nonmaterial matters and makes him question all the values he had previously held in highest esteem. His willingness to face reality, even when unpleasant, carries him through the crisis, but he sets out alone on world travels that are in essence a search for his own identity and for meaning in his life.

Marise grows up in almost complete isolation from her own age group, her sensitive nature fostered and fulfilled by immersion in the most immaterial of the arts, music. Her contacts with practical life and with earthly reality disgust rather than attract her, as she sees them through the eyes of the family servants in France. She learns to hide any expression of what she really feels, and she is determined not to be "taken in" by life.

Fortuitous circumstances bring Marise and Neale simultaneously to Rome, where each finds in the other the aspect of life that was previously lacking. In a decision reminiscent of the author's own, they return to Ashley, Vermont, to live. Neale is to run the factory he has inherited from his great-uncle there, and Marise will be near Aunt Hetty, whom she visited as a child.

As she started work on *Rough-Hewn,* Dorothy wrote to Alfred Harcourt:

> What I want to do is to make, by means of the European frame, the American scene visible to eyes that look right through it as a rule. . . .
> It's going to take more hard work than any thing I ever did, because of this Chinese-puzzle question of equilibrium and balance and construction. I don't want Neale's life too closely, in detail to counterbalance Marise's — the counter-balance must be spiritual, and not material — and yet apparent to all but a stupid reader's mind.[30]

While, in detail, Dorothy did not want Neale's and Marise's lives to exhibit an exact balance, in structure the book presents a precise situation of balanced construction. There are seven sections in the novel. The first, third, and fifth tell Neale's story; the second, fourth, and sixth follow the development of Marise. In the seventh the threads of their lives are brought together and joined. The idea of predestination is contained in a quotation on the title page, "There's a divinity that shapes our ends . . . ," and this plan, required by the purpose of the novel, is carried out in its structural development.

Rough-Hewn was written to explain *The Brimming Cup.* In *Rough-Hewn* the author shares with her readers her own mental image of the main characters of *The Brimming Cup* and the invisible background elements of their actions, which are only hinted at in the novel of their adult years.

The problem around which the plot thread is wound is the difference between "European" (here "French") and "American." It is the same problem that Dorothy treated in *Gunhild* and in a number of her short stories. For her, "European" meant a society that places great emphasis on social distinctions, telling "necessary" lies to please others or protect oneself, and preserving deliberately a clear distinction between the superficial image one presents to the outside world and the real person one keeps safe within a protective shell. "American" in the guise of Neale is midwestern America, for although Dorothy places him in Hoboken, New Jersey, and West Adams, Massachusetts, temperamentally Neale is the vigorous, productive, direct, and openly ambitious product of the American Midwest. He has neither the sharpness of the New York businessman nor the dry taciturnity of the New Englander. He is bluff and direct in all his dealings with problems and people, and large in body and spirit. To his college acquaintance Livingstone, an American who has become a professional European, he seems "rough" and "hard." To Marise the harmony between his surface actions and his inner personality is incredible and like a breath of cleansing wind that blows away the evil cobwebs of her troubled childhood.

In earlier narratives Dorothy had taken for granted that these differences between European and American culture were familiar to her readers, and she had referred to them in unconscious assumption that the terms "European" and "American" would call to other minds the same images that they did to hers. In this book she explains the bases on which the differences rest, the life experiences that produce the contrasting outlooks on life. From the standpoint of plot development, of suspense and holding quality, *Rough-Hewn* is the weakest of Dorothy's novels. She herself called it "a plotless book."[32] As a study of contrast between Old World and New World cultural patterns and of the strengths and weaknesses of each, there is in the book much that is thought-provoking and fine.

10
The Feminist Novels:
The Home-Maker and *Her Son's Wife*

Dorothy Canfield always insisted that she was not a feminist. "I was never a feminist," she wrote. "It was my older generation, my father and mother who were. I was rather (as it often goes in generations) in reaction from their extreme zeal for 'women's rights.' "[1] She was honoring her father's views, she said, when she accepted an invitation to a dinner in her honor in 1922:

> The Author's Club of New York is giving a dinner for me on the twenty-third . . . I accepted this invitation only because Father belonged to that club for a long time and was always very unhappy (you know that he was very much of a "feminist") that they did not recognize women writers. This is the very first time they have offered a dinner for a woman writer and they are going to continue to do so from now on, so they say. How many doors are opening up everywhere for women! But it is all the same to me whether the door is opened or remains closed! What is the use of all those dinners "in honor of someone!" All that is important is to do one's work well, and dinners don't help you in that — on the contrary![2]

Although Dorothy was not a militant, crusading advocate of women's rights, it is clear from her writings and her life that she saw no reason why women should be spared the responsibilities and rewards of meaningful work and active citizenship. Her next novel, *The Home-Maker* (1924), is a thoughtful exploration of the conflict between the needs of the individual and the straitjacket standards of society. She had touched on this theme in earlier works. Daniel Rankin's "radical" statements in *The Squirrel-Cage* bring up the problem. Molly in *The Bent Twig* illustrates the tragedy possible when a solution is not found. Yet, although these earlier works indicate the hazards of the useless woman, neither suggests a positive solution. In *The Home-Maker* Dorothy struggles with the problem, faces realistically the demands of the social environment and the needs of different temperaments, and comes up with a solution, one that was, however, not wholly satisfactory to many of her readers.

The book is divided into four parts. In Part One the reader is introduced to the Knapp family: Evangeline, Lester, and their three children, Helen, Henry, and Stephen. Evangeline is a compulsive housekeeper, first seen angrily scrubbing a line of grease spots from her kitchen floor. She is a woman created to deal with big problems and confined to the world of petty troubles. Her husband is a failure in the business world, and so they must live in the poorer part of town. Her two older children are sickly, with nervous ailments and delicate lungs and stomach; but the youngest, Stevie, is a rebel, defying his mother with all the force of his infant naughtiness.

Evangeline Knapp is determined never to complain about her husband and always to be "a good mother." She creates a home in which tension is the most ever-present emotion, and where fear of her displeasure fills the hearts of those closest to her. She hates every moment of her housekeeping, but she drives at it because she sees it as her duty. Her real talents are shown to the reader as she deals competently with one problem after another in a meeting of the church guild, but neither she nor anyone else there questions her decision not to head up a fund drive, when she says, "I'd *love* to! . . . But I mustn't think of it. . . . My first duty is to my home and children."[3]

The pattern of life in the Knapp household is sharply changed when Lester Knapp falls from a neighbor's roof and breaks his back. The "fall" is not wholly an accident; Lester is on his way home after losing his job, when a fire on the icy roof of the neighbor's house gives him the opportunity to escape the necessity of facing his failure and Eva's reaction to it.

Part Two shows the business world through the eyes of an enterprising young businessman, Jerome Willing, who has just taken over the Emporium with great plans for that store's future. One of his unpleasant initial duties has been the firing of incompetent employees, in particular Lester Knapp. When Evangeline Knapp comes into his office to apply for a job, Jerome is pleasantly surprised by the business sense she displays. He employs her first in the stockroom, but by rapid stages she advances to sales and then to supervisory positions. She is absorbed in her new work and happy—so happy and absorbed that details of life at home entirely escape her notice.

The new arrangements at home make up the third part of the book. Lester is now able to sit up in a wheelchair and to do anything except walk because he is paralyzed only from the waist down. With the children he works out a variety of ingenious dodges for keeping the house neat, such as spreading the kitchen floor with newspapers during the day, a covering that they take up just before Eva returns home. Together Lester and his daughter Helen learn to cook from the cookbook, to the great delight of both. He always has time now to play with the children and to share with them the stories and poetry with which his mind is filled. He has time to think, too, about just what each of the children needs for happy and healthy growth, emotional as well as physical, and this interest gives him the will to live and the sense of being of some worth in the world. The children thrive like plants in the sunshine under his sympathetic care. Even Stevie's rebelliousness melts in the warmth of the new understanding and affection that surround him. Helen blossoms into robust health, and Henry's delicacy of appetite and digestion disappear.

Part Four begins with Evangeline's promotion at the Emporium. Her salary will now be twice what Lester was receiving only a short time before. She thinks happily of the luxuries she will be able to provide for the children and for Lester, college for the children, perhaps a new Ford for the family so that they can all go to the country for picnics together. Everything is going splendidly at home, and everyone is happy.

Gradually, a dark cloud appears on the horizon and spreads over the family as, one after another, the main characters come to the realization that Lester might get well again. Nothing stands in the way of his recovery now except psychological factors, the doctor assures an old aunt of the family.

The realization that Lester is cured strikes Evangeline as she looks lovingly down on her sleeping husband and sees him move one of his "paralyzed" limbs in his sleep. The implications of what she sees stir her to panic.

Like a person shut up suddenly in an airless prison, she ran frantically from one locked door to another, beating her hands on them, finding them sullenly strong, not even shaken on their cruel steel hinges as she flung herself against them. If Lester got well, of course he could not stay at home and keep house and take care of the children — no able-bodied man ever did that. What would people say? It was out of the question. People would laugh at Lester. They would laugh at her. They would not admire her any more. What would people say if she did not go back at once to the children? She who had always been so devoted to them, she whom people pitied now because she was forced to be separated from them. Every one had heard her say how hard it was for a mother to be separated from her . . .

For one instant, an instant she never forgot, Evangeline knew for the first, the only time in her life, a gust of cold, deadly contempt for herself. It nearly killed her, she who had tried so hard all her life to keep her self-respect, she who had been willing to pay any price so that in her own eyes she might be always in the right.[4]

Horrified, she finds herself praying that her husband will not get well! Lester's realization of his cure is even more traumatic that Eva's. A curtain catches on fire from the flame of a candle near Stevie's bed. Lester springs from his bed to seize the curtain and extinguish it before it falls on the face of the sleeping child. He finds himself standing in the middle of the floor in a state of exalted shock:

> As actually as he had seen and felt the burst of flame from the curtain, he now felt himself flare up in physical ecstasy to be standing on his own feet, to know that he had taken a dozen steps, to know that he was no longer a half-man, a mutilated wreck from whom normal people averted their eyes in what they called pity but what was really contempt and disgust.
>
> He was like a man who has been shut in a cage too long for him to stand, who has crouched and stooped and bowed his shoulders, and who suddenly is set free to rise to his full stature, to throw his arms up over his head. The relief from oppression was as rending as a pain. It was a thousand times more joyful than any joy he had ever known. His self, his ego, savagely, grimly, harshly beaten down as it had been, sprang up with an exultant yell.
>
> The flame of its exultation flared up like guncotton, as the curtain had flared.
>
> And died down as quickly crushed and ground to blackness between giant hands that snatched it to one side as it dropped down towards Stephen's unconscious upturned face.[5]

The realization of what his getting well would mean to the family, and particularly to Stephen sleeping as peacefully unconscious of the flaming curtain as of the deeper psychological disaster it symbolizes, plunges Lester into an abyss as black as Eva's. He realizes that he is the one who has the capacity to care for the children, not their mother. He sees that

> Eva had passionate love and devotion to give them, but neither patience nor understanding. There was no sacrifice in the world which she would not joyfully make for her children except to live with them. They had tried that for fourteen dreadful years and knew what it brought them. That complacent unquestioned generalization, "The mother is the natural home-maker"; what a juggernaut it had been in their case! How poor Eva, drugged by the cries of its devotees, had cast herself down under its grinding wheels — and had dragged the children in under with her.[6]

Lester, too, realizes that the only way for the children to have a fair chance is for him to remain a cripple.

Over his head Tradition swung a bludgeon he knew he could not parry.

He had always guessed at the presence of that Tradition ruling the world, guessed that it hated him, guessed at its real name. He saw it plain now, grinning sardonically high above all the little chattering pretenses of idealism. He knew now what it decreed: that men are in the world to get possessions, to create material things, to sell them, to buy them, to transport them, above all to stimulate to fever-heat the desire for them in all human beings. It decreed that men are of worth in so far as they achieve that sort of material success, and worthless if they do not. . . . Why, the fanatic feminists were right, after all. Under its greasy camouflage of chivalry, society is really based on a contempt for women's work in the home. The only women who were paid, either in human respect or in money, were women who gave up their traditional job of creating harmony out of human relationships and did something really useful, bought or sold or created material objects. As for any *man's* giving his personality to the woman's work of trying to draw out of children the best there might be in them — fiddling foolishness! Leave it to the squaws! He was sure that he was the only man who had ever conceived even the possibility of such a lapse from virile self-respect as to do what all women are supposed to do. He knew well enough that other men would feel for such a conception on his part a stupefaction only equaled by their red-blooded scorn.[7]

The story ends with the visit of the doctor, who is to make some "very special tests which might be conclusive as to the possibility of recovery."[8] In a decision that makes the medical man complain inwardly, "Why did any honest man ever take up the practice of medicine?"[9] he announces: " 'I now realize that it would be very dangerous for Mr. Knapp ever to try to use his legs. Crutches perhaps, later. But he must never be allowed to make the attempt to go without crutches. It might be — .' He drew a long breath and said it. 'It might be fatal.' "[10]

The happiness of the family has been preserved, but at tremendous cost. Lester's sacrifice, and the lie on which it rests, are known to him, to Eva, to his old aunt, and to the family doctor — that is, to all the major adult characters. Only the children are saved from the knowledge and hence from the taint of it. For the adults the solution of the social problem the book presents is a sacrificial one, requiring not only Lester's freedom and self-respect but the integrity and self-esteem of the others as well.

The author was dismayed that the book was taken as an argument for women's rights. She complained of "the way the book's been misunderstood and the way it should be taken, as a whoop not for 'women's rights' but for 'children's rights.' "[11] Its writing caused Dorothy more mental anguish than any of her earlier novels. For the first time, she did not share a work in progress with John. Usually, Dorothy had shown John chapters or sections as she wrote them and had asked for his suggestions while the work was still in process. This time, however, she wrote the book completely alone.

She and John left for Europe immediately after sending the completed manuscript to the publisher, and she reported to Alfred Harcourt: "I was more pleased than I can say that the people around the office like The Home-Maker. I wrote that book in such a vacuum, without anybody's knowing anything about it, without even John's reading it till it was quite done, and then our coming away directly on top of its first typing . . . I never have had so little comment of any sort on any book of mine."[12]

After writing *The Home-Maker* Dorothy was exhausted. She wrote to Alfred from Europe, "I've laid your letter away with my copy of the Mss. to work over when I get *rested*. I'm tired from the strain of writing the intense thing. That horrible first part nearly killed me to write and John to typewrite. I never wrote anything that carried me away emotionally so wholly — I feel as though I'd been on a prolonged bat of some kind and were just coming to, slightly."[13]

With the revised manuscript, sent back four months later, Dorothy wrote, "I haven't changed a thing of the essentials, as you'll see, but I've gone over it with a file, scales, chemical tests, tuning-fork, and all the other implements of the trade, as far as its outer garment goes."[14]

A marginal note in a letter to Alfred Harcourt a year later is even more indicative of the inner turmoil the book caused her: "I dreamed last night that you wrote me The Home-Maker had fallen flat, been savagely reviewed, nobody liked it and all the booksellers were returning the copies they'd taken! What possessed me! I never had such a dream in my life before."[15]

When an English agent seemed to be slow in placing the narrative for serial publication, Dorothy and John were sure that she must have overstepped the bounds of propriety. "Mr. Cape has never reported aye-yes-or-no about the Mss. of 'The Home-Maker' which I sent him to see if he could place it serially," she wrote to Alfred. "John surmises that any Englishman would be so overcome with horror at the very conception that a man might do better in the home and a woman out of it, that he could find no words in which to speak of such a blasphemous work."[16]

From France, where they were traveling, Dorothy wrote again, evidently worried about the reaction her book was drawing: "I haven't heard anything about the Home-Maker, except some heated letters pro and con which have already made their way here. One of them just raised the hair on my head . . . a woman in Massachusetts wrote me wildly that she would give her life if I had only written the book earlier, for her husband committed suicide last winter . . . an artist with no business ability, trying to make a living for her and her six children."[17]

In spite of Dorothy's fears, the book was evidently accepted by the American reading public, for it stood among the ten best-selling novels of 1924.

In *The Home-Maker* Dorothy brought to full fruition the radical ideas about work for women that she had suggested in *The Squirrel-Cage* and *The Bent Twig*. After having described them in this extreme situation, however, she laid the problem to rest, and it never appeared directly in another novel.

It was easy for critics to misunderstand Dorothy's message about work in this novel because of the unconventional situation it portrays. Like her father, however, Dorothy was not so much impressed with the injustice to the oppressed in society as with the waste of human resources that resulted from placing people where they did not belong. With respect to oppression, Lester Knapp is clearly as "oppressed" in the business world as Evangeline is out of it. The moral of her story is not that women should be put into commercial employment but that each individual should be placed in that spot where he or she is most productive. Only in such an arrangement can everyone be content and can children grow and thrive. It is a tragic commentary on the weakness of society that the only acceptable means to effect such a division of labor is for Lester to simulate illness and to make the consequent personal sacrifices.

The flaming exultation of Lester Knapp and the subsequent despairing realization of the effect his regained health must have on his children finds a vivid symbol in the burning curtain that threatens the sleeping Stephen. This scene could also be an echo of experiences in the author's own life. The offer of an academic career, which caused her "to jump with joy" until she realized how much her parents needed her with them, must have been such a time. The situation in which the first joy of a goal attained turns to ashes in the mouth of the successful aspirant, when the consequences of that success are fully realized, becomes a recurrent theme in Dorothy's later works and may well reflect personal frustrations in her own complicated existence.

The novel is structurally much tighter than its immediate predecessors. Limited to one family in one small town, and also to a relatively short span of time, the problem of the best use of human resources is given full and effective treatment by means of one example. The reader is then left to draw his or her own generalizing conclusions. The author demonstrates but never preaches, and only occasionally does she bring in a peripheral character like the aunt to give an outside view of the family's affairs. Her technique is rather a series of striking "before" and "after" pictures, vignettes of home life that by their vividness remain with the reader and suggest some of the possibilities open to human beings outside of the usual patterns of society. By its breaking of old idols, it is a book to stir the mind to still further flights of social imagination.

Of her next novel Dorothy wrote to Alfred Harcourt, "I doubt if you or any man will be able to get into it, at all. But I bet Ellen and a lot of other women will."[18]

The main character of *Her Son's Wife* is John Bascomb's widow. Mrs. Bascomb, like her predecessor Eva Knapp, is a paragon of housewifely and motherly virtue in her own eyes and in those of the community. Since her husband's death, when their son Ralph was three, she has supported Ralph and herself by teaching school. Ralph is now through his course at the university and is scheduled to enter law school in the fall.

Mrs. Bascomb is a woman who is accustomed to being in charge of every situation, especially of her son's life. Ralph has never given her a moment's trouble, she reports, remarking, "I've always been proud to show Ralph to my friends."[19] Her son's sudden, secret marriage to a girl from the poorer section of a neighboring town fills her with consternation, although she bravely welcomes the young couple into her home.

Everything about Lottie is offensive to Mrs. Bascomb. The household becomes a battlefield where "Mrs. Bascomb was perpetually amazed that any one always right as she was, could be made so often to appear in the wrong."[20] Instead of having everything in its place, as she has always had it in the past, Mrs. Bascomb now must cope with Lottie's slovenly ways, especially burdensome to her as they affect the new grandchild who has too soon joined the household. Part 1 ends with Mrs. Bascomb's departure from home to a job and an apartment in a neighboring town.

Part 2 describes Mrs. Bascomb's tranquil life in her new setting, where she is free to attend all the meetings and lectures she wishes and to enjoy her former assured social position. She is shaken from this serenity by a chance encounter with her grandchild. Dids, as she is always called, looks out of her small, dirty face with her grandfather's eyes. These eyes have a special significance for Mrs. Bascomb and are a recurring element in the novel.

The first time John Bascomb's eyes appear in the story is when Mrs. Bascomb shows a locket picture to a young woman who is her choice for Ralph's wife. There the eyes are described as "deep" and "steady"[21] and looking at his widow "as if there were disappointment in that well-remembered deep gaze of his."[22] As she looks at the picture, Mrs. Bascomb remarks, "I was very much afraid of him. I still am . . . , the way you are of your conscience."[23]

The second encounter with John Bascomb's eyes is when the newborn baby is placed in her grandmother's arms. "She turned back a fold of the blanket and looked down unlovingly on the new strange person in her house. . . . As their gaze met, John Bascomb's widow woke from her long nightmare. The eyes were John Bascomb's set under John Bascomb's brow."[24]

In Part 3, Mrs. Bascomb swallows her pride and returns home for the sake of Dids. She makes herself small and humble and submits to all Lottie's cheap whims so that she can infuse a breath of wholesomeness into Dids's life. However, all that she can do seems at first to be insufficient to counterbalance the unwholesome influence of Lottie. Lottie has become very heavy through overindulgence, and her feet and back bother her so much that she often has her meals in bed. The meals without Lottie are relaxed and pleasant times in contrast with those eaten in her complaining presence. The sections ends when Mrs. Bascomb casually thinks to herself, " 'Oh, if Lottie could only take *all* her meals in bed!' And with the thought, so naturally, so lightly, so almost casually slid from one half of her life to the other."[25]

Part 4, the most crucial and controversial section of the book, begins with the visit of Dr. Pell, a quack doctor whom Mrs. Bascomb remembers from the time he spent in her schoolroom as a "frightful little gutter-snipe"[26] with a hand that was "grimy, chapped, and given to appropriating what did not belong to it."[27] Maurice Pell has grown into a man with a "broad, swarthy, rather battered face,"[28] "a white smooth hand"[29] into which hers sinks "as if into a feather bed,"[30] and a "rich voice rising and falling with preacher-like flourishes at the end of his phrases"[31] as he intones meaningless formulas filled with medical and scientific terms.

In Dr. Pell Mrs. Bascomb has found the tool with which she can keep Lottie in bed and away from Dids. The monstrous realization that it would be possible to talk Lottie into being really bedridden and so to remove her from active influence on her little granddaughter's development "towered above her now like a djinn let out of the bottle."[32] For Dids's sake Mrs. Bascomb feigns a real concern for Lottie's health and begins on a course of deception. The toll that this course takes shows itself externally in a number of ways.

When Ralph returns home, he finds Lottie in bed, Dids playing happily with her dolls, and his mother's face wearing such a grim expression that the insane thought passes through Ralph's mind that "Mother looks as though she had killed Lottie."[33] Later that evening, Ralph is puzzled to see his mother pause in the midst of washing dishes to scrub her hands with a stiff vegetable brush, and he is awakened by a noise in the night to see a sight that makes a cold chill run down his back: "There, in her nightgown, her white hair in curl papers, her thin withered face bent over the wash-bowl, stood his mother washing her hands."[34] The next morning Ralph mentions that an older associate has commented on the resemblance of Dids's eyes to those of her grandfather and asks to see the locket his mother always has worn, only to learn with surprise that she is "not wearing that any more" but "only took it off last night."[35]

Having taken the fateful step, Mrs. Bascomb does not turn back. She supplies Lottie with all the luxuries that will make her imprisonment enjoyable, a victrola and all the latest popular records, a mystery story, easy needlework, jigsaw puzzles, cosmetics, boxes of candy, and wonderful refreshments whenever her friends come to call. She even has a sunporch built onto her room where she keeps flowers growing in profusion. In her attempts to keep Lottie happy, Mrs. Bascomb explores her daughter-in-law's personality, and what she discovers is an immense surprise. She had regarded the woman who married her only son as her natural enemy, a sinister and powerful force. When she finally makes the effort to know her, Mrs. Bascomb finds at the base of Lottie's nature "an incoherent triviality which went beyond her powers to imagine . . . because nothing ever happened inside Lottie every break in the ghastly monotony of her life must come from the outside."[36] Turning her attention to supplying interest from the outside, Mrs. Bascomb is able to accomplish her purpose and to give Lottie a more interesting life as an invalid than she could achieve for herself as an active person.

Part 5 is told from Dids's point of view and relates her experience of growing up in the home her grandmother provides for her. This life is full of the kind of growing experiences that encourages inner as well as outer development. Dids is surrounded with friends and activities and soon shows herself to be a natural leader. When she reaches her senior year in high school, she becomes the first girl to be elected senior class president. Only briefly is she drawn to the life represented by Lottie, when she discovers the powers of physical attraction,

> that walking along the street with one of the big boys, she had only to look at him in a certain way . . . and in a minute or two, no matter how hard he was talking about baseball, he'd stop, and look back at her in a certain way, and walk closer to her so that they touched each other as they stepped. Then they'd both be tingling from head to foot, and laughing a great deal over nothing, and not really know what they were saying, at all. It was *frightfully* interesting. And it made everything else that had been in her life seem flat and stupid and insipid. Lessons! Basketball! Granny!

Piano practice! Skating! Poetry books! Dids could hardly remember when she had been such a child as to put her mind on such things.[37]

From this dangerous path she is rescued by another encounter with her grandfather's influence, which hangs like a brooding spirit over the whole course of the novel. An out-of-town speaker at the school notices Dids because of her resemblance to her grandfather, who was his college room-mate and dearest friend. When he asks her if she is John Bascomb's grand-daughter, he pronounces the name in such a "tone of sacramental affection" that she is startled and can only nod in silence, "her eyes fixed on his, receiving from them with the avid haste of youth seeking its own, more vital material for the construction of her House of Life, than in weeks of ordinary life."[38]

This encounter with her grandfather's spirit is reinforced for Dids when her grandmother learns that the speaker is now at the railroad station about to take a train. She hurries Dids into her coat to rush with her through the streets, the station, and out onto the platform in search of the distinguished man. "Dids followed along, horribly embarrassed and ashamed of Granny. What would a distinguished, famous man like Dr. Levering think of them, crowding themselves in on him like this? And Granny so old and plainly dressed, with one of her most awful hats on. Dids wished earnestly that she had not come along, that she could disassociate herself from Granny and not share in the awkwardness which was before them."[39]

The emotional meeting between the two old people, united by their love for John Bascomb, is a revelation to Dids: "So this was what it meant — to love."[40] Dr. Levering observes, "I have been living with him in memory all this day, because I saw his spirit look out of his granddaughter's . . . I was thinking about that clear deep look of his. Wonderful to find it still living, in a new human being. . . . At the moment you came up to me, I was thinking of him and asking myself if I had lived so that I would not fear, now, to look once more into John Bascomb's eyes."[41] When Mrs. Bascomb recoils with a cry of pain, as if he had struck her, Dr. Levering says, "Why, Mrs. Bascomb, *you* certainly would be proud to look into his eyes, with such a splendid girl as you are bringing up to inherit his spirit."[42] Granny's wild question, "She *will* be like him, won't she?"[43] and Dr. Levering's affirming kiss on her forehead are a turning point in Dids's life.

In Part 6 all the threads of the story are drawn together. Ralph has now changed from a routine job he disliked to the sportswriting career that fits him. Dids's new maturity is tested against an encounter with her other grand-father, Lottie's father, who comes to spend his last days with the Bascombs. "She never seemed to shrink from being seen on the street with the shabby old workingman, answering unabashed the greetings of her friends in his barbarous bad grammar. . . . There was apparently nothing in her heart at this time save a burning and indignant compassion."[44]

The book ends with Dids's departure for college and with Mrs. Bascomb's tardily found affection for Lottie, for whom in her own new maturity she is able to feel "pity and love."[45]

As Dorothy started work on *Her Son's Wife,* she wrote to Paul Reynolds,who was eager to arrange a contract for it, "It has no love story, and is not in the least light or cheerful. I feel it very deeply, and hope it may amount to something, but whether it will be fit for a magazine is another question."[46] She outlined her plot: "The story turns . . . on the development and strengthening of a character, in this case after forty-five, the age when most people are set for life. [This was, it should be noted, Dorothy's own age in the year of her writing.] A woman of forty-five meets calamity in the person of an unfit wife for her only son, and struggles through great sorrow and misery, to an immensely deeper understanding and self-abnegation. It's sad, but not futile."[47]

Dorothy dreaded beginning work on the book, calling it "that new novel, which will certainly kill me to write."[48] After Reynolds had made an advance serial sale, she wrote, "It throws me into rather a gloomy state of mind to know that now I really must write that all-fired serious story, which seems, from a distance as though it would be the death of me. . . . I really dread starting work on it, and would be glad to know that I have really plenty of time for it."[49]

When Paul Reynolds suggested that the consciousness of a deadline helped authors to keep at their work, Dorothy responded with considerable annoyance:

I do protest against being lumped in with loafing authors who don't work unless they're hurried to it. No sir, by gracious, that is not me. Nobody *can* hurry me, unfortunately, and I really don't need it, if the work is on the right track. It usually ends by carrying me off my feet so that I can't think of anything else, and eat, sleep and breathe it twenty-four hours of the day, whether anybody even knows that I'm working on it or not. If it's not on the right track (whatever that mysterious process is) no amount of having promised it can get it out of my skin.[50]

A note to Alfred Harcourt a little later reports, "losing my grip on reality every once in a while, and feeling my feet slide from under me, as I slip altogether into the world where my characters live, rather than the real one up here. It's rather scaring—like any sort of hallucination."[51]

The year turned out to be an ideal one for working on a novel. In March Dorothy wrote:

> I've been wrestling like Jacob with the new novel, and have had a magnificently quiet winter in which to work—deep snows, the house empty all day (for Jimmy was at school, Mr. Fisher in the Legislature at Montpelier, and Sally far away at boarding school) and I have worked harder and with less nervous strain than ever before. It has turned out something which I have *felt,* terrifically, and still feel too deeply to have much idea how I have succeeded. . . . I think it will be a story which women will be interested in, (I hope which they will feel deeply) but I don't believe that it can interest any man. They have for too many generations had the possibility and the habit, of putting on their hats and melting away out of the house, when family relations got too uncomfortably tense. I rather imagine that they will put on their hats and melt away from the book at about the third chapter. But I hope that women who have had, for generations, to stick it out with no escape, may have a certain horrified interest in the story.[52]

When the serial began to appear, Dorothy could see that she had indeed communicated her feelings to her readers. In a note to Alfred Harcourt she reported:

> I am getting more letters about "Her Son's Wife" as it appears serially, than about any other serially published book of mine. I had so little idea how people were going to take that story, that I find them rather interesting. . . . Most of them speak, almost with alarm, of the intensity of feeling in it. Somebody wrote me yesterday that "the book shakes and trembles with the feeling in it." And somebody else wrote me, "I simply *loathe* reading it, but the instant it comes into the house I must sit down and plunge myself into wretchedness with Mrs. Bascomb."[53]

Dorothy's fears that writing the book might be too much for her seemed to be realized in the winter of 1925–26. On January 1, 1926, she wrote to Paul Reynolds, "I've been quite under the weather and still have a fluttering heart as a result of infection."[54] A week later, she will still feeling the effects of illness and reported, "I write this painfully by hand because the staccato motion of the typewriter sends my pulse too high for comfort."[54]

The selection of a title created special problems for Mrs. Bascomb's story. Dorothy wrote to Alfred Harcourt:

> The relations of mother-in-law and daughter-in-law are not the subject of this novel, in any general sense; but the obligation laid upon a

member of the older generation to sacrifice herself for a member of the younger, when she realizes that she is the only hope of the child. As far as Lottie interferes with Mrs. Bascomb's doing what's best for Dids, their relations are the subject of the book. But if there had been no child, they wouldn't have had any relations at all. So I'd like some title which would suggest what seems to be the vital point of the story, the relation on the one hand of Mrs. Bascomb to her fine husband (the best influence in her life and one which determines her character) and her relation to his grand-daughter. So here are my four suggested titles . . . John Bascomb's Widow, John Bascomb's Granddaughter, Her Son's Wife, or, and this last would be my favorite, "Every Man to His Heritage." This phrase comes from a sentence in Proverbs, which runs, "I will bring them again, every man to his heritage, and every man to his land." . . . You can see without my explaining, in how many ways this would refer to what seems to me the real subject matter of the novel, the rescuing of the heritage of John Bascomb from destruction or at least from deformity.[56]

In spite of the author's own stated emphasis, however, her publisher selected the title that focuses attention on the relationship between Mrs. Bascomb and Lottie.

Her Son's Wife is dedicated "To the memory of Aunt Phebe's spirit." This is the same aunt who was the model for Aunt Nancy in *Gunhild.* She had spent her last years with Dorothy's brother Jim and died in June 1924, just before Dorothy started work on the novel.

William Lyon Phelps, the noted critic, had high praise for the book. He wrote to Alfred Harcourt, " 'Her Son's Wife' is Dorothy Canfield's master-piece and it is also *a* masterpiece. It is a profound, subtle analysis of human character and human life and a very remarkable book. I predict that it will win Pulitzer Prize for 1926. It deserves it."[57] The novel did not win the Pulitzer Prize, but it did attract very favorable critical attention both in America and in Europe.

Dorothy was flooded with letters, "so many — all very intense, divided in-to two sides; — those who loathe Mrs. Bascomb and think she is a murderess — red-handed and I am as bad for allowing her any comfort in life; and those who can't understand why Mrs. Bascomb should even feel an in-stant's compunction for doing the only possible thing."[58] With amusement she reported that "Rupert Hughes writes me that he was so astonished and pleased by the unexpected turn in 'Her Son's Wife' with Mrs. Bascomb's discovery that Lottie is not a Jezebel but only a moron (my phrase not his!)."[59]

When William Lyon Phelps compiled his volume *Selected Readings from Much Loved Books* in 1940, he included a three-page passage from Dorothy's novel, introducing it with the comment: *"Her Son's Wife* is her best book. When two men fight over a woman which they are doing somewhere at this moment, it may or may not be exciting; but when two women fight for a man, it is thrilling — because there are no rules. Even as the great zoologists (I have heard) can from one bone reconstruct an entire prehistoric animal, so can any woman from one hat describe the appearance, character, personality, and previous experience of its female owner."[60] The passage that drew such praise was the description of Mrs. Bascomb's first realization of Lottie's personality when "she stepped into her hall and saw hanging on her hatrack a bright green hat, of an eccentric shape, made of very shiny, varnished, coarsely braided straw, which she recognized as one of the cheap models of that season. . . . The air was heavy with perfume . . . the sort of perfume that would go with that hat."[61]

This book is the most realistic of Dorothy's novels. To an extent beyond any of her earlier works, she has here described the everyday environmental circumstances of ordinary people struggling with the problems of living with each other. No sordid detail of living or dying is too distasteful for the author; none is treated for its own sake, however, but rather for its contribution to the understanding of the personalities involved. Phelps selected Lottie's green hat as a detail from which Dorothy Canfield drew a whole personality. He could equally well have taken a number of other details, from the dirty dishes piled in the sink or the blisters on the fine old mahogany table to the fashionable tight shoes, for every external detail of Lottie's existence reflects an inner personality trait. The same use of indicators and motifs accompanies the description of other characters, so that the interaction of personalities plays on both the psychological and material levels.

An interesting thematic aspect of the novel is the development of character in a woman beyond the age when such development is supposed to take place, a growth brought on by love for her dead husband and the determination to give a granddaughter who resembles him the chance she deserves. Eva Knapp of *The Home-Maker* had only one moment when she realized how far she was from her ideal; Mrs. Bascomb has repeated moments of such insight, and they contribute to the deepening and maturing of her personality.

Most of Mrs. Bascomb's moments of self-awareness come in connection with her son Ralph. Her personal growth from the enjoyment of power over a dependent son to the realization that "a mother is not a person to lean upon, but a person to make leaning unnecessary,"[62] is accomplished through searing moments of vision, agonizing periods of humility, and finally genuine selfless love.

The novel won high acclaim in German-speaking Europe. In a review in the Swiss journal *Der Bund,* Maria Gleit called "*Her Son's Wife* probably one of the most significant books in world literature."[63] In 1949 a small volume appeared in Germany, *Güte, Wissen, Verstehen, Drei Lebensbilder grosser amerikanischer Erzieher,* containing an essay on Dorothy Canfield Fisher by Dr. Dora Edinger. This critic remarks on the similarity of solution in *The Home-Maker* and *Her Son's Wife,* in both of which sickness is used as a means to achieve an end.

> Only through his "escape into sickness" is it possible to retain the exchange of roles for the good of their children. . . . The same solution of an "escape into sickness" is also chosen in the later book by the strict and self-righteous heroine. She consciously assumes guilt, in suggesting to her morally weak daughter-in-law that she lose herself in the role of a chronic invalid. This is the only way out of an otherwise hopeless situation, in which a whole family would be destroyed. Dorothy Canfield Fisher, descendant of strict New England Puritans, has the moral courage to show that for mature human beings responsibility for one's own actions must take the place of a conventional concept of sin. She insists, however, that the full price for such a decision must be paid with one's own happiness.[64]

A similar insight is evident in an article by Edward A. Post, "The Neo-Puritanism of Dorothy Canfield,"[65] in which he cites Dorothy Canfield as an example of "an essential, organically American tradition of 'responsibility.'" He sees this as a natural element in the steady current coming from the earliest American beginnings, "a continuity of momentum through Puritanism, Quakerism and Transcendentalism that never died out and that has been deepening its stream, especially in the novels of Dorothy Canfield." In her novels he finds "practical realism" — that is "a paralleling of idealism and a functionable application of it," or in another light "the empiricism of John Dewey reduced to practicable human terms." According to this concept, "the significance of life is achieved by growth from within; self-discipline through meeting life head-on is a just inheritance of a pioneer people." Professor Post uses *Her Son's Wife* as the example on which to base his arguments, and he points out that Mary Bascomb is at the beginning of the novel "disciplined from without . . . by the conventional and stereotyped Puritan formula of dignity and propriety." As the plot develops, "all of her neat Puritan maxims are shown to be but a lifeless fabric of unreality which brings calamity upon the person who leans upon them instead of achieving the necessary fiber of character from within." He finds in Mary Bascomb "a symbol of the metamorphosis through which religion must go to transmute its pre-established formalism, however ordered and dignified, into a vital humanness that grows from the very germ of life deep within."

Professor Post's evaluative comment on the quality of Dorothy Canfield's work is curiously reminiscent of her own evaluation of the French author Augier (cf. p. 25), when he says:

> Because the detail in her work is rich and full, it is none the less highly selective and everywhere relevant—artistically related to theme. To characterize it as autobiographical or documentarian—and hence realistic only in a practical sense—is to miss the disciplined architectonics of her novels, all the more artistic because decorously clothed with the flesh and blood of life. It is this very fidelity to life itself that leaves its meaning to be integrated by the reader's consciousness. It is truth to be discovered that we are offered; and beneath the surface the currents are determined by the channels of deeper truth, gradually taking direction and course and momentum as the stream deepens in its progress.

Dorothy liked this review and felt that, for once, her work was being understood as she had intended it. A marginal note to a copy of the article exclaims: "I was so much pleased by the complete understanding of this man . . . of Her Son's Wife. Not a single idea or detail I put in that has been missed."[66]

Dorothy's Danish friend, Mary Westenholz, wrote to her, comparing *The Deepening Stream* with *Her Son's Wife,* "I still think 'Her Son's Wife,' though I do not like it best, is the most powerful book you have written. You lead your heroine through defeat, crime, humiliation—not into a happy marriage—but, accompanied by a hymn of victory, at last to the beginning. To this the end of 'The Deepening Stream,' of which I am so fond, sounds like a beautiful song compared to a Symphoni."[67]

The Home-Maker and *Her Son's Wife* are the first novels not set, at least partly, in Vermont. It may be no accident that they immediately follow two of her "most Vermont" novels, *The Brimming Cup,* and *Rough-Hewn,* for, in a letter to her cousin Arthur Canfield, Dorothy wrote, "I'm glad you like The Brimming Cup's Vermontness. It certainly is very Vermont, so much so that I wonder if real Westerners can 'get' it. I notice that most of the letters I get about it from enthusiastic readers come from Maine or Massachusetts or somewhere else in New England. But I don't *want* to be limited to being a New England writer! Me, born in Kansas!"[68]

11
Two Views of a Vermont Village:
Bonfire and *Seasoned Timber*

"He likes it. I think he thinks it is the most *interesting* story I've ever done, 'attachant' in the French sense of making you keep turning the pages over pretty fast to see what is coming and what is going to happen."[1] So Dorothy reported her husband's estimate of her next novel, *Bonfire.*

Her publisher sent her with amusement a different reaction from a rural library in upstate New York: "Harcourt, Brace and Company has just learned from an irate patron of the Nyack Public Library, N.Y., that the aforesaid library has banned Dorothy Canfield's new novel, *Bonfire.* She was told by the librarian that 'we aren't going to have that. It's about a bad woman who led men astray. You don't want to read it.' "[2]

Dorothy had been criticized for the "good" pictures of married life she had given in *The Brimming Cup* (1921) and *The Deepening Stream* (1930). In *Her Son's Wife* (1926), the marriage portrayed was an unsuitable one, but peripheral to the main story of the child and her grandmother. However, in 1933, in *Bonfire,* Dorothy set a "bad" marriage in the very center of her novelistic stage and created in the character of the wife one of her most interesting fictional personalities.

Bonfire is set in a sprawling Vermont community made up of four different areas within its isolated mountain valley. While all go under the general name of Clifford, there is a great difference between The Street, which has "subdued to cleanliness and decency its corner of the epic mountain magnificence of Windward County,"[3] and Searles Shelf, with its "wild, bold, backwoods, lawlessness."[4] Clifford Four Corners is a depressingly poor section, containing "only epilepsy and hopelessness and dirt and incest and imbecility."[5] The Other Side is "the road of prosperous dairy farms and apple orchards, of clean red-cheeked boys and girls, and well-read, hard-handed, hard-headed men and women."[6] It was nicknamed "The Other Side" by "a sharp-tongued rector of St. Andrew's, exasperated by the un-Samaritan aloofness from other people's troubles of the well-to-do church-going families who lived along it."[7]

The novel is divided into six parts. In the first part we are introduced to the main characters, particularly Anna Craft, through whose eyes a good deal of the action is seen. The story opens with Anna's return from Paris, where she has been working for two years as a private nurse after spending the ten years before as district nurse in The Valley. As she walks up the street from the station, she greets, and the reader meets with her, the other people of The Street who are to play parts in the story. There is Cora Ingraham, spinster schoolteacher, who is devoted to M'Sanna; Isabel Foote, an almost-grown-up young neighbor; Fred Kirby, the birthmarked pastor of the Anglican Church; and others. This device for introducing the persons of the narrative is an effective one, and by the time Anna reaches her own home the reader has met all but two. These are her brother Anson, who is about to return from medical training to take up his late father's practice, and Lixlee, a poor orphan from Searles Shelf.

Lixlee is a totally primitive siren, whose path through the pages of the book is marked by the emotional disasters she causes. In portraying Lixlee Dorothy was interested, as she had been with earlier characters, in showing how a human being develops into a particular kind of person. This emphasis — and also her annoyance with reviewers who practically ignored the rest of the characters of the book — is expressed in a letter to Alfred Harcourt: "But I'd *like* not to have the book spoken of as though Lixlee were the only character in it. And oh *how* I would like somebody to mention the fact that here is a siren who did not spring full-fledged from the head of Venus, so to speak, but started a human being with human feelings, and gradually by the force of circumstances and her own (at first hardly recognized by herself) gift for being alluring, was pushed into the role of siren."[8]

Anson Craft, Anna's brother, returns to Clifford without enthusiasm. He would much prefer to be engaged in research in a laboratory, but his self-respect demands that he make money to repay his sister for her sacrifices in putting him through medical school. He gradually becomes reconciled to his rural practice when he sees in it a chance to study hereditary heart disease, using a combination of his father's and his own records.

Meanwhile Anna, who has lived only for him and is now delighted to have him back with her, is oblivious to his real problem and thinks of securing his contentment in a happy marriage to her wholesome young neighbor Isabel Foote. Anna Craft, as district nurse, is involved in the lives of all the inhabitants of the valley and in trying to improve the quality of life, especially for the poorer people there. To give the children in the outlying districts a chance for a high school education, she initiates the idea of a cooperative residence near the academy. This will require town funds, and her campaign for votes for the project takes so much of her attention that she fails to notice that Anson is spending more and more time at the home of two aged sisters where Lixlee is working. The night before the town meeting, where the vote on the cooperative house is to be taken, a mysterious shot strikes both young Doctor Anson and Lixlee. Anson subsequently marries Lixlee in the hospital, where they are recuperating from their wounds.

The marriage of Anson and Lixlee is not a success. Lixlee, the personification of primitive passion, is bitterly disappointed when she finds that Anson is devoted to his medical career as well as to her. She proceeds to make his life miserable in an effort to take revenge on him for what she regards as his broken promises of total devotion. She also destroys a number of other relationships around her and finally leaves Anson for the wealthiest bachelor in the village, with whom she flees to Europe. Anson's personality is completely ruined by her actions. He loses interest in his research and becomes obsessively absorbed in competitive sports. His studies of hereditary heart ailments are continued only by the efforts of Isabel Foote, whom he marries after a divorce from Lixlee.

During Anson's gradual disintegration, his sister Anna's personality has been expanding and developing in her work for others and in a belated realization of her love for Fred Kirby, the Episcopal minister. They finally find each other against the symbolic background of a brilliant display of northern lights, which dwarfs them both in its magnificence.

The final chapter of *Bonfire* shows most of the main characters gathered together at a party in the cooperative student house, awaiting the return of the high school team from an out-of-town game. Anna's experiment in bringing rural young people to town for their education is a success, and she has found personal happiness in her marriage and motherhood. In a final symbolic scene, she looks up from caring for her baby and sees Anson capering foolishly in the street at the head of the victory procession for the returning athletic team.

Alfred Harcourt thought that Dorothy might develop a little more sympathy for Lixlee. After reading part of the manuscript, he wrote to her:

Anson is clear. Lixlee is just first-rate. I think the book might stand a paragraph here and there to arouse a little more sympathy for her and her problems. She is not just a hell-cat. I have heard and observed that a marriage where the woman is considerably more strongly sexed than the man is pretty sure to be hell. You make perfectly clear what a hell it is for Anson. The reader isn't quite sure that you understand what a hell it is for her. But the picture of what these driving impulses do to her is clear and unforgettable.[9]

Dorothy replied:

> I can't tell you how glad I am that you see that Lixlee is not just a wild-cat, but a human being with a heart and with pride of her own, totally misunderstood. A short chapter near the end will perhaps make the reader more aware of her side of it. Though I do not want ever (this just technical) to have anything shown from her side. She is the only character, you'll have noticed, whom you don't see from the inside. I wanted the reader to make up his own understanding of her from what he sees of her, just as he would in real life.[10]

John did not wholly agree with Dorothy's way of presenting Lixlee. "John says," she wrote to Alfred,

> if I wanted people to realize that about Lixlee — that she really *was* an ignorant girl at first, that she really was terribly in love with Anson, and that her life broke right in two (just as much as if she were a "virtuous" woman) when she found that he was incapable of loving her as she loved him — that I should have told them so in the character of the author. But I hate that sort of telling. When you show characters acting — oughtn't your readers to draw their own conclusions from their actions as you present them? Well, maybe some of them will. You certainly did, when you first read it — I remember your speaking about the tragedy that her marriage was for *her*, as well as Anson.[11]

And in another letter she wrote, "Novel-writing seems to me to depend on the ability to create characters and set them in action."[12]

There are several rather technical discussions of medical research in the novel, and Dorothy wanted to have them scientifically accurate. She first talked over these matters with Dr. Russell, the family physician in Arlington, and then sent the manuscript to a heart specialist in Poughkeepsie for a further opinion before letting it go to the publisher.

Another problem for the author was how to give readers as accurate a mental picture of Clifford and the relationship of its various sections as she had herself. "One of the most important chracters in the story (for me) is Vermont, the locality, the valley, the community," Dorothy wrote to Paul Reynolds. "I mean it to take the part of a character in the reader's mind."[13] To help accomplish this visualization, she had her Vermont neighbor, the artist Wallace Fahnestock, draw pen-and-ink sketches of The Valley for the inside covers of the book.

In a letter to Professor Edward A. Post of Boston University, who had written asking her some questions about *Bonfire*, Dorothy gives some of her own ideas about the novel. She refers to

a point I think vital—the difference between Anson's rebellion against convention, which, like that of most young and inexperienced rebels, was based on the illusion that you can have your cake and eat it too, be primitive with all the splendid untamed force of the primitive, but—at will, *his* will—return to take on when he thought necessary the obligations which the truly primitive does not recognize at all. Lixlee was truly primitive—perfectly willing to pay the price (ignoring of obligations, deceit) to attain primitive immediate satisfaction. I do not conceive of the gap between Anson and Lixlee as being caused wholly by the economic gap between The Street and Searles Shelf. There was in it to my mind something worse, Anson's (unconscious) deceiving of her and of himself, and his (again unconscious and muddle-headed and ignorant and young and inexperienced idea) that a balance and equilibrium could be struck and kept between them when he gave only a part of what he *said* he was willing to give, and Lixlee really was willing to give all—and so expected all. . . . I feel something false in poor Anson's attitude towards Lixlee, a crack in his character (very common) and so feel the catastrophe would go deep with him—to the roots—hence the disintegration of his character into Babbitism in the last.

Lixlee was in reality rather dumb, not much mind, any amount of passion and *pride*. But, according to her lights, she lived fully up to the obligations she assumed. Anson was keenly intelligent (*in his profession*) but put so little thought on his relations with Lixlee that he could think (see Page 188 where he complacently tells himself that with his work and with a lover like Lixlee *waiting at home* to renew his vitality . . .) that he can use the whole of another human being to minister to a part of his needs—that a human being can "wait at home" to renew *his* vitality, —that is, that life can be suspended in the other except as he needs her. He needed Lixlee's physical magnificent power to love, and he thought he could pick that out of her life, and leave the rest. See Page 206 when—just *once*, he really thought of what their love meant to *her* and not only to him. In other words he (implicitly) refused her the right to a whole life. The point is, of course, and he instinctively knew this, that all the rest of her personality was just dumb, ignorant, limited, dull mountain-girl. But you can't kill off or ignore the parts of those you love that don't suit you, without danger, and without cruelty. My feeling was that there was something fundamentally wrong and selfish in Anson's attitude that weakened his character so that he did go to pieces when the crash came. A scientist friend of mine (a research chemist) greatly interested in Anson and recognizing (so he says) many of his own reactions in him, assures me that in ten years time Anson will have recovered from this reaction into the commonplace, (which by the way he recognizes as true, and says what I feel too, that many and many a Babbitt we see at forty is victim of the mistakes made in his youth when, fumblingly and awkwardly like poor Anson, they tried to break out a new path of their own, and got hurt so much in the process that they shrink back to the middle of the highway ever since). You see it was not merely (as the old doctor thought) that Anson's wife deceived and ran away from him. *He* had been divided, not whole, in his relations to her, so there was poison in the wound.[14]

Edward Post had commented not only on the characters but also on the narrative style, and he remarked on a change of pace, a speeding up toward the end of the story. Dorothy reacted to this comment by saying:

Your acute eyes saw of course, what nobody else noticed, a change in movement in the sixth part. . . . It's a fundamental problem in writing novels — if you take a subject deep enough and rich enough to be worth the essence of heart's blood you pour into it, it would simply take the space of an encyclopaedia to give all of it the same development. The convention allows one to hasten the last part — and wisely I think. If you have done your work of character depiction well enough (which evidently in your case I had not) you can trust your reader to do some — considerable — developing of his own, going on from the data you have given him up to then. If he *knows* M'Sanna, as I hope he does, he'll know without my telling him what things mean to her — what she'll feel when she hears poor Henry Twombly has shot himself, etc. The best one can do then (without going to War and Peace length — and even that you'll remember, resorts to just simple statement of facts at the end) is to hope that the reader's mind has been enough stimulated to thought and that he knows the characters well enough to make his own comment.[15]

As Dorothy finished writing her novel, she felt her usual optimism and confidence. She wrote to Alfred Harcourt at this stage that she was "in the last revisions and having a wonderful time — still in the warm comfortable period of thinking that *this* time I'm going to come nearer to it than before."[16] After the book was published, she experienced her usual disappointment in her achievement. To Edward Post she wrote: "My theme — that passion, since always embodied in a human being, cannot with justice ever be enjoyed without a realization of the *humanity* of the person giving it — is such a deep one that it is perhaps not surprising that I wasn't equal to it. But of course 'a man's reach—' "[17]

This comment of Dorothy's drew a contrite apology from Edward Post, to which she replied, "But I consider, you know, not that you 'failed to find what you should have,' in the 6th part of Bonfire, but that I failed to make it evident. Novelists are not permitted the chance to scribble long letters of 'explanation.' *The novel should need none.*"[18]

Dorothy was always pleased when a reader recognized some of the artistic literary devices she had employed in her novels. She congratulated Edward Post for recognizing that the kitten in the story that "went wild" was a symbol for Lixlee.[19] She was even more pleased with Alfred Harcourt's perceptive praise of the book, when he wrote after receiving the major part of the manuscript, "In many ways, I think it's the best novel you have ever thought of writing—really interesting characters, a completely realized scene, and every once in awhile just the best writing you've ever done. The walk that Anna and Fred take through the sleeping village to see if there is a light in Anson's place with the Northern Lights at the end is, under all the circumstances you've built up, just splendid."[20] Dorothy replied to this: "And *how* nice that you thought the Northern Lights scene successful! It is the climax and turning point of the book, and it shows the old hand you are that you picked it out as such, even without having the last part to read."[21]

A review of the British edition of *Bonfire* noted its realistic ending with approval: "It is a happy ending with a difference—peace after storm, a rest made more enjoyable by the exertions which preceded it; in fact, the only sort of happy ending that we feel is credible to the reader and well merited by the actors."[22]

A criticism of this same ending by an American professor brought forth an unprecedentedly full description of the author's intention and plan in writing the book. Professor Arthur H. Quinn of the University of Pennsylvania had written to Dorothy, saying, "I felt that the hero should have done something more essential and important at the end than the leading of an athletic parade!"[23] Dorothy responded:

I could lay my head down on my desk and weep that you should think that poor broken Anson Craft was the *hero* of "Bonfire," he whom I intended as the ne plus ultra of a failure, the blackness of his defeat the night against which the soaring triumph of the *heroine* of the book, his sister Anna, rises on a parabola of glorious happiness into the only heaven her generous soul could know, fulfillment and hope for some of life's disinheriteds!

I intended the pattern of the book to show the decline into defeat and failure of Anson, for I can't imagine any failure more abject than a grown man of brilliant intelligence who can get joy *only* in the adolescent triumph of an athletic team of boys; and the rise from disheartenment and apparent hopelessness (as far as personal happiness goes) of a great-hearted woman whose passion was to open prison doors and let out those unjustly shut up inside.

At the beginning of the book the line of Anson's life starts high in promise: vital, intelligent, established in the finest profession known to humanity, with a beautiful young girl in love with him; Anna's position in life seems a poor thing far below the boldly up-soaring curve of his, for she is no longer in her first youth, not beautiful, she is convinced that she has inherited melancholia, she has found no joy in her attempt to "do as she pleased" when she left her laborious position in Clifford to go to Paris, to easy well-paid work. But because Anson's attitude towards life is materialistic, cynical, non-generous, everything he touches turns to ashes, and it is the very violence of his failure which breaks Anna's reflex-habit of not taking the personal happiness then at her hand, and sets her free for personal joy. I refer here to the scene where Anson has the attack of angina, and startles Anna into an emotional crisis in which she realizes her love for Fred Kirby. This, in my visualization of the pattern is the point where Anson's descending and Anna's ascending lines cross.

Anson loves and marries in a materialistic reaction from all that makes love and marriage more than bodily love; and is betrayed to misery by just that, when poor dumb Lixlee takes him at his word and honestly tries to live as though bodily love were the supreme good. But no, the spoiled boy must have his cake and eat it too. He must have physical love as the supreme emotion, but it must *not* be supreme at the moment when his professional training makes him will to put something else first. Poor trapped bewildered Lixlee would have been better off with the wild man from Searles Shelf who *did* set his passion for her above everything else, and who meant what he said, as he showed when he killed himself at the end when she went away forever from Clifford.

When in your analysis of "Bonfire," you said the "ending is weak," it gave me a literal start, for the last chapter of that book is — for me — by all odds the most powerful and satisfactory I've ever written, almost too symmetrical and yet, I thought true. You see Anna's life soaring in blessedness — she is not only happy herself with an adored and adoring husband, a lovely child (why did you suppose I wrote the little vignette of her child asleep upstairs and the closed bud of the adolescent country girl getting her first intimation of the beatitude of maternity from looking at her?) with a second child on the way, but — equally important for her great soul, her darling project of rescuing those ignorant, poverty-stricken young people from the back-roads farms *is a success,* as you can see from the way those Merrill young people react to it.

I was church-thankful as I wrote, because I had for heroine a woman of so large a nature as to be incapable of that complacent satisfaction with her own personal satisfaction and happiness (or sorrow over her own personal unhappiness) which is all that most heroines of novels can (apparently) feel. She is in a kind of heaven on earth, Anna Craft is, there in Dewey House which is giving those needy adolescents what she had risen from the nether hell of personal unhappiness to fight for at the Town Meeting. And from the lighted windows of that heaven of fulfillment she looks out on poor Anson in the dark capering foolishly like David before the ark (why did you think I had him actually prancing with all sense of dignity gone, with a woman scorning him as she looked down on him from a window above, except to make my readers think of the gambling King David and another woman looking down on him?), and then across her heaven falls the shadow of perplexity and wonder (which is the beginning of a wider wisdom) at the unguessable complexity and confusion of human existence, where everything turns out so differently from what you expect, where you yourself who never tried for happiness, nor hoped for it for yourself, are drowned in bliss and your cherished brother who had it all in his grasp, is broken and defeated.

I *meant* her confession of bewilderment at the very end, to suggest to the reader (if he were subtle enough) that she was on the brink of realizing that she herself was a prime factor in Anson's defeat because she gave so immoderately to him all her devotion — so that she is on the brink of a new kind of wisdom, a new painfully acquired lore of living which will enable her hereafter to "be devoted" more wisely and to realize that even in devotion the necessity of keeping things in right proportion still exists.

Well, I never before, I think, tried to defend a book of mine from criticism. I see their faults so clearly I always take for granted that criticism is justified. But when I defend I rather go into it with all my might, don't I? I really didn't know what you meant by saying the end was "weak," and wanted to ask you. Your letter speaking of being disappointed in the end to which "the hero" had come, was a revelation to me of how totally you had (so it seems to me) mistaken my meaning. Was it all my fault that you did, do you think? Where was it that I failed to make that meaning clear?

Was I mistaken in thinking that I was strong enough to take on as "heroine" the kind of woman who in real life goes almost invisible, quite unrecognized? Did I risk too much in defying the unwritten literary convention that the person in the book who has the most vivid sex-experience is necessarily the central figure?[24]

Bonfire had hardly appeared in print before publishers were pressing Dorothy for a new novel. All her novels had been published by Harcourt, Brace and Company since Alfred Harcourt had left Holt in 1920 to go into business for himself. From time to time other publishers wrote to Dorothy suggesting that they might be able to offer her more favorable publication terms, but she consistently refused them. Now in the mid-1930s, however, she was one of the most popular American writers, and Alfred was anxious to secure the contract for her next novel even before she started writing it. An early indication that a new novel is on the way comes in an answer to such a request: "Yes, I do believe I see enough clear time ahead of me to make at least a start on that new novel. But let's wait before anything so concrete and definite as a contract, till I've made at least a beginning. Maybe it won't go! I'll tell you later."[25]

The new book was to have the same setting as *Bonfire,* but the center of the action would be in the local high school. A new group of Clifford people would be the main characters, and those central to *Bonfire* would now be peripheral. As she prepared to begin the actual writing, Dorothy wrote to Alfred Harcourt, "Yes, I'm just about to begin writing (I've been working on it in my mind for a long time) on a novel, laid in Clifford, Vermont, again and concerned with the old Seminary and the group of people of which it is the center. The Lord only knows how it'll go. It'll probably take forever. But the pot is just about ready to begin boiling."[26]

Work went slowly, and Dorothy wrote apologetically to Alfred Harcourt in 1936: "The novel progresses with my usual slowness—a good deal interrupted by living, as my novels always are."[27] In February 1938 she reported again, "The novel gets on slowly—delayed not by any lack of interest on my part—I'm in the usual author's naive fever of intense interest in every detail of it—but because I'm so pestered by a thousand demands on me to be a public character."[28] By the summer the novel had acquired a tentative name: "I'm working on 'Long May Our Land Be Bright' (I don't like Portrait of a Man of Decency any more than you do) as much as I can, with the keenest interest and delight in it,"[29] and by September she was nearing the end: " 'Long May Our Land Be Bright' and I are still wrestling together like Jacob at the ford, but I hope to be through with it by the first week in October—and unless I run into some special snag which I don't expect."[30]

The tentative title taken from the song "America" did not really suit the author, however. Dorothy wrote to Alfred: "I don't like it, myself, because it does mislabel the book, giving a disproportionate emphasis to what is only an incident in the portrayal of a man."[31] She further objected that "it would misrepresent the book, and that the (I admit quite probable) commercial advantages can't compare with other values involved."[32] After considering and rejecting a host of other titles, Dorothy wrote again to Alfred:

> Here's a suggestion which I really believe is the title we've been looking for. It's from a poem of George Herbert
>> Only a sweet and virtuous soul
>> Like SEASONED TIMBER never gives etc. etc.
> How about
>> *Seasoned Timber?*
> I think it expresses T.C., expresses the process that has taken place — that takes place with everybody in full maturity (if he's any good) expresses the difference between the strength of maturity and the strength of youth."[33]

Before writing anything down, Dorothy felt that she had to have a clear picture of the setting of the story. Among her papers at the University of Vermont is a folder with this note on the cover: "Notes — on location of seminary, budget, history etc. made before *Seasoned Timber* was begun. Very little of this data was ever directly used in the novel. But some such detailed information about the basic facts of a situation needs to be in the author's mind before anything substantial and firm in texture can be written."[34]

In connection with these notes, it is revealing to read Dorothy's statement to Edward Post, written as she was completing *Seasoned Timber:*

> I never can use notes or anything outside the novel when I am writing a novel. I always solemnly go through the same farce when I begin one. As I think about it — a process which often lasts six months or a year before I put pen to paper — a lot of ideas come into my head, and I often write them down. And I look over notes taken in between times and think "Now that's just to my purpose," and put that with the other notes. There they are in a folder, all ready for use, when I sit down, my heart in my mouth, in a panic, in an excitement, in a certainty of failure, in a wild hope of success — this time! — to begin work. But there they stay! I have the complete notes, entirely unused, for every novel I've ever written! The point is that when you are writing a novel, you are not yourself but inside the skin of each of the characters. And your notes are taken by yourself. So of course they don't exactly fit, ever! Such-and-such an observation is not what Timothy Hulme would have thought of, felt, but what Dorothy Canfield felt, when she was thinking, about him. So that observation doesn't fit, and gets left in the folder. But of course all those notes have left an impression on the mind of the author. . . . And of course they are in the book, though never literally. What's in the book is what the characters

would have made of such an observation.[35]

Seasoned Timber is the story of Timothy Coulton Hulme, known as "T.C.," the middle-aged principal of Clifford Academy, a school which is a curious hybrid between private academy and public high school in the little mountain village of Clifford, Vermont. Timothy's development takes place in two stages, and both play against a steady background of school and community activities. The first is the late-blooming love of T.C. for young Susan Barney, who has just begun teaching in the schools of Clifford. T.C. is a widower, forty-four years old when the book opens, the sole support of his ancient and eccentric aunt. It is a complete surprise to him when he finds himself falling in love with Susan, and he welcomes the light and life this affection brings into his existence. Susan's fondness for him grows, and he seems about to win her as his wife, when his nephew appears on the scene, and Timothy's anticipated joy gives way to a deepening and maturing experience of renunciation.

When the pain of his loss is at its height, a threat to the school forces Timothy to forget himself and to devote all his energies to a life-and-death struggle for the principles he holds most dear. A wealthy trustee of the academy has died, leaving a million dollars to the school on three conditions: 1) that it raise its tuition, 2) change its name to his, and 3) exclude Jews. Another quarter million is available if girls are also excluded. A new trustee must be elected, and the acceptance or rejection of the gift will be decided by that trustee's choice. T.C. and his friend Mr. Dewey lead the campaign to elect a trustee opposed to the gift. The temptation to take the gift is great and the campaign is close, but it ends in a triumphant majority for the principles of democracy, and the gift is rejected.

The election fight was the incident that caught public attention when the book appeared in 1939. Anti-Semitism was a contemporary problem, and international concern about German Fascist activities was growing. The news events in the background of the book were the contemporary dispatches of the day, and the principles the book so stoutly defends were the same ones that sent young American men to Europe and Asia in a war that was to cost the author the life of her own son.

The story is, however, not primarily a treatment of contemporary problems but the same kind of study of late maturation of character that Dorothy gave in Mrs. Bascomb of *Her Son's Wife*. T.C., like Mrs. Bascomb, must abandon completely any thought of happiness for himself before he can win a larger personal fulfillment. "It is the story of the development of a human being," Dorothy told an interviewer, one who "didn't find it any easier to be honorable than anybody else, but he came through both these trials (personal and public) triumphantly, retaining his dignity and his integrity."³⁶

The "Hulme" of T.C.'s name is the same as the middle name of Dorothy's father. Although setting and physical characteristics for Timothy Hulme are very different from those of James Hulme Canfield, so many of the most basic traits are the same that it is clear that Dorothy intended to pay tribute to her crusader parent. T.C. is as concerned with giving a chance for a good education to the boys and girls in isolated mountain communities as Dorothy's father was with making sure that every child in every village in Nebraska had the opportunity to enter "The Golden Door" of the state university. There is an echo of President Canfield's concern with the coeducational opportunities for women at Ohio State University in T.C.'s rejection of the suggestion that Clifford Academy exclude girls. Librarian Canfield's sulfurous diatribes against the concept of "gentleman and scholar" have a fictional counterpart in T.C.'s campaign against the corruptive million-dollar gift to the academy.

Discrepancies in physical appearance between James Hulme Canfield and T.C. are consistent with Dorothy's creative ethic. Some years earlier she had written to Paul Reynolds: "I'm in a perfect impasse — all the stories I want to write won't do because they would seem too much like putting real people and their troubles into print — friends of mine, I mean."³⁷ Another time, in a letter to Alfred Harcourt commenting on a new novel — where the young author had kept too close to an actual portrait of a real person — Dorothy wrote:

> Of course the young writer has done as inexperienced writers so often do, stuck literally to details which have nothing to do with the success of a character's depiction. It must be perfectly easy to change the external aspect, for instance, of the teacher . . . making him fat if he is thin, dark if he is red-haired etc. — which is quite sufficient to throw most people off the track. I'm writing to tell you this, hoping that it is not too late to make such changes (unimportant to the book's literary quality) as would make the story harmless to the defenseless people who would suffer in feelings and perhaps in purse, if it came out as it is.³⁸

T.C. is tall and slim, with aristocratic hands and thinning hair; James Hulme Canfield was short, stocky, and swarthy, with thick black (later snow white) hair and striking black eyes. This is just the sort of obvious physical change in appearance that Dorothy had suggested in the case of the young writer above.

There are other names in *Seasoned Timber* that come from Dorothy's family, and each name seems to carry with it some traits of the original owner. So Susan Barney, the young woman whom Timothy loves, bears the same family name as Dorothy's grandmother Martha Barney. Martha turned her back on the security of her Vermont home to follow her pioneer husband into the wilderness. Susan Barney in the novel rejects the "safe" old stone house of her ancestors, and the secure life with T.C. that it symbolizes, for a free, almost gypsy life with Timothy's nephew, a builder of "flimsy wooden houses" that you can fit to your own needs "when you feel like having more windows or another door."[39]

Susan's sister Delia has the name of Dorothy's maternal aunt, of whom she wrote: "Delia Camp Fletcher was the youngest of the 'Camp girls' — my mother's sisters. She married a businessman and lived in Clear Lake, Iowa, and Minneapolis, Minnesota. Unlike my mother, she held to the New England tradition of great interest in details of the family history, and — more static than any of her volatile, changeable, sisters, — kept records of a good many of them."[40] Delia of the novel is ambitious and methodical, with a good mind for details.

Eli, the young man with a combination of "stern Doric dignity"[41] and "business sense . . . more'n his little finger than you and me in our hull bodies," according to one of his associates,[42] has the name of Dorothy's clergyman grandfather, Eli Hawley Canfield, who led his church into areas of social betterment. When the fictional Eli of the novel campaigns for the good of the school and extends his bus route into outlying districts, he is "ablaze with a simple faith in 'education' . . . . In every one of these tall, rusty-haired, bashful, rustic boys and girls, only a little younger than he, he saw himself — poor, overlooked, forgotten, excluded from the civilization around him. He fought for their chance as he had for his own."[43] Again the setting and the specific details of appearance and mannerism are different, but Eli the grandfather had also burned with a desire for an education, and later with zeal to give others the chance he had had. From what appeared to be an inescapable environmental trap, he had, like the fictional Eli, become "*some*body".[44]

Another autobiographical note is a reference to the Vermont wild-flowers, arbutus and hepaticas. Timothy mentions them in answer to a question put by the mother of a prospective student, "Tell me, do country children — still go out in the woods in May to pick wildflowers?"[45] Timothy has spent all day in New York, beaten about by its impersonality and commercialism, and the wild-flower names sound "unreal" to him even as he pronounces them. "What were hepaticas and arbutus?" he muses. "Nothing real, surely, like merchandise for sale. He could not remember how they looked."[46] The same contrast between the very present city and the distant country had many years earlier given a special quality to the hepaticas that were John Fisher's courtship present to Dorothy.

In the introduction to *Raw Material,* Dorothy wrote of the family habit of making speeches to oneself. In *Seasoned Timber,* T.C. pauses by the edge of a snowy road, still burning with a missed opportunity to say something meaningful to a group of students about the threat of fascism, and suddenly

> his floundering, halting, qualifying ineptitude melted away in the exquisite illusion of triumphant mastery which comes when a man is talking to himself. In the fool's paradise of the inner colloquy, with a docile and admiring interlocutor who is eagerly receptive, who requires no tiresome proof of what you say, who never doubts, never misunderstands, for whom your confusion is crystal clear, who is never mocking, always sympathetic — what masterstrokes can be dealt, what glorious victories won! Timothy expanded guilelessly in the certainty that inspiration had at last come to him, that now he knew perfectly how to say what he wanted, and strode off from cloud to cloud, hurling thunderbolts.[47]

The speech that Timothy then delivers to his imagination would have done credit to Dorothy's crusading educator father, with his faith in free trade and his belief in human equality despite economic differences, when he thunders:

> Laugh in the faces of the Fascist priests who chant the new Black Mass when they tell you boys and girls that democratic government means nothing but license for the money-getters. The impudence of them to use that line of attack, with their marching and countermarching pauper-slaves, no better off economically than economic serfs have always been. . . . The enormous idiocy of too-great wealth and too-great poverty, doesn't it come because a primitive way of handling one side of life has hung on into our emerging civilization, where it's no longer useful — the vermiform appendix of modern society? . . . It is not enough to be alone. Nor to be together. . . . Don't let yourselves be cheated out of the rich complexity of the human birthright. See, there is the goal before you, to fight for both.[48]

The inclusion in the novel of the attack on anti-Semitism made it too controversial for serial publication. When Paul Reynolds reported one editor's objections to the plan for the novel, Dorothy replied:

> Yes, I thought that probably putting in so living a controversial subject as race prejudice would not be to her editorial taste. She is probably quite right — the readers of her magazine wouldn't like to have such a red-hot poker picked up in their presence. Yes, that part of the story is an essential part of it. T. C., a highly intelligent man feels all through the first part of the story that he has been out of the real battle-field of human life, has been off in a safe corner, where there are no red-hot pokers lying around.

His love for Susan is partly a fumbling reach for something to fill that void. Then when the ugly modern octopus flings a tentacle so far afield that it reaches his quiet little corner, his chance comes to strike a real blow — at a real risk to himself — for the cause of decency and human dignity. And that sends him on into the next phase of his life, very much more satisfied — feeling that he has after all made his life count for a good cause. So you see, the story would lose its point if that strong element were left out. But I think it quite possible that most editors would react . . . that it is really too disagreeable to subject to think about — (of course one of my purposes is to make people, comfortable in their own remoteness from the problem think about it!) — and to be mentioned in an audible voice. . . . I hope I've made myself clear on the Jewish question. I think race prejudice is creeping in insidiously to American life . . . I'm ashamed of it, and I think most decent Americans would be ashamed of it, if they stopped to think about it. T. C. is a decent American. Q.E.D.[49]

Dorothy sent the manuscript before publication to Harry Scherman, who wrote enthusiastically that she had succeeded in an "achievement of reality . . . the kind Henry James succeeded in,"[50] and that T.C. was "the first Jamesian character, almost, that I can think of in any book — since James."[51] He went on to say that "Timothy himself has haunted me as a creation," and he reminisced about an earlier era of which he was reminded by *Seasoned Timber*: "What a different day that was in novel-writing, when we could all really get worked up by the *people* in books, not the problems — the social problems, anyway. When they remained in the consciousness — really forever, like people one knows, in unusual circumstances."[52]

When *Seasoned Timber* arrived at the offices of Harcourt, Brace and Company, the younger editors joined with the Harcourts in their enthusiastic reception. Alfred wrote to Dorothy, "The boys agree with Ellen and me that this is your best novel *so far*."[53] Alfred thought that it should be tried once more for serial publication, so Dorothy sent it again to Paul Reynolds with the comment: "Mr. Harcourt is so (rather unexpectedly to me) enthusiastic about this novel I'm just finishing, and so *sure* that it will make acceptable serial material that I'm sending it to you . . . although after your total lack of any success with it some years ago, I've little idea you'll find an editor interested."[54] In spite of Alfred's enthusiasm, only part of the novel was ever published serially. This was the story of the campaign against the gift to the academy, which appeared in *Scribner's* and *Scholastic* magazines and then in book form as *The Election on Academy Hill*.[55]

Seasoned Timber was translated into French with a title that stresses the individual side of the story, *Ce Coeur a tant de Peine* (This Heart Has So

Much Trouble).[56] John Fisher wrote of the novel that "success here called for persuading the reader (against all romantic tradition) that Timothy's apparent failure was actually a success in forcing him into the life-activity suited to his age. The whole thing is a highly technical set of variations on a theme — the theme being Emerson's, 'When half-gods go, the Gods arrive.' The problem was to get the reader's mind to underline the word just before: 'HEARTILY know, when half-gods go.' "[57]

In many ways *Seasoned Timber* is a summation of Dorothy's novelistic work. Neither she nor anyone else knew that this was to be her last novel. She was sixty years old, but like her book she possessed a kind of mellowed strength. John Wright Buckham wrote of the book:

> It is itself a piece of seasoned timber, a masterpiece of the art of fiction, having the soundness and maturity of form and content such as only exceptional insight and a trained and experienced hand can produce. If something of the brilliant *aper-çus* and the engaging ardor of the earlier books is wanting, it is more than made up by the breadth of outlook and fecundity of wisdom, combined with thrilling and sustained interest, that characterize this truly notable novel. It has both the dramatic movement and the integral unity of an enduring work of human value and literary art.[58]

One device by which the effect of inner unity is produced in *Seasoned Timber* is the tracing of two lives, whose lines intertwine in ways significant for both. The opening scene shows Timothy Hulme answering the door reluctantly to one of the less-promising students in the academy, Eli Kemp. In this encounter Timothy is conscious of his own superiority, of his background in the upper-class Hulmes (spelled with an *l*), from whom he has inherited an ivory-headed cane and an embroidered motto "Noblesse oblige." He is equally conscious of the contrast this background makes with "Eli's worthless, drunken, bee-hunting, and muskrat-trapping father, his dull-witted, feeble mother, the foredoomed futility of Eli's poor efforts to educate the brains he did not have."[59]

By gradual stages Timothy throws away his aristocratic differences from the people around him and becomes one of them. When, near the end of the book, some students come to borrow his cane for a play, it is not to be found, and "he had no recollection of it at all. It must have been months ago since he had last used it."[60] As the cane has gradually and unconsciously slipped into disuse, so have Timothy's habits of aristocratic thought. Eli has meanwhile been climbing upward through the social structure, until Timothy sees his uncanny ability for making money as a threat to society and begins to discuss altruistic economic philosophy with him.

Always the educator, and now an increasingly selfless one, Timothy himself has grown to maturity and inner peace. Eli represents the disadvantaged students who need him most. A symbolic scene closes the novel, where Timothy sits by his namesake, Susan's baby, and senses his unity with all humanity.

Timothy's inner peace is not an experience of religious asceticism, however, and Dorothy hotly protested the first design for a book jacket, which showed a New England village church. "You should have seen the first sketch," she reported. "It has a narrow-chested church on the center of the design. I said to the publishers, 'That isn't a Vermont church, it is a Massachusetts church, and besides, there is no church in this book!' "[61] Timothy's peace is rather "the tranquility of one who has come to a goal."[62]

Part 4

The Short Fiction

"The writer is not born with more capacity than other people for seeing color and interest and meaning in life. He is merely so made that he cannot rest till he has told everybody who will listen to him the impression that life has made on him. This is the queer mainspring of creative literature."

Raw Material

12
Early Collaborations:
Hillsboro People, The Real Motive,
Fellow Captains, The Sturdy Oak

In the same Vermont valley with Dorothy Canfield, but sixteen miles away in the town of Dorset, lived another author, Zephine Humphrey, and halfway between them in Manchester lived still another, Sarah N. Cleghorn. Of the three Robert Frost once wrote: "One of these is wise and a novelist, one is mystic and an essayist, and the third is saintly and a poet."[1] All three had published volumes with Henry Holt, and when he visited Vermont in June 1908 he decided to invite the Fishers, Zephine, and Sarah to Fairholt, his home in Burlington, for the weekend. It was a first meeting for the three authors, and from that time on they became fast friends. In her autobiography Sarah wrote:

> Especially have we shared with each other whatever we might be writing, or even projecting; and in this way all Dorothy's novels, back to and including *The Squirrel-Cage,* have been familiar to Zephine and me long before the publisher saw them. Weighting down her three or four chapters with apples to keep them from blowing away, as we sat on the grass in Zephine's orchard, Dorothy would read us, in her rapid, lucid easy manner, an early draft, perhaps a little angular, with events not mellowed yet by detail nor fully shaded with sidelights and shadows — not deepened by reflection; and the next month she would read us the same chapters in second, third or seventh draft, coming out now in rich complexities of deed, thought and character.[2]

The three young women remained fast friends, and when Dorothy visited the Montessori schools during the winter of 1911–12, Sarah and Zephine were with her in Rome.

The friendship with Sarah Cleghorn was an especially deep and meaningful one for Dorothy, so much so that when her little daughter was born in

1909, she named her Sarah and asked Sarah Cleghorn to be godmother. For the sensitive single friend this was an overwhelming compliment. "When I heard her name," she wrote later, "and that I was to be her godmother, I felt an extraordinary sensation — I was drenched with thrilling and incredulous vainglory. And not for a moment only, but every time I thought of it for years. It's one of the great and lasting elations of my life."[3]

Sarah Cleghorn was a convinced socialist and an active member of the socialist movement in America. Her love and devotion for Dorothy, together with her concern with social problems, gave her a rare insight into Dorothy's work, which she expressed in the following evaluation:

> It's always illuminating to see Dorothy in process of stabilizing all she writes by her constant re-pinning of it fast to the common lot, to generic human experience. Her greatest achievement, to my way of thinking, lies in her power to stand firmly on this realistic ground while at the same time she pulls a possible future right through the present. It's a thing teachers sometimes do, but they seldom know how they do it, and I'm fairly sure Dorothy doesn't know how she does it. Teachers do it for individual children, whom they know fairly well; Dorothy does it for an unknown multitude. In her public speaking there's the same double reflection of the audience — a picture soberly true, yet expanding under its own eyes, in full daylight, into a whole category of its possibilities. . . . Nobody could single out the influences strongly affecting American life for the first quarter of this century without including Dorothy's novels. They seize the reader by an intimate hand and take him at once on an incursion and an excursion. Readers have learned to expect that her next novel will take them a little farther still into their possible selves.[4]

Sarah Cleghorn had published poetry in many of the leading magazines of her day, but her most widely quoted piece of verse is probably the quatrain that appeared first in Franklin P. Adams's column in *The Tribune*:

> The golf links lie so near the mill
> That almost every day
> The laboring children can look out
> And see the men at play.[5]

When Dorothy's first collection of short stories, *Hillsboro People,* was published in 1915, it contained, in addition to eighteen narratives by Dorothy Canfield, eight poems by Sarah Cleghorn.

The common element in the stories of *Hillsboro People* is their Vermont setting, many of them laid in the mythical town of Hillsboro, a transparent disguise for Arlington, Vermont. Using this fictional setting, Dorothy contemplates in narrative form the human scene before her.

There are a number of themes that run through this collection of stories. A defense of rural, homespun, "genuine" values against the "artificial" standards of materialistic, fashionable, urban society is the basic element of several of them, including "Petunias — That's for Remembrance," a tale that Eleanor Roosevelt once named her "favorite story."[6] Other tales, however, admit that rural life is not the answer for everyone, and that the narrow valley can stifle as well as liberate personality.

At about this time Dorothy was herself worried about the effect on her literary art of isolation from urban circles. When she went to New York, editors and fellow writers urged her to remain with them. It was always a relief to her to return to the quiet surroundings she loved, yet she respected her urban friends, and their warnings worried her. In February 1916 she wrote to Paul Reynolds:

> I tell you, it seems good to get back to big pines and long, still nights, and rosy children, and welcoming farmer-neighbors! I just snap my fingers at Mr. Gilman Hall and his reiterated advice not to "hold myself so aloof from literary atmosphere" but to go down to the city for a couple of months a year and foregather with editors and other writers, for the purpose of keeping in touch with what's going on in "that world." Seriously, do you think there is anything in that sort of advice — for me at least? I'd really like to know.[7]

Reynolds answered her reassuringly, "I don't think it's important for you to foregather with the editors and other people down here in New York. I think they probably do an author more harm than good."[8]

Other aspects of life in *Hillsboro People* are the worth and dignity of personalities outside the social mainstream, and the deceptive quality of superficial appearance, which may mask a very complex reality. The thread that runs through the whole collection, however, is the indomitable nature of the human spirit, a potential strength that can rise to superhuman levels when faced with necessity. In some tales this quality serves as a talisman against despair, in others it gives an example of the purest selfless devotion, but in every case it has the capability of taking the readers, in Sarah Cleghorn's phrase, "a little farther still into their possible selves."

"The Artist," a story of the subjection of a fine artistic talent to the demands of a life of service to others, drew this comment from Henry Holt on its first appearance: "I have just read your 'Artist' in March Scribner's. Heavens, how you are growing! Every girl ought to have a big husband and a little baby if she has any literature in her: they fetch it out most wonderfully."[9]

One story, "A Drop in the Bucket," may have been written with Sarah Cleghorn in mind. It tells how the tales of a socialist cobbler neighbor stir a conservative New England spinster to travel to Chicago to bring back some victims of society's inhumanity to share her life in Hillsboro. Sarah had become an ardent socialist, and she campaigned actively for social reforms. Although Dorothy could not find answers along the same paths, she felt a great deal of interest in her friend's activities. Once she wrote to her, "I wonder if I ever told you that it was my father's intention to devote his energies after he retired from Columbia to two objects — the amelioration of prison conditions, and the abolition of child labour. You can just think with what poignant sympathy I read anything you have to say about prison amelioration."[10]

Henry Holt, who brought out *Hillsboro People,* wished to publish a second collection the following year. This volume also contained poems by Sarah Cleghorn and short stories by Dorothy Canfield. The title, *The Real Motive,* suggests a thematic basis for the collection, a contrast between the apparent and the real, but this theme is not borne out by an examination of the contents. Only the initial sketch, "The Pragmatist," and two of the subsequent tales ("A Sleep and a Forgetting" and "A Good Fight and the Faith Kept") have hidden motivation as a dominant aspect. The others are a motley group, varying widely in theme and narrative quality, and including three stories ("The City of Refuge," "An Untold Story," and "The Sick Physician") that Dorothy valued but that had not been accepted by serial publications.

After making her selection of stories for the book, Dorothy wrote to Alfred Harcourt:

> My own impression of "The Real Motive" collection is that it is more uneven than Hillsboro People. It has quite a few stories which I think are better than anything in H. P.; but then again it has some others which maybe aren't so good. It's simply distracting to try to decide about the lighter ones — whether they're good enough to be permanently preserved! Just because they're lighter is no reason why they're not good, if they *are* good — but when you come on one after reading one of the very serious, deep-going ones, why, you feel it's pretty trifling — at least that's the way some of them strike *me* — but you said to leave them in to temper the tone of the whole volume — anyhow to leave them in till you and some other critic outside the Fisher family had seen them. So they go down to you.[11]

Among matters treated in the narratives of *The Real Motive* are social distinctions in the midwestern academic community and in the business world, the opposition of the values of "art" to the values of "life," several love stories with differing conclusions, and a sketch of the maturing influence of a new baby on its mother. This last story, "Vignettes from a Life of Two Months," is almost the only piece of fiction Dorothy wrote in the six months following the birth of her son James Canfield Fisher in December 1913, a period during which repeated apologetic notes from Dorothy to her literary agent Paul Reynolds promised stories that were not forthcoming. After "Vignettes from a Life of Two Months" was sold, Dorothy wrote on May 15, 1914, "I shall try to put the real baby a little more to one side and so some writing soon."[12]

In lieu of new stories Dorothy had earlier sent Reynolds "The Sick Physician" and "The City of Refuge," which she labeled "the ones which the various editors who saw them characterized as 'queer,' by which they may mean 'too serious' or quite simply 'not well enough written.' "[13] Neither of these stories is a light or amusing piece of fiction. The main character of "The Sick Physician" kills herself while performing an operatic suicide scene, and "The City of Refuge" presents dramatic art as a monster that devours the human qualities of those who achieve its successes. Reynolds was not able to sell these stories, and he wrote to Dorothy about the problem of marketing pessimistic fiction, "A story where things go to smash is always difficult to sell, because people like to be amused, rested, comforted when they read. Their daily life generally gives them all the smashing they need — or at least they think so."[14]

In 1916 also appeared another collaborative work by Dorothy Canfield and Sarah Cleghorn, entitled *Fellow Captains*. The idea for this volume was Sarah's, and an early title that was later discarded was "Home Grown Secrets of Serenity."[15] The curious little book opens with a list of "loquentes personae," the members of "the fortnightly club," which means, we are told, that "five neither young nor old American women had settled themselves in wicker chairs on the porch for the twice-a-month conversations in which, for a good many years, this group of life-long friends had talked over their differences of opinion."[16]

There is no particular attempt to hide the identity of these speakers, called Anna, Sarah, Emily, Mildred, and Dorothy. Dorothy is described in the list of persons as "a housewife, mother, and novelist, who was, with odd inappropriateness, trained to special knowledge in Old French philology, and still preserves a leaning towards analytic ways of thought, united with considerable courage in pursuing them, and accepting their conclusions."[17]

Dorothy begins the discussion by reading a "fantastic parable"[18] she has just finished writing. The parable is entitled "The Secret of Serenity,"[19] and after the reading a lively discussion develops among the friends about the merits of different approaches to the problems of life. This discussion is followed by two final sections of the book: "Sarah's Collection" and

"Dorothy's Note-Book." The first of these contains original verse by Sarah Cleghorn, poems employing the power of suggestion to induce desired states of mind. The second gathers together Dorothy's favorite quotations, which range from brief, pithy aphorisms to beloved passages of poetry and present an interesting revelation of the personality of the author herself.

Dorothy was asked to participate in another collaborative effort, *The Sturdy Oak,* which appeared in 1917. Woman suffrage was a burning political issue at this time, and it was decided to ask fourteen leading authors each to contribute a chapter to a composite novel that would aid the campaign to give women the vote. The proceeds from the serial and book sale of the novel were to be devoted to the suffrage cause. The editor, who was to solicit and coordinate the chapters, was Elizabeth Jordan, and the fourteen authors were Samuel Merwin, Harry Leon Wilson, Fannie Hurst, Dorothy Canfield, Kathleen Norris, Henry Kitchell Webster, Anne O'Hagan, Mary Heaton Vorse, Alice Duer Miller, Ethel Watts Mumford, Marjorie Benton Cooke, William Allen White, Mary Austin, and Leroy Scott. *The Sturdy Oak* was subtitled "A Composite Novel of American Politics by Fourteen American Authors" and is, as its introduction claims, "a very human story of American life."[20]

The main character of the story is George Remington, "Aged twenty-six; newly married. Recently returned to his home town, New York State, to take up the practice of law. Politically ambitious, a candidate for District Attorney. Opposed to woman suffrage."[21] To convert George to the side of the suffrage cause, his antisuffrage views are followed to their logical conclusion. He publishes a statement proclaiming a man's duty to protect his women relatives, and immediately an assortment of dependent women move in on him and his young wife.

Dorothy was assigned Chapter 4 of the narrative, in which the invasion of the Remington home takes place. Her description of events is accomplished with a delightful irony of understatement, a shade of Vermont humor that contrasts amusingly with the style of some of her more discursive fellow authors. As in many of her other narratives, her attention is focused on the contrast between superficially correct behavior and underlying feelings, here with highly comic effect.

The book as a whole is a museum piece, containing as it does within the covers of one volume examples of the contrasting styles of contemporary authors, all writing on the same theme.

13
From World War I:
Home Fires in France, The Day of Glory,
Basque People

During her years in France, Dorothy sent a steady stream of articles and stories home to America for publication. These were written partly to arouse American sympathy for the French and partly to raise money to support the relief work in which Dorothy was engaged.

Among the things she sent to Paul Reynolds were a series of war sketches, which she regarded as "better work than any short stories I've ever done."[1] One of these, "La Pharmacienne," became longer than she had planned, as Dorothy developed her interest in the underlying reasons for character and action. She wrote about it:

> It is a study of a Frenchwoman, typical nice, housekeeper, good-mother variety, who is hard hit by the war, living in the war-zone, and is little by little transformed out of being a house-cat into being one of the stern, unconsciously heroic obscure heroines of France. To my mind the study has value because nobody has said a word as yet about the *processes* by which all this unexpected heroism has been evolved out of the French people. There has been a great deal of exclaiming and admiring, but I have a notion that most Americans don't *realize* by what hard and bitter and horrible phases the Frenchwomen have had to pass before they emerged from being just nice home-keepers into being guardians of the public weal, as they are to so great an extent in the deserted villages and towns. And I don't think American women realize at all how many of the little prettinesses of life the French women have had to leave behind, and leave behind forever — I don't think ever ever they can be so foolishly important as before. All this, I find, can't be said, even using suggestion ever so freely, in a short sketch.[2]

Of another of the sketches, "The Permissionaire," W. A. Wolff of

Everybody's Magazine wrote to Dorothy:

> I wrote to Collier's that it was the finest story I'd seen come out of the war — I amended that to say it was the best short story I'd ever read. I do think so. I congratulate you, and I envy you, and I owe you my thanks for the loveliest and most heartrending and inspiring thing I've ever seen in words. And everyone I know feels as I do. It would have done your heart good to see the Collier bunch when they got the story — and to see them going around now, in their sinful pride.[3]

In 1918 *Home Fires in France* was published, a collection of stories in which the anguish of a war-torn country is portrayed in vignettes of the people whose sufferings Dorothy shared. In answer to her mother's comment on the moving quality of this volume, Dorothy wrote, "I'm glad to know that you wept over it, for I wept over some of those stories, and went to bed *sick* after working over them. It would be a pity if I hadn't communicated some of that emotion."[4] William Lyon Phelps read the book in galley proof, and Alfred Harcourt reported to Dorothy, "When Professor Phelps returned the proofs, he said, 'It is a wonderful book. I think it is bound to make a powerful impression in America. It is a remarkable interpretation of the French people to Americans. No one except a born novelist could have written such a brilliant book.' "[5]

The Americans entered the war, the tide was turned, and Dorothy and the children could return to Versailles in October 1918, a month before the end of the war. Six months later the Fishers sailed for America, and in May 1919 they were back in Arlington, Vermont. Later the same year, Dorothy's second book of war stories, *The Day of Glory,* was published.

In portraying the war Dorothy focused her attention on plain men and women in whom the horrors and crises of an invaded homeland uncovered new strength of spirit. The series of sketches that make up her two war books display a search for the springs of strength in these ordinary people.

The "home fires" in France are the hearth fires of both France and America, for in this collection Dorothy tries to explain the two nations to each other and to reconcile their differences. She does this partly through confrontation and argument, as in the encounter of an American and a French druggist in "A Fair Exchange" or the story of the American buyer in "Hats." In "The Permissionaire" and "La Pharmacienne" she shows French people in situations that parallel those of American life, but where their behavior is typically French and thereby different from that of their American counterparts. In "A Little Kansas Leaven" and "A Honeymoon . . . Vive l'Amérique!" those positive American qualities which most puzzle the French appear in fictional form.

Whereas *Home Fires in France* is a French-American book, skillfully showing that the war is an experience of people and hence deserving of human sympathy and understanding, *The Day of Glory* is an antiwar book, whose title was chosen in obvious irony. In this second, much slimmer volume of war tales the war itself in all its horror is brought home to the reader. The inanity of the conflict and the personal agony of the participants provide the dominant tone, a much darker mood than that of the earlier book. The keynote here is the courage of silence and resignation—a sharp contrast with the stories of the earlier collection, which showed the power for active heroism lying dormant in the human spirit.

The first story in *The Day of Glory,* "On the Edge," reports the mixed ecstasy and agony of the all-too-brief home leave of a soldier and the struggles of a young wife and mother with emotional and physical burdens too heavy for her to bear. She is repeatedly pushed to the edge of hysteria but always drags herself back once more to go on.

Dorothy said of "On the Edge" that "it pretty nearly broke my heart to write it, but as usual I haven't any idea as to whether the emotion will penetrate the words and get to American readers."[6] She sent it to John at the front and reported, "He thinks it the best one of the series, and was so painfully impressed by its truth and dreadfulness that he said he almost reverted to the school of those who said such sad things ought not to be written! And he is anxious to have it appear in the book."[7] To Alfred Harcourt, who was handling the publication of the book at Henry Holt & Co., she wrote, "I sent over a story recently to Reynolds 'On the Edge' which personally I think the best one I have done—but then, stories are like babies, the youngest is always the pet!"[8]

The second story, "France's Fighting Woman Doctor," is a vignette of a heroic woman who was called by mistake to the front, took her full share of the burdens of war, and returned to organize a training program for military nurses. Then follows a piece entitled "Lourdes," which is really a pair of sketches, describing the famous shrine in the afternoon, when long lines of cripples, many of them victims of the war, pray for the blessing, and in the evening, when the joyful, light-bearing pilgrims ascend the hill through wind and rain.

The difficulty of writing at all in France at that time is shown in Dorothy's letters about the Lourdes sketches. She had written to Paul Reynolds from Guethary in May 1918, "As for the material for fiction stories, that I always have with me, like the poor. But I have to have a certain amount of leisure to get that out, and peace of mind about the children, and a well-regulated life etc. etc., all things which in war-time are mighty hard to get."[9] In September she wrote, "I have been to Lourdes, to the big annual pilgrimage there and on my return found my little boy slightly under the weather, just enough to make me spend a sleepless night. That's about the only occasion I have to write, nowadays, and I set down on paper two impressions of Lourdes."[10] A footnote to the sketches themselves is added in a letter a month later, "I particularly meant the torch-light procession to be a symbol of humanity, and not a dispiriting symbol either."[11] The final impression with which the sketch ends bears this out: "Last of all I saw a strong young man whose light had been extinguished, holding out his lifeless candle to that of an old, poor, bent woman who, patiently, patiently, offered him her tiny, living flame."[12]

The subject is again the war itself in "Some Confused Impressions." The reader is shown the American soldiers in France; they appear through the eyes of the French, and the French through theirs, always separated by the language barrier. "It Is Rather for Us to Be Here Dedicated" is a grim sketch, in which the sacrifice symbolized in the body of an American soldier, lying where he was killed in a French field, is contrasted with the inhumanity and greed of French citizens in a nearby town. The clear implication is that the sacrifice was not justified. The final sketch, "The Day of Glory," is a portrayal of the French reaction to the signing of the armistice, a time when a new sense of brotherhood was felt among the common people. The little volume raises many questions, and the answers, as indicated in the personalities described, are confused and frequently pessimistic.

One of Dorothy's most frightening war experiences was her little daughter Sally's bout with typhoid fever. When Sally had recovered sufficiently to be moved, Dorothy took her from Paris to the warm, sunny Basque country for a long convalescence. There Dorothy became acquainted with the French Basques, whom she found in many ways similar to her beloved Vermonters. In isolation they, too, had developed pride in their own traditions, self-reliance, and a distrust of "city people." Robert Frost once said of Dorothy that "the Basques she lived with and wrote about read to me like Vermonters,"[13] and Dorothy herself included the "Basques from St. Jean-Pied-de-Port" among those "people who wouldn't know how to find Vermont in a geography book and yet who have a natural affinity for what we think of as our way of life."[14]

When Dorothy first described the projected stories to Paul Reynolds, she said that the collection would be "a little like The Home Fires in France material, only without Hamlet —, that is, without the intensity of war-feeling."[15]

Basque People, which appeared in 1931, contains eight stories about the

Basque country and its people. They are told as Dorothy experienced them, by a French-speaking outsider living in the area. Four of them are told to this narrator by a Basque schoolteacher, a woman "who had been born and brought up in a remote Basque-speaking valley in the Pyrenees, had had a few years' training in a normal school of the region, and after that for twenty-five years had taught school in this little settlement of fishermen and small farmers tucked in between the Bay of Biscay and the Pyrenees."[16] These firsthand experiences are interspersed with four other narratives about Basque traditions.

The collection is in many ways similar to the volume of Vermont narratives *Hillsboro People*. The Basques, like the Vermonters, are pictured as defensive of their simple way of life and opposed to more sophisticated urban patterns. The first story, "At the Sign of 'The Three Daughters,'" is told to answer the often repeated tourist's comment "But the Basques have no art."[17] The answer is the same as that Dorothy has given in her writings about Vermont: "Is there no poetry that is not written but lived?"[18]

The simplicity of Basque life, away from the expensive entertainments of urban centers, is given charming expression in a description of the arrival of the traveling puppeteer in the Basque village, "Vive Guignol!" This is also a story of the way that the Basques can put important matters, even if they are only the children's enjoyment of the annual visit of Guignol, ahead of official rules (here school schedules) artificially imposed from outside.

A more serious tale of the resistance of a Basque community to the artificial pressures of outside officialdom is found in the final story of the collection, "The Majesty of the Law." It tells of a witchcraft trial in 1609, when the fishermen of the community return from the sea just in time to save their wives from punishment at the hands of the court and to run the French judges out of town.

There are three love stories in the collection, two of them involving competition between native and foreign suitors for a Basque hand. Two stories of Basque emigrants complete the number, one of a local boy who has become rich in Argentina, and the other of an American schoolteacher of part Basque ancestry who returns to her ancestral home.

This last story involved Dorothy in an argument with her sister-in-law about literal truth versus fictional truth. In the tale she describes a cave with ancient paintings and tells of primitive religious rites performed by country people. "If you read the story called "An Ancestral Home,'" Dorothy wrote to Alfred Harcourt,

You'll remember that the old Basque woman made a sort of libation of bread and milk to the spirits of her ancestors, and the American great-niece discovered a cave with paintings presumably done by her ancestors. Now all that is imaginary — fiction. Betty Fisher is shocked by that, says when an author is read in the high schools of the country she must stick to truth not fake things etc. What do you think? Why can't I invent that part of a story as well as any other? This is not a volume of ethnology or anthropology I'm writing, but stories. And the Basque worship of the remote past is well represented by that story, even if it isn't literally true.[19]

Dorothy must have won the argument, for the tale appears in the published collection with the libations and the cave paintings included.

The strong presence of the past, the independence, the material poverty, and the distrust of outsiders are reminiscent of Vermont traditions, but there are other traits shown in the collection that are uniquely Basque:

the strangeness of their racial isolation, not only unrelated to the European Aryans all around them, but to any other of the races of mankind; their legendary vitality which has outlasted the Romans, the Goths, the Moors, feudalism, monarchy, industrialism; their passionate clinging to incomprehensible old folkways; the oddness of the fact that unlike all other peoples they never seem to have roamed and migrated to and fro, but (since they are probably descendants of the Pyrenean cave-dwellers) are the only human beings in the history of our race who took root where they were planted.[20]

The problem of a title for the collected Basque sketches was debated back and forth by letter between Dorothy and her publisher. Dorothy and John suggested this list: *Along the Biscay Coast, Berets and Espadrilles,* and *Between the Sea and the Mountains,* with the subtitle *Children of the Eskualdunak,* using the Basques' own name for themselves.[21] Then Dorothy's brother Jim suggested "The Land Lost to Satan," from an old Basque legend. "You may remember," Dorothy wrote to Alfred Harcourt,

the story that Satan once noticed that the Basques were getting on too well, that he had no hold on them, and went down to live in the Basque country to get them under his hold as well as the rest of humanity. He stayed for seven years studying the language, because of course he couldn't influence them if he couldn't speak their language, and by that time he had learned the Basque word for "yes." Then he stayed seven more and had learned the Basque word for "no." But by that time he had forgotten the word for "Yes," so he gave it up as a bad job and left them in peace.

She went on to say, "It's not only a mildly amusing racial legend, but it is significant of the attitude the Basques have about themselves — that they somehow have a better grasp on *how to live* than races that are smarter than they in many other ways."[22]

John questioned Dorothy's enthusiasm for the Basques, and she responded to his skepticism with spirit. "Mr. Fisher says I'm as hipped on the subject of the inherent interest of the Basques as Sir Walter Scott was about the Scotch," she wrote to Paul Reynolds. "And I say if I can hypnotize a hundredth part as many people into thinking the Basque interesting as Scott fooled folks into thinking the Scotch lore was important, I'll send up rockets."[23]

Of all the reviews of *Basque People,* Dorothy found one published in Italian in *Il Popolo di Roma* by the Italian scholar Adriano Tilgher "the most understanding one . . . in any language."[24] This reviewer had written: "Put together subtle observations, amiable irony and gentle satire. Add to this a strongly bitter pessimism, a taste for fables and legends. Enrich it with a rough carving of actions and characters, and the finished product is a recent book *Basque People* . . . the happy marriage between 'old' and 'modern.' "[25]

14
Two Do-It-Yourself Collections:
Raw Material and *Made-to-Order Stories*

In the decade following World War I, Dorothy Canfield published two unusual collections of short prose narratives, *Raw Material* (1923) and *Made-to-Order Stories* (1925). These volumes offer an invitation to readers to have the fun of being authors themselves. In the introduction to *Raw Material* the author writes:

> It is for the active-minded people who enjoy doing their own thinking as well as watching the author do his, that I have put this volume together. When life speaks to them, their hearts answer, as a friend to a friend. They are my brothers and my sisters. They practice the delight-giving art of being their own authors. They know the familiar, exquisite interest of trying to arrange in coherence the raw material which life constantly washes up to every one in great flooding masses. And they do this for their own high pleasure, with no idea of profiting by it in the eyes of the world. They work to create order out of chaos with a single-hearted effort, impossible to poor authors, tortured by the aching need to get the results of their efforts into words intelligible to others.[1]

To explain what she means by being your own author, Dorothy gives three illustrations, provided by her clergyman grandfather, her college administrator father, and her own experience as a novelist.

Of her grandfather she writes:

> My clergyman grandfather always said that he never enjoyed any sermons so much as the ones he preached to himself sitting under another clergyman's pulpit. When the text was given out, his mind seized on it with a vivid fresh interest and, running rapidly away from the intrusive sound of the other preacher's voice, wove a tissue of clear, strong, and fascinatingly interesting reasonings and exhortations. Grandfather used to say that such sermons preached to himself were in the nature of things much better than any he could ever deliver in church. . . . "I am not

obliged to hold the wandering attention of their muddled heads by a series of foolish little rhetorical tricks or by a prodigious effort of my personality. I can just make my sermon what it ought to be."[2]

Dorothy's father was a dynamic public speaker, although not a preacher, and she reports a similar experience on his part:

When a speaker began an address, he always fell into a trance-like condition, his eyes fixed steadily on the other orator, apparently giving him the most profound attention, but in reality making in his mind, on the theme suggested by the audible speaker, a fluent, impassioned address of his own. He used to say that he came to himself after one of these auto-addresses infinitely exhilarated and refreshed by the experience of having been speaking to an audience which instantly caught his every point, and which, although entirely sympathetic, was stimulatingly quick to find the weak spots in his argument and eager to keep him up to his best. Afterwards he dreaded an ordinary audience with its limping comprehension, its wandering attention, its ill-timed laughter and applause.[3]

This process continues in Dorothy Canfield herself, who reports:

The stories I told myself were infinitely superior to anything I ever got down on paper. Just as my father had been the ideal audience for himself, so I was my own best reader, a reader who needed no long explanations, who caught the idea at once, who brought to the tale all the experience which made it intelligible. Two words with the grocer's boy, delivering soap and canned salmon at the back door, and I was off, author and reader galloping along side by side, on a story which made not only my own written tales, but other people's as well, seem clumsy, obvious, and wordy. A look on an old cousin's face was to me — like a text to my grand-father — a springboard from which author and reader plunged simultaneously into the sea of human relationships, sensing in human life significances pitiful, exalted, profound, beyond anything that can be drawn out with the loose-meshed net of words. Did I sit idling in a railway station, my great-uncle, who died before I was born, stood there beside me, expounding his life to me with a precision, a daring abandon, a zestful ardor which would wither and fade if it were transferred to the pages of a book.[4]

Dorothy goes on to say that she has come gradually to realize that not everyone shares this experience with her. "I have occasionally come across people whose eyes are too weak for the white brilliance of reality," she writes,

who can only see life through the printed page, which is a very opaque object. Such people — and they are often cultivated, university-bred — will say, quite as if they were uttering a truism: "Of course characters in books — well-written books — are ever so much more interesting than men and women in real life."

They perceive the fateful mixture of beast and angel in the human face only in a portrait gallery; for them the birds sing, the winds sigh, and human hearts cry out, only at a symphony concert; they depend on books to give them faintly, dully, dimly, at third-hand, what lies before them every day, bright-colored, throbbing, and alive. It is a mental attitude hard for me to understand but it does exist. I have seen them turn away from a stern and noble tragedy in the life of their washerwoman, to the cheap sentimentality of a poor novel, which guarantees (as a fake dentist promises to fill teeth without pain) to provide tears without emotion. I have seen women who might have been playing with a baby, laughing at his inimitable funniness, leave him to a nurse and go out to enliven their minds by the contemplation of custard-pies smeared over the human countenance.

We are so used to this phenomenon that it does not seem strange to us. But it is strange — strange and tragic. And I do not in the least believe that the tragedy is one of the inevitable ones. I think it is simply a bad habit which has grown up as the modern world has taken to reading.[5]

Dorothy blames this unimaginative approach to life partly on writers,

because the new medium of cheap printing let loose on the world the innate loquacity of writers, unrepressed by the limitations of the human voice. Other people have not been able to hear themselves think since Gutenberg enabled writers to drown out the grave, silent, first-hand mental processes of people blessed by nature with taciturnity. The writer is not born (as is his boast) with more capacity than other people for seeing color and interest and meaning in life; he is born merely with an irrepressible desire to tell everybody what he sees and feels. We have been hypnotized by his formidable capacity for speech into thinking that he is the only human being on whom life makes an impression. This is not so. He is merely so made that he cannot rest till he has told everybody who will listen to him, the impression that life has made on him. This is the queer mainspring of creative literature. The writer cannot keep a shut mouth. To speak out seems to be the only useful occupation. But there is no reason why other people who have other useful things to do should miss the purity and vividness of a first-hand impression of life which they could enjoy without spoiling it, as an artist always does, by his instant anxiety about how much of it he can carry off with him for his art, by his instant mental fumbling with technical means, by his anguished mental questions: "What would be the best way to get that effect over in a book?" or "How could you convey that impression in a dialogue?"[6]

Of *Raw Material* itself she says:

In this unrelated, unorganized bundle of facts, I give you just the sort of thing from which a novelist makes principal or secondary characters, or episodes in a novel. I offer them to you for the novels you are writing inside your own heads, before I have spoiled them by the additions, cuttings, stretchings, or twistings necessary to make them fit into the fabric of a book. . . . I have treated you just as though you were that other self in me who is my best reader. I have given you the fare I like best. And I have faith to believe that you will enjoy for once being able to move about in a book without a clutter of explanations and sign-boards to show you the road the author wishes you to take. . . . I am only handing you from my shelves a few more curiosities to set among the oddities you have already collected, and which from time to time you take down as I do mine, turning them around in your hands, poring over them with a smile, or a somber gaze, or a puzzled look of surprise.[7]

The "oddities" that Dorothy Canfield collected in *Raw Material* are not so much events as people. Some of them are members of Dorothy's own family, and the stories she tells of them are part family legends and part her own reminiscences. Among these are her two grandfathers and her great-grandmother. There are also "Uncle Giles," who managed to live a life of indolent ease at the expense of his more energetic relatives, and "Uncle Ellis," whose private record of family abuse contrasted sharply with his benevolent public image. Other characters come from Dorothy's French experiences. There is a sketch of a French schoolteacher, whose personality expands to meet the demands of a war crisis and then shrinks back to its former narrowness; a radical French newspaper editor whose life is ruined by the inheritance of wealth; and a favorite professor who taught linguistics in Paris. Two stories feature her own children, one set in Vermont, the other in Paris. There are several that deal with passing styles in art; two that describe curious recluse characters in Vermont; and a few that defy categorizing altogether.

Before they appeared in book form, Dorothy sent the sketches to Paul Reynolds to see if he could find a market for them in the magazines. With them went a note, saying, "I think Mr. Harcourt wants to publish them in a volume next spring. So if somebody doesn't arouse himself and appreciate them at their real lofty merit, we're done—can't dispose of them serially at all! Oh well, such are the ups and downs of our profession. I've had a lovely time writing them, and I do really think there is freshness in them, even if old stick-in-the-muds of conventially-minded magazine editors can't see it in that bonny light."[8]

Dorothy had learned to be skeptical about magazine editors in experiences like this one: "This happened to me once," she wrote to Céline Sibut,

a magazine, having asked for a story, kept it a long time, then refused it, saying that it was too gloomy and not well written. After two years, the editor was changed, and I was again asked for a story. I sent the same one. The new editor accepted it, published it with many fine illustrations in the first number under the new editorship. The former editor (the one who turned it down) saw that and came to reproach me: "Look, that is a superb story! It has set them and their business afloat. Why didn't you ever send something like that when we were the editor of the magazine?" Yes, like that. And I didn't let on. I kept the funny thing for my own consumption, to laugh at inwardly, murmuring to him some vague excuse. The race of editors![9]

Dorothy had doubts about the market appeal of the *Raw Material* sketches because, as she wrote, "I see as I look them over, that as usual, I have not a single time treated the subject which is always dear to magazines, of how two young people fall in love."[10] Among the sketches Dorothy had, of course, her own favorites, and she was amazed when *The Outlook,* which had taken some of them, started off its series with "Old Man Warner," the story of an old Vermonter who lived out his days in rugged independence on his isolated hill farm, instead of with the story of a more unusual character like the Parisian "Professor Paul Meyer." She wrote to Paul Reynolds, "You know I was rather disappointed that The Outlook chose Old Man Warner to start that series. Well, they seem to know more about it than I did, for I don't think I ever had more letters about anything I ever published."[11] And a few days later she reported again, "Oddly enough every letter I've had about that has come from men. Women apparently don't see anything in it. well, between us, I can't quite see much in it, myself."[12]

The second collection of narratives from this era resulted from a storytelling game Dorothy played with her little son Jimmy. After *The Home-Maker* was published in 1924, Dorothy was very tired, and she answered her publisher's inquiry whether she were writing another book by saying:

You ask if there's another book on the stocks—nossir, I've been truly resting and lying fallow, feeling that I needed to do it. I'd been putting out a lot of stuff, you know, since we went back from France after the war. It will do me good to be just a human being again. As a matter of fact I have not, of course, been able to keep my pen from paper entirely, but what I've set down has been something so different from anything I've ever done that I doubt if you could call it a "book on the stocks." It's this: for years now, ever since Jimmy could talk, we have "run" a series of what we call "Jimmy's made-to-order stories." He hates the banality of the usual book-story where he sees from afar the same old tricks about to be turned, and invented this way of getting stories that are bound to be unexpected. He gives his own recipe — "I want a story with a puppy and an ice-berg and a churn and a little boy and a dozen marbles." Thus avoiding the usual story of a puppy with a tin-can tied to its tail and a brave little boy-scout who rescues the poor thing which turns out to belong to the millionaire Lady Bountiful of the village or something of that sort. You can imagine that stories constructed with the ingredients which Jimmy gives out, are unexpected if nothing else. The whole point about them is that the unexpectedness must be in the incidents and not in the telling which is always matter-of-fact and serious. It has made a little narrative recipe which has amused Jimmy and Sally for a long time. I must have told a thousand of them, more or less. They run off as fast as you can talk, you know, since you are bound by none of the usual rules of narrative. Well, in Switzerland, last Christmas time, I happened to tell one about an angry polar-bear which got the children to laughing so that they had the idea of setting it down for other children to laugh over. I didn't think myself that any of the real flavor of it could be decanted into cold print, and realized, what Jimmy and Sally don't, that most of their charm for us consists in the fact that they are a family tradition. But to please them I did put it down, and four others of the four days afterwards. I sent them along to Mildred Batchelder of the Horace Mann School, as the best judge for that sort of thing I know — with many years of experience with children of about the age of those for whom these stories are told; and also a woman of ripe literary judgment. I told her that if she found, after trying them out on assorted children in the Horace Mann School, that they "went" to send them along to Reynolds, to see if he could perhaps place them with St. Nicholas. In the same mail with your last, which came in yesterday, I had a letter from Mildred, saying the stories had had an immense success, and another note from Reynolds saying he had received them and would see what he could do with them (Reynolds' usual effusive epistolary style). If you think it's worth while, you might get them from Reynolds, if he still has them in his hands, and see if you think there's a volume in them for children's use. I could write any number needed, goodness knows. Perhaps Ellen would look at them. Her judgment might be better than yours, in that matter. I remember she had a good flair for children's books. Personally I haven't the least idea whether they're not too trivial to consider. John thinks I've taken leave of my senses to have written them down at all.[13]

Alfred Harcourt wanted to see the stories and asked for Dorothy's carbon copy of them. In her reply she still expressed doubt of their value for publication as a book. She wrote:

Yes, I have a carbon copy of those "Made to Order" stories. I'll send them along to you, although I am not at all sure that they are anything to your purpose. They were set down very hastily, almost like a stenographic report of just the way they were told to the children. I haven't corrected them, or even considered them since then, because they seem pretty fantastic as reading matter for anybody but Jimmy and Sally who are used to them. If they are published, I shall want to go over them carefully, and simplify them as to vocabulary, for I have an idea there may be some rather "literary" words in them which were all right for Jimmy and Sally, but do not really fit the tone of the stories. It would be my idea to have them almost altogether in Anglo-Saxon monosyllables, so that they would be easy to read for children like Jimmy not gifted in that line.[14]

The introduction to *Made-to-Order Stories,* subtitled "According to the Recipe of a Little Boy of Ten," sets the tone for the collection: " 'I do hate fairies in stories,' said Jimmy; 'they're so foolish. And I hate things that couldn't possibly have happened. And I despise a story that tries to teach you something without your knowing it. And all that's why I like Mother's stories. But the thing I like best of all about them is that there isn't ever any moral to them.' 'No, nor any sense,' said a grown-up. 'Yes,' said Jimmy, 'that *is* another nice thing about them.' "[15]

The first story to be written down, "The Angry Polar Bear," begins this way:

Jimmy came charging in from school, shouting, "A dog, and some sand, and a polar bear and — and an elephant, and some water."

While his mother was thinking over this, he went off to get some bread and butter. When he came back, chewing hard, he added thickly, "And a little boy."

"Oh, that one!" she said. "The one about the little boy who lived quite close to the Zoological Garden, so that he used to go and play there, the way you play in our yard." The tone of her voice showed Jimmy that the story was beginning.[16]

The basic formula remains the same throughout the collection, but the resulting tales show a range of diverse delights from "The Pony-Cart" through "The Upside-Down Moral" and "Jombatiste and the Forty Devils" to "The Very Last Story of All." In this "very last story," Jimmy discovers that he can be his own storyteller and make up his own stories "to order."

15

The Educator:
*Fables for Parents, Nothing Ever Happens
and How It Does, Tell Me a Story*

In 1935 Dorothy's publishers urged her to make another collection of her stories into a book. A first hasty attempt to gather together narratives that had appeared only in magazines did not turn up a group with a cohesive theme, however, so the matter was dropped. Those were very busy years for the Fishers, and their interest in new projects was not great. A steady stream of stories and articles was pouring from Dorothy's pen, and she was constantly in demand as a public speaker. John had become active in Vermont politics and had served several terms in the legislature from his home district, a course of public service that culminated in his being named chairman of the Vermont State Board of Education by Governor George Aiken in 1939 for a term of ten years.

Fables for Parents finally appeared in 1937, a set of stories grouped about the central theme of parenthood. Dorothy had serious doubts about publishing this collection. To reassure her, Alfred Harcourt sent her a memorandum from one of the younger members of his editorial staff, Sam Sloan. It read:

I feel strongly that these stories are worth publishing and that there should be a good market for them. They are perceptive and sensitive and consistently interesting. It's so good to find somebody for whom there are positives as well as negatives in life. There is already a nucleus of a market for the stories, not only because they are by Dorothy Canfield but because of the reception which FABLES FOR PARENTS have already received. It's time for us to be publishing another of Mrs. Fisher's books and this one is worthy of her. I read them all looking for trouble and trying to find ones to throw out. "The First Evening Out" and perhaps — because it did not seem to me to fit in so well with the motif of the collection (Fables for

Parents) — "Murder on Jefferson Street." But A. H. does not agree with this, and his arguments are persuasive.[1]

Alfred added his own comment to this memo: "Needless to say, the collection struck me as a book really worth publishing. I quote Sloan's report, both because I trust his judgment and because as a representative of the younger generation who doesn't know you personally, I think you're apt to take his judgment as a little less prejudiced than mine."[2] Except for a rather lengthy discussion in letters back and forth about the particular stories to be included in the volume, the matter was now settled, and the book proceeded toward publication.

The volume is divided into three sections. Section One contains five stories that deal directly with the problems of parenthood, in the various stages from new mother to grandparent. Section Two contains four stories that are more subtle in theme. All treat hidden inner reality, and each has a poignant quality that comes from its particular contradiction between the apparent and the real. The eight stories of Section Three have the least obvious connection with parenthood. They are, Dorothy wrote, ones that "open the doors of the imagination to certain overtones of peculiar significance to parents."[3]

Two of the stories in the last part of the collection deserve special mention, "The Murder on Jefferson Street" and "An Unprejudiced Mind." The first mention of "The Murder on Jefferson Street" is in a letter from Dorothy to Paul Reynolds in 1931: "I have a short, rather grim, story laid in American life I'd like to write. . . . The general theme is one which has always aroused me to deep feeling, the harm done by what is called 'teasing' — that is the enjoyment in causing another pain. I'd like to show something of the poisonous harm done by this when directed to a gentle and non-combative temperament."[4]

Paul Reynolds was a practical man who knew that it was more difficult to market a pessimistic than an optimistic story. He wrote to Dorothy, "I am a literary agent earning my living by selling stories and naturally the more stories that I get that I think will sell, the better I like it. . . . I often think of a story under this caption: — A trouble and its solution."[5] He went on to suggest that, in life, experience worked out well as often as badly, and so a happy ending was not necessarily "unnatural." "People read magazines for entertainment, and if they can have a natural happy ending they prefer it to the reverse. I always think of a dressmaker, say, in Fall River, who is having a desperately hard time to make both ends meet. Her eyes are tired out at ten o'clock at night, but she grabs up a magazine to rest herself before she goes to bed. She naturally doesn't want to read a story like this."[6]

Dorothy had, however, something she wanted to say, and her story was a vehicle for that message. As John Fisher said of her work later, "After the very first years when she was practicing her scales she never wrote anything just because it might be bought by some editor looking for 'light summer reading.' "[7] She defended the ending of "The Murder on Jefferson Street" as essential to the story and suggested:

> substitute for your tired Fall River dressmaker reading the magazine of an evening, the young mother of three children one of whom is getting crowded out from light and air by the other two. I admit the Fall River dressmaker might find such a story a frost, but I still think the mother, dimly concerned about the under-dog among her children, might find it *quite* interesting. A happy ending would take all the meaning out of the tale—the man who has just skimmed through over a grade crossing ahead of the train feels more like turning to wave his hand derisively to the engineer, than like making a solemn resolution not to take such a risk again, don't you think?[8]

Editors apparently agreed with Paul Reynolds, however, and the story was generally rejected. Finally, Dorothy called it back to rework and shorten it. Four years later, a letter to Paul Reynolds shows that she is working on the story again: "I'm once more laboring over 'The Murder on Jefferson Street,' trying to rearrange it again and get it in shape to send you."[9] John was less than encouraging in this struggle, but Dorothy was determined to do what she could with it. "Mr. Fisher says I'm just pig-headed to go on working on that story," she told Paul Reynolds. "But there's an idea in it I'd like very much to get expressed. And I hate to give up beaten, too. Maybe I am pig-headed. Anyhow, I'm still spending morning after morning on it, and will send it to you before so very long."[10]

Before she could send the revised version to Reynolds, however, an editor of *Story* magazine asked to see it. "I'll soon have The Murder on Jefferson Street ready," she wrote to Paul Reynolds,

> but I think I'll send that first to one of the editors of "Story"—who has expressed an interest in it. She is the wife of the head of the Book of the Month Club, and was visiting us not long ago when I happened to mention how long I had had that story, and how much work I have put on it, with no idea that any magazine would take anything so long, and so somber. She said she'd like to see it. So—because I'm pretty sure no other editor would be interested at all, I'll send it first to her. Then if they find it unusable, I'll put it again in your hands for a while, probably to retire it to the good old bureau drawer retreat, afterwards.[11]

Dorothy had been buoyed up in her work on "The Murder on Jefferson Street" by the encouragement of some of her friends. When it was accepted by *Story,* she wrote to Alfred Harcourt:

> Do you happen to remember a longish short story of mine you read a year or so ago, called "The Murder on Jefferson Street." You and Ellen liked it, I remember, which pleased me very much, for I'd taken any amount of trouble with the writing of it, and couldn't find a magazine that would even consider it because it was a so sad, and "morbid study of insanity." (I hadn't tried many because Reynolds was so sure nobody would look at it.) Well, I got it out in January and put a lot more trouble on it, and sent it to "Story" without trying any other magazine. And they've just written they like it and are going to print it in June. I thought you and Ellen would be interested.[12]

"The Murder on Jefferson Street" appeared in June 1935 in *Story.* Before the end of June, Dorothy reported to Alfred Harcourt that "Angus Burrell, of the Comparative Literature Department of Columbia, wants to use 'The Murder on Jefferson Street' in an anthology of 'Great American Novelettes and Short Stories.' "[13]

Harry Scherman hailed this story enthusiastically:

> I don't know when I have been so moved by a story — not for *years*! . . I'm so, so seldom now caught and utterly wrung as I was by this, and as it seems to me I used to be more often. I think it's just masterly, and I'm proud for the human race you're alive to see such things in people and write about them. — I know you'll think it's just friendship to talk so, but it isn't. "Masterly" was the one word that kept recurring to me, as I read — particularly at one thing you seemed all the time to be doing sharply and clearly — something which novelists ought always (it seems to me) to do, and which most of them don't even seem to *try for* — namely, to show how our motives of what-other-people-think-of-us are almost the most powerful of all springs of action, and not only are these whims ordinarily in large part mistaken and wrong, but as in this case actually the very reverse of what people *do* think. — The whole thing is a beautiful touching plea for charity and understanding, and I'm sure nobody will be able to read it without seeing the mote in his eye and being somehow different afterwards. It's just fine![14]

"An Unprejudiced Mind" had a different beginning. In the late 1920s one of the most talked-about new books was Judge Lindsey's work on companionate marriage,[15] which proposed that the incidence of divorce might be reduced if young people lived together as married for a trial period before legalizing their relationship. The controversy stirred up by this proposition filled newspapers and magazines, and Dorothy was asked in October 1927 to contribute an article stating her opinion about it. She refused and the matter was dropped. Almost a year later, however, she sent to Paul Reynolds a piece she called "a queer little sketch which I wrote to please myself."[16] She went on to say: "It is—though nobody could see the connection without being told, my impression of what I hear about companionate marriage. You know several magazines asked me last year for my 'opinion' on that proposed institution. I haven't any opinion, which can't be had without much more exact and accurate information about facts than I possess. But this little sketch gives my impression."[17] The story, which relates a young composer's encounter with a pretty green snake, has clearly Freudian implications, but direct connections with companionate marriage are not superficially apparent.

Fables for Parents is not, on the whole, as amusing and entertaining a collection as earlier volumes of Dorothy's stories. The optimism is not as bright, and the realism sometimes borders on the bitter. The literary quality is uneven also, and some of the individual tales are weakened by too obvious didactic intent. The volume contains, however, especially in the third part, stories that belong to the author's best and most serious narrative work.

Two collections of stories with explicitly didactic intent followed the *Fables for Parents.* The first, a volume for children entitled *Nothing Ever Happens and How It Does,* was jointly authored by Dorothy and her friend Sarah Cleghorn. The seven stories that Dorothy contributed to the collection are all designed to help children to see beneath the surface of human life. They are didactic, but in the sense of deepening the reader's understanding, rather than in recommending any specific course of action.

The second is a book of stories for parents to tell to children. Each of the tales in *Tell Me a Story* appears in a longer and a shorter version. The reason for the dual treatment is that the book is not meant for the children themselves to read, but for an adult to tell to them. The shorter version is given for younger children, whose span of attention is shorter, or for children who are unaccustomed to listening to stories. The longer version contains a more complicated and elaborate telling of the same material. Suggestions are made throughout the stories for sound effects or pantomime, which may make them more effective.

16

The Last Anthologies:
Four-Square and *A Harvest of Stories*

In 1949 Harcourt, Brace and Company brought out another collection of stories by Dorothy Canfield. Alfred Harcourt had left the firm in 1942, but in correspondence with Donald Brace, the remaining one of the original partners, Dorothy discussed which stories should be included and admitted her difficulty in writing the autobiographical preface he had requested. "You haven't got the Preface yet," she wrote after the stories were already in his hands. "I'm finding it a hard assignment. You know I don't often, ever in fact, talk about myself or my work. It really is an impossible task. The Archangel Gabriel couldn't do it, and always steer a straight course between false modesty, which is sickening, and taking-your-work-too-seriously, which is horrid."[1]

She stipulated that she should have a chance to revise the stories, and she used this revision as a theme for her introduction to the volume. In it she wrote:

> During all of my life as a writer — half a century long it is, now — readers have been helpful advisers to me. . . . I don't share the feeling of those writers who say they write solely for themselves. It doesn't seem to me that I am unlike people who read my books — how should I be? What I write is an invitation to those with whom time has proved that I have much in common to join me in reflecting on the human life we all lead. They are an indispensable part of the effort to feel the essential quality of the doings of men, women, and children. Here is the place to acknowledge with comradely appreciation the spoken explicit, and unspoken implicit cooperation given me by readers in the revision and re-writing of these stories.[2]

Dorothy's own feeling of oneness with all the people who read her stories had been growing since her earliest writing days. She had consciously worked to pull away from stilted, academic language and thought and to move into closer understanding and communication with other people. For one of her early stories, she put a subtitle "Told in Prakrit," and to Paul Reynolds's question she replied:

> Prakrit is the familiar "women's talk" variation on Sanscrit. They wouldn't let Hindu women in the old days have schooling enough to use Sanscrit, the language of the learned folks. Consequently the women soon developed a rapid, easy-going, home-talk of their own, which *they taught their sons* (a detail not foreseen by the learned gentlemen!) and as a result of which Sanscrit rapidly became the stiff, dead, formal, "literary" language, and was soon dead and buried as far as actual use by living people was concerned. The "literature" in Prakrit is lots more living and authentic than those solemn old Sanscrit chants (so it seems to me) and I've been amused sometimes to reflect that very likely the same sort of thing is going on now.[3]

The title Dorothy chose for the new collection was *Four-Square.* Her publishers wondered if that was a biblical reference, and she responded rather brusquely that she was "anything but a religious-minded author,"[4] and that the quotation was from Tennyson. Subsequently, the explanatory lines were printed just before the title: ". . . that tower of strength/Which stood four-square to all the winds that blow."

The significance of the title becomes evident from a survey of the stories that make up the collection. The tower of strength which can stand up to all the winds that blow is the human spirit resting on the base of a strong inherited tradition. This is a group of stories about human beings—plain, ordinary people, but the kind that make one glad to be human, because human in them means strong enough to meet the problems of life. Dorothy was seventy years old when *Four-Square* appeared. She had enjoyed success and she had suffered personal tragedy. She was well acquainted with the winds that buffet human beings, but also with the springs from which strength is mysteriously replenished.

Seven years after *Four-Square* another anthology of Dorothy's stories appeared. As its title indicated, this was to be the last collection, *A Harvest of Stories* from the writings of a master narrator. The stories were not this time, as in earlier collections, those printed previously only in magazines but included many that had appeared in book form as well.

Harvest is divided into three main categories: "Vermont Memories," "Men, Women—and Children," and "War." The Vermont stories are selected as a distillation of Vermont personality, stories that illustrate the traits of this region which Dorothy loved and honored. The second section could be subtitled "How the behavior of men and women affects the future of children," for into it Dorothy put the best of her stories that deal with this problem. The section entitled "War" contains a small group of antiwar sketches. They show the horror and brutality of war itself, as Dorothy saw and described it in two world wars, but the final sketch of the Hessian soldier who has become part of a Vermont community is a plea for reconciliation.

In the Prologue to this book, Dorothy wrote a tribute to her mother's influence on her life. Dorothy's mother had been a troublesome element in her daughter's development, and Dorothy was conscious more of their differences than of their similarities. She generally thought of herself as "Vermont" like her father, and of her mother as a kind of opposite anti-Vermont personality. In this introductory sketch, however, Dorothy considers what positive influence, if any, her mother had on her literary career. She comes to the surprising conclusion that she became a writer because of her mother's influence. She sees her mother as a person who welcomed the life that was the life for her. "She did not say a frowning 'No' to aspects of human existence she did not wish to admit as valid. Rather she ignored them, did not see that they were there. She turned a glowing, ardent welcome to what she was willing to recognize."⁵ Dorothy sums up her mother's influence: "After all, what she's always done . . . is to reach for the only stars she sees. What better can any of us do than to reach for our own stars — and know which they are?"⁶

In the remainder of the Prologue, Dorothy explores the ways by which she came to recognize her "own stars" and became sure that she "was born to be a teller of stories."⁷ She concludes that "in the obscure labyrinth of the inner world, it is comforting to be sure of anything."⁸

The original selection of thirty stories was made by the publishers. Then Dorothy and John went over their list to make "any revisions which the passage of such a very long period of time since they were written might make necessary."⁹ They found only three stories that should be omitted, the first because of historical inaccuracy, and the other two for literary reasons. Of these last two Dorothy wrote:

I think the publishers chose them because they thought, perhaps, that they sounded rather more "knowing" and sophisticated than some of the plain, homespun ones of everyday people, because they were laid in France, and had illicit love in them, and a complicated cosmopolitan plot, which (such was my guess) publishers thought might serve to prove to readers that Mrs. Fisher is after all not just a plain homebody. But there had always been something about those stories which to me seemed rather mechanically well done than really flowing from a vital stream of life — I am sure you know what I mean, the sort of story which goes on sounding synthetic no matter how elaborately bolstered up it is by technical devices of narration.[10]

These rejections recall the young author, just starting out, who wrote home idealistically from Norway that she "did mean to try honestly to have the ideas . . . true ones, and to try and move people to more than a passing interest in a certain verbal dexterity."[11] In fifty years Dorothy Canfield had held with persistent tenacity to this ideal of integrity in her work.

Dorothy knew that this collection was a serious one, much darker and heavier in tone than some of the earlier volumes of short narratives. She objected to having it advertised as though it were a happy, optimistic book, a course that might attract readers only to disappoint them. She wrote to he publishers:

> I don't like, *for this collection,* the pleasant, genial sentence quoted from the Herald Tribune, to the effect that the reader feels better after reading my stories. I realize that this is the tag or label often affixed to my writing — I haven't protested against it and don't now — except that for this selection of my stories I think it gives so inaccurate an impression of what the reader will find in the volume that it would be really bad business to hang out that sign, as anything is bad business which claims too much. There are too many stories in this volume which rather portray the puzzling, or tragic, or disheartening aspects of human nature and human life.[12]

Perhaps her own view of life had been sobered by many years of living and personal suffering. She did not feel that the balance of stories needed revision simply because it did not tip toward the cheerful. "There are, I think, plenty of stories in 'The Harvest' which are written out of the author's warm consciousness that human beings are often lovable and heroic as well as cussed and self-seeking and that human life often is sunny as well as dark."[13]

Part 5

Public Service and Nonfiction

"Hope and faith in the possibilities of human nature."
Dorothy Canfield Fisher Papers

17
The Writing of Nonfiction

Dorothy Canfield Fisher never became a classroom teacher, and she told a friend once that she wanted to be thought of as "a very hard working and intensely serious writer of fiction."[1] All through her life, however, she served on a variety of educational boards and wrote didactic articles in support of causes in which she believed.

"I feel about articles that they interest me, often to write," she observed in 1920; "that when I have no special piece of fiction on hand, I might as well be writing articles as doing anything else; and that they often afford me an opportunity to help directly in some cause in which I am interested."[2] Although article writing supplemented her income, Dorothy never took her articles as seriously as her fiction, and she commented on one occasion to Paul Reynolds, "I don't believe I could ever have the nerve to ask a fiction price for that sort of work. It's really not worth it — doesn't take it out of the writer's innards as fiction does."[3]

In the summer of 1919, shortly after Dorothy had returned from war work in France, Paul Reynolds wrote to ask if she would like to do a series of articles on education for the *Delineator*. "I'm much interested in the possibility of doing a series of articles on child-training for the Delineator," she replied,

> but I'd like to know a little more in detail about it, before I decide, and to
> have them know a little more in detail what my ideas are. Here's my side. I
> would not care to write any specific, detailed educational advice, such as
> whether "children should begin to train for a vocation at fourteen, or six-
> teen, or twelve." In fact I don't approve of that sort of specific advice
> from anybody. It's like a doctor's saying that eggs are "bad" for people or
> "good" for people, when as a matter of fact they're good for some *folks*
> and bad for others. But I would like to set down *some* ideas on the fun-
> damental principles which should enable parents and children to decide
> wisely *for themselves* what's the best thing to do. I'd like to consider some
> pretty deep subjects, that question of individual sovereignty as against

ultimate obedience to the state, which we all dodge and evade, but which is the crux of our conduct and the way we train our children — I'd like to speak as vividly as I can about the need to keep the *inner spark alive,* at no matter what effort, rather than to attain "efficiency" as success — . . . the war has made me feel very deeply on these subjects.[4]

After the three articles for the *Delineator* were published, Alfred Harcourt suggested that more be written so that a collection could be brought out in book form. In Dorothy's reply she revealed how she and John worked together in writing them:

We said about all we have to say in those three, and it would be padding to add more. You note I say "we" consistently in speaking of them. John wrote them as much as I. We worked over them together, as we are apt to do for articles of all sorts, first I, in a rough draft (or John first) then the other fellow revise, then the first one revise his revision — discussions at table till the family get sick of the sound of the things — slowly they get themselves done . . . very differently from the silent, secret heat with which fiction is achieved.[5]

In the light of this description of collaborative writing, it is interesting that Dorothy never mentions John's work when she discusses these articles with Paul Reynolds, who marketed them for her. The closest she comes to involving John is in an initial comment: "I have been talking over with my husband the last letter about the Delineator articles. We both think it would be well worth while to try them, the three of them as you suggest."[6] She goes on to say:

If, as you say, Mr. Tower is not afraid of radical ideas, he won't be afraid of my articles. Tell him that one of the things I want specially to emphasize is the danger of too great unanimity, that fatal unanimity which made it possible for the German Government to invade Belgium without arousing any protest among the people, who *individually,* we know to have been as capable as most other folks of realizing the iniquity of that action. I want to emphasize the fact that we not only ought to bring our children up to be their own masters, but that we *must* do so, to prevent their falling into the hands of unworthy masters. . . . I would like, in those articles, to speak of certain elements in the training of French children which might interest us, and to our profit. Everybody is convinced now, after the long strain endured by the poilu that there must be something worth while in the French way of doing things, and I'd like, as I go along, to mention some of the differences in the way they manage children, just as stimulating ideas, for I don't think they could be applied literally to American children.[7]

There were so many things to say that Dorothy and John found themselves exceeding the suggested word limit. "Would you ask them please," Dorothy wrote to Paul Reynolds, "how long they really want those articles. I'm killing myself to keep them down to nearly 5,000 words, because *I do not* want *them cut.* If they must be cut, won't you please ask Mr. Tower to send them back to me, and tell me exactly how much he wants taken out, and I will do it myself. On the other hand, I would like very much to know if they could print them longer, for I would find it easier to make them 6,000 words than 5,000."[8]

Although John played an active role as collaborator in the writing of articles and as editor of Dorothy's fiction, his name never assumed the commercial worth in the market place of hers, and in June 1923 Dorothy wrote to Alfred Harcourt, "John and I have gone into partnership (legally I mean) in rc income-tax business, under the name of 'Dorothy Canfield,' so please have checks made out to that name."[9] This arrangement lasted ten years, and then another letter announced, "We've given up that legal partnership arrangement which turned out to be more bother in account-keeping than it was worth."[10]

A corollary to the different arrangements under which fiction and nonfiction were written in the Fisher home was that works of fiction were always published under the name "Dorothy Canfield," whereas nonfictional articles and books consistently appeared by "Dorothy Canfield Fisher."

18
The Montessori Books

When Dorothy returned from her visit to the school of Dr. Maria Montessori in Rome in 1911, she burned with the crusading zeal of her educator father to tell American parents and educators what she had seen. The first report of her observations appeared in 1912 in *A Montessori Mother.* There she told how she had found in the Casa dei Bambini in Rome an experimental school where children learned to be independent mature human beings by participating in and gradually assuming responsibility for adult activities. The "educational toys" that have become a commonplace in America today were a new and essential part of this schooling. The children tied knots in cords and buttoned buttons into holes on large frames. They learned the intricacies of arithmetic, first on objects and then as abstract concepts represented by symbols. One of the most impressive facets of the whole experiment was the evident contentment of the children in this educational environment.

In Rome Dorothy had watched children from two-and-a-half to six years old, busily and happily learning in apparently complete freedom to perform the tasks necessary for personal independence. The pleasure in learning shown by the children and the background position of the teacher in the learning situation made a deep impression on Dorothy, who was then a young mother herself. Her highly trained mind and her experience in the Horace Mann School in New York fitted her for an analysis of what she saw and for the application to the American scene of the best in the new methods. Because she felt that the American school system was too bound by tradition and by its own educational hierarchy to accept new ideas easily, she directed her book at the American mother, who was in a position where she could most readily use the new ideas with her own children in her own home.

In Chapter 9 of *A Montessori Mother,* which treats the application of the Montessori philosophy to American home life, Dorothy writes: "We are simply, at last, to include children in humanity, and since despotism, even the most enlightened varieties of it, has been proved harmful to humanity, we are to abstain from being their despots."[1] Further on in the same chapter she asks: "How, practically, concretely, at once, to-day, can we begin to avoid paternal despotism over little children?"[2] She answers her own question: "To begin with, by giving them the practical training necessary to physical independence of life. . . . The child must *learn how* to be independent, as he must learn how to be anything else that is worth being, and the only excuse for existence of a parent is the possibility of his furnishing the means for the child to acquire this information with all speed. . . . Help that is not positively necessary is a hindrance to a growing organism. . . . Unnecessary restriction in a child's life is a crime."[3] The impact of these ideas can be seen in a review in the journal *Public,* which commented that "no better book for making a radical out of a conservative can be found than this one."[4]

The publication of *A Montessori Mother* brought a flood of letters from women all over the country asking for advice on how to apply the Montessori ideas to the education of their own children. The immediate result of these inquiries was *The Montessori Manual,* which appeared in 1913.[5]

Dorothy published another Montessori volume, *Mothers and Children,* in 1914, a book that, in the words of one review, "gives the wisdom of an expert in the language of a friend 'just talking.' "[5] Then, in 1916, appeared another practical book on raising children, *Self-Reliance,* subtitled "A Practical and Informal Discussion of Methods of Teaching Self-Reliance, Initiative and Responsibility to Modern Children."

19
Translations:
Papini's *Life of Christ* and Tilgher's *Work*

Shortly after World War I, Dorothy undertook a task that proved to be one of the most distasteful of her literary career, the English translation of Giovanni Papini's *Life of Christ*. It was a book that had attracted international attention because of circumstances surrounding its writing.

Giovanni Papini had started, as an atheist, to write an account of Christ the man; during the course of his research and writing, however, he became a convinced Christian and ultimately a monk. His prose is elaborate and wordy, emotional rather than intellectual. To Dorothy, who had struggled for years with the problems of literary style, Papini's flamboyant excesses were distasteful in the extreme. She tried to remain faithful to the original work, but she found it repeatedly necessary to cut down the length and elaborate quality of the prose to "make it more acceptable to English-speaking readers, so much less tolerant of long descriptions and minute discussions than Italians."[1]

While working on the translation Dorothy consulted her cousin Arthur Canfield, a professor of romance languages at the University of Michigan, and a letter to him indicates some of her troubles with the job. "Very much obliged for the help about the Italian," she wrote. "I enclose two copies, and will be glad of any suggestions. I suspect that certain of my troubles come from my lack of sympathy with Papini's style, or thought. I detest the flamboyant, verbose style, and never have had any patience for sensual, men-of-the-world (Huysmans is one who always makes my bristles rise) who get converted to Catholicism so's to have some new sensations. So I daresay I'm not a good choice as translator."[2]

Dorothy's hectic schedule, and particularly the struggle with the translation of Papini, took a toll on her strength. In October 1921 Alfred and Sue Harcourt came to Arlington for a visit. John and Dorothy "had hurried our heads off to get the manuscript ready to give him when he left,"[3] she wrote. The struggle was too much for Dorothy, for that very day she fell desperately ill. At first the doctor thought that it was diphtheria and feared for her life, but laboratory tests showed it to be only a serious case of tonsillitis, and by spring she was regaining her customary vigor.

When Paul Reynolds asked for a copy of the Papini translation to see if he could place it serially, Dorothy was very skeptical. Who would want to have such a religious book in a magazine? Then, when he succeeded in marketing it for $1500, she was amazed and wrote to Alfred Harcourt, "Isn't old Reynolds the crafty animal! What do you think of that? I all but passed away."[4]

In the fall of 1922 Dorothy was reading proof for the book version of Papini's work and again shuddering with revulsion at the sight of the book. To Paul Reynolds she wrote in November, "It seems to me that I've done nothing but correct proofs since the beginning of time. For the first time in my life my eyes begin to feel the strain. Many of these proofs are of that accursed translation from the Italian. What a wretched mess that thing has been — all except the magnificent sale you made of a serial version of the horrid thing!"[5] In December she reiterated her objections to it: "The work on Papini has been a strain because I've disliked the book so intensely, I suppose."[6]

Dorothy's translation of Papini's *Life of Christ* appeared in book form in March 1923 and went through one printing after another. Alfred Harcourt, who published it, was delighted, but Dorothy could not overcome her aversion. "I'm glad it's selling," she wrote to Alfred. "You deserve to make something out of it, though I still think the book deserves no readers."[7]

Eight years later, Dorothy gave Papini's work rather negative credit for contributing to her understanding of the importance of the Jewish tradition. "I hated that book and its raw spirit of rancor," she wrote in 1931, "but I really owe it a great deal, because in Papini's endeavor to show that Jesus owed nothing to Jewish tradition, he informed me that Jesus owed everything to it."[8]

When Alfred Harcourt wrote to Dorothy about translating another Italian book, *Homo Faber* by Adriano Tilgher, she reacted with guarded interest. Her mother, now in her eighties, was a constant care and worry, and she and John were planning to spend the summer in Europe. She wrote to Alfred, "I'm sort of translation-shy, of course, after Papini, but I would like to look at that book Homo Faber. It is the kind of work I feel more like doing from now till we sail, than any creative work. I can't get poor mother out of my mind long enough to live myself into the creative state of mind."[9]

The subject of the book, the significance of work in human history, interested Dorothy, and she finally decided to undertake the translation. It was still unfinished when she left for Europe, and she carried it with her to finish there. From Kirchzarten bei Freiburg she wrote to Alfred at the end of July as she sent the completed manuscript:

> Here's the translation, plentifully watered with brow-sweat and heart's blood and other effects of the LOT of work put on it. . . . The accursed thing has taken any amount of effort to get it into even passably readable English. . . . I thought on reading it once rapidly that it was interesting, and as most readers will look at it in the same way, maybe they'll like it better than I do, after toiling and poring in exasperation over every paragraph and phrase. . . . We've done nothing this whole month but work on this thing. (And I thought I had it almost ready on leaving home!)[10]

When Dorothy received a copy of the published book the following January, she wrote to Mr. Chase at Harcourt, Brace and Company, "I'm quite astonished to see what a real sure-enough book you've made it appear. On that horrid thin Italian paper, with the crowded pages, it looked like not much more than a pamphlet. But when I came to struggle with the translation of it, I became aware that it was a good deal more than a pamphlet all right!"[11] This was during the depth of the depression of the 1930s, and Dorothy wrote later in the month to Alfred Harcourt, "The author's dark misgivings about the future of capitalistic society don't sound so imaginary as when I first read them."[12]

This second translation from the Italian was very different from Papini's book. In Tilgher's work Dorothy found a book about humanity that "cast back over that long, dark, confused procession, a light which shows at least which way it is moving."[13] In her translation, entitled *Work, What It Has Meant to Men through the Ages,* she made "a free translation, which aims at rendering the spirit rather than the letter."[14]

Tilgher's book describes the different points of view about work held by men from the Greeks and Hebrews to the present day, concluding with an analysis of the present situation and with speculations about the future. It traces the concept of work as a punishment and its gradual transformation into the place of honor as the very essence of human existence, but it speculates that work may be losing its prime place to recreation and that this may be a sign of incipient decadence.

Dorothy found much in Tilgher's book to interest her. Two of her novels, *The Squirrel-Cage* and *The Home-Maker,* are directly concerned with the economic world. In another, *The Bent Twig,* the father of the heroine is a professor of economics, and the man she marries is involved in an economic experiment. From the time when Daniel Rankin suggests in *The Squirrel-Cage* that work is a man's most valuable possession and that he ought to share it more equitably with women, the place of work in human lives claims Dorothy's attention. Because Tilgher's book corroborates on the whole Dorothy's earlier views about the nature and importance of work, it is difficult to say just how much her translation of this book played a part in her own literary development. Perhaps its greatest significance for her is summed up in her statement in the Introduction: "The value of the book is not as a mine of exact information about facts, but rather as an extraordinary clarification and quickening of the ideas inside one's head."[15]

20
Adult Education and the Book-of-the-Month Club

Dorothy Canfield felt that her interest in adult education was a legacy from her educator father, who "used to say that there was no use educating people if, after their commencement, they used their diplomas as a weapon to ward off more learning."[1] It was in the last years of her father's life that Andrew Carnegie began to give money for public libraries across the land. The Carnegie Corporation also promoted the American Association for Adult Education, which assembled information on America's reading habits. Dorothy, who was national president of this group for a while, "was horrified, . . . by the shockingly poor showing which the United States of America made in comparison with other countries. We ranked along about with Patagonia," she recalled later, "in the number of books bought and read."[2]

So when the president of the Carnegie Corporation asked her to write a book about adult education in America, using data collected by their researchers, Dorothy willingly agreed. She described the project in a letter to Paul Reynolds:

> Some weeks ago the President of the Carnegie Corporation made me an interesting proposition, in regard to some material gathered by field workers of theirs. Convinced by many signs both here and in progressive countries abroad, that adult education is the next great move in democracy's battle to maintain itself, they have been for some time, conducting an investigation in the field of adult education in this country.
>
> The experts whom they have employed (many of them distinguished educators) after an intensive survey of their various fields, have brought in detailed, statistical technical reports, which Macmillan's is to publish as books. What Mr. Keppel wished me to do was to write out of this gold-mine of new material, a book which would be intelligible and interesting to the thoughtful part of the general public. The aim of the Carnegie Corporation is to focus and concentrate the now existing great (but diffused, hap-hazard and casual) public interest in this matter, which is so vital to

the further progress of our country, and to divert towards adult education more really intelligent and disinterested efforts than are now being made by the various elements working in it.[3]

Dorothy found the material interesting but not easy to put into simple, readable form. "The material is singularly glutinous with statistics," she wrote to Paul Reynolds. "I don't wonder they want somebody to get it in intelligible shape for them."[4] Later, she wrote to Alfred Harcourt of "being deep deep in the chapter on Museums, and afraid to take my eyes off'n it for fear it would instantly relapse into its original chaos if I do."[5] In a postscript to this letter she commented with feeling, "Gee whiz, what a job this book is!"[6] However, as she continued to try to distill out of charts and technical reports their real significance, she reported, "It is juicier material than I thought at first, now I've had it soaking for a while, and dripping with the sap of pure raw strong Americanism — which note I mean to keep strong (and raw)."[7]

In 1927 the book was published as *Why Stop Learning?* and Dorothy regarded it with considerable satisfaction. When Harcourt, Brace and Company composed a little biographical booklet on her life and works in 1929 and sent it to her for approval, she said, "On the last page, I wish you'd put in a little more mention of 'Why Stop Learning?' I'd like not to have people forget that book. I've said some things in it I'm glad to have said."[8]

The book is, for the most part, a summary of the reports from which she was working, but in the final chapter, "Some Last Guesses," Dorothy speculates about the impact of adult education on the future:

> Just as it is probably sensible not to expect the millennium as a result of widespread long-continued mass instruction, so it is probably just as well not to fear that its only result will be the integral triumph of mediocrity. If worse comes to worst, I daresay that a certain few of our descendants will be able to create lives of tolerable civilization and distinction, no matter what intellectual barbarity lies about them, just as a few of each generation has always managed to turn that trick. Perhaps that is the best we can expect.
>
> But perhaps not. Perhaps more widespread education really will solve some of our new difficulties, will be a help in those more complex lives suddenly wished upon simple beings who are not given time gradually and biologically to adjust their brain-cells to complexity. Perhaps it will help our children and grandchildren to cope with that second hardship, the disconcerting appearance in lives unprepared for it, of the priceless perilous treasure of leisure time. In spite of our sensation of hurrying

there is now vastly more leisure time than any other generation ever had. Not only are these fewer hours spent in work, but most work is much less physically exhausting and much less interesting. Hence less time is taken in resting from the effects of it, and in thinking about it afterwards. Millions of human lives and human minds have new blank emptinesses which only a few in the race ever encountered before. This is certainly one of the forces which drives people to this new reaching out after more excitement, more sports, more entertainments, more material possessions, more noise of any sort to fill the place in their lives formerly occupied by long hours of toil. The rising tide of suicide would seem to indicate that they are as yet not wholly successful.

That same rising tide may indicate another lack of our modern life, the absence of any generally recognized motive for living. . . . More bitterly than food, or shelter or love or occupation, human beings need a goal, a compelling reason for going on. The more time they have to think the more drastic is this need, the more horrifying that dead absence of a purpose in life which is really the absence of religion, of faith. It is possible that we are now (and have been for a half-century or more) seeing the emergence of a new faith, a new belief — namely that there are in humanity glorious and beautiful qualities which it is the duty of every man to protect and cherish, both in himself and in others, qualities splendid enough to make their protection worth any man's devotion.[9]

Dorothy was just beginning her work with the Carnegie material when a letter arrived that significantly changed the course of her life. Years later, in a lecture, she described this event and its consequences. She had long felt, she said,

a deep concern about the necessity for a wider distribution of books among the citizens of a democracy . . . when twenty-two years ago I received a letter from a New York office signed by two names I had never seen before. The letter described the workings of a book-club — an organization of which until that moment I had never heard in my life. I was asked to be on a committee of selection, the other members of which were Henry Canby, an old friend of mine, William Allen White, a former student of my father's, Christopher Morley, everybody's friend, and Heywood Broun whom I had known from the time he had been a high school boy at the Horace Mann School. The idea of distributing books through a book-club was to be tried out. Would I accept membership on the Committee of Selection?[10]

Dorothy could see a good many reasons for not accepting the invitation.

Some of them were personal; she had, after all, a full and busy life already. "Anyhow I didn't like the name very well—"The Book-of-the-Month Club. As if there would be *a* book of the month which would suit all readers. It sounded to me (as it has sounded to many another person since) as though there were something presumptuous in the idea of assuming to choose other people's reading for them."[11]

While she was still considering whether to agree to serve, Dorothy happened to go to New York on a shopping expedition.

It was a Saturday afternoon on a fine clear day in spring. Not realizing what this would mean for the shopping industry, I got myself transported to Macy's, stepped inside and asked for the counter where sheets and pillow cases were being sold—that being my prosaic errand.

The big shop was alarmingly (to my eyes) crammed with milling crowds of bargain-crazed women. There must have been some sort of a bargain sale going on in the sheet and pillow case department, for a frenzy of the purchasing mania surged five or six deep around the counter where I wanted to go. I was literally afraid to risk my small person amongst them. I gave it up, decided to send by mail for what I needed, and made my way, very precariously, to a door through wildly swirling eddies of impassioned shoppers.

Out on the sidewalk, the situation was no better. It was the first warm spring afternoon in New York, and everybody was out. I crept along as best I could, hugging the side of the building closely, turned at 34th Street, found the crowd just as great there, and when I reached Fifth Avenue, stopped, really thunderstruck. For Fifth Avenue was by far the most crowded of them all. The sidewalks were full, crammed with human beings to the curb, the street itself was full of automobiles, bumper to bumper. One could have walked without falling, from roof to roof of the automobiles, and from head to head of the people on the sidewalk.

A bus came along—this was in the days of the double-decker buses on Fifth Avenue. The seats on its high open roof looked to me as a floating henhouse would look to a person swept away by a flood. I struggled across the street and up the steps of the bus to the top, sank down in a seat and from this safety looked up and down on that thoroughfare of commerce. For a Vermonter, to see, as far as the eye could reach, nothing but people closely packed together, all of them bent on either buying or selling, was startling. . . . "No wonder," I said to myself, "that businesses try to get themselves established in New York. This must be now the greatest buying and selling center of the whole world. You could sell *anything*, with so many buyers stepping on each other's heels."

After a few blocks, I remembered that my daughter, then in college, had asked me to buy a Spanish dictionary for her. Brentano's was in the neighborhood. I decided to stop there as we passed, buy the dictionary and have it sent. I saw the familiar bookstore front show up; I rang the bell, climbed down the steps; fought my way across the street between the crowding automobiles; fought my way across the sidewalk between the crowding people; flung myself on the swing door — and found myself in a slumberously peaceful atmosphere like that of a remote country churchyard on a sleepy summer afternoon.

I had been wrong in thinking that you could sell anything here. Not books. Piles of beautiful new books lay on the counters. Sedate salespeople stood behind these piles. The silence was exquisite. The impression of passive repose was like a spell. A dignified person approached me asking if he could be of use to me. In a hushed voice I inquired where the dictionaries were. He motioned me courteously up the steps to the mezzanine. When I arrived on that floor, I found that I was the only customer visible.

Well, I went home to Vermont and wrote an acceptance to the people who were trying to organize a new method of selling books — the mail order method, which has worked well in other fields. It looked as though it would be worth while to try almost any other possible method, in addition to the methods then in use, to distribute more books to the American reading public. It began to be obvious to the eye that the generation to which my father and Melvil Dewey belonged had made a grave miscalculation, not about libraries and books but about human nature. They had assumed a spontaneous, lasting, continuous interest in books and intellectual life, which doesn't seem to exist, any more than a spontaneous interest in being good seems to animate human nature. They had assumed that to have books freely accessible would be enough. Evidently the distribution of books of decent quality to an adequate percentage of our population is a wheel which can't be rolled forward and up hill, unless all kinds of shoulders are set to it with determination and much ingenuity.[12]

The work on the board of selection was demanding and stimulating. At first she and her colleagues tended to underestimate the taste of the American reading public. "I was really disconcerted at that first meeting," she reported,

by our total ignorance of what the American reading public will read. All five of us had been in active literary work all our lives, yet we found we had only the dimmest notion of the tastes of the bigger American reading public, and that dim notion turned out to be quite inaccurate. . . . We all thought that it might be possible to send out, in addition to plenty of readable and agreeable novels, perhaps one or two nonfiction books a year. Our guess — at that first meeting — was also that it would certainly be necessary to send out a number of detective stories every year, or the reading public would turn away.

That's all we knew! The fact is that the nonfiction books selected are as numerous as the novels, and in many years more numerous. And only once, when we sent out *The Omnibus of Crime,* have we ever sent out a detective story as a Book-of-the-Month Club choice. Somewhat shamefaced at our lack of faith in the reading public of America, we soon found out that those who were interested in securing books in this new way, did not want any novels at all except those of first-rate quality.[13]

In 1954–55 the New York Times Oral History Program conducted a series of interviews with persons who had served on the early Committee of Selection of the Book-of-the-Month Club, recognizing it as an important element in American cultural development. These interviews were later transferred from tape recorder to typescript and were stored in the Columbia University Oral History Collection. The interview with Dorothy Canfield Fisher contains over a hundred pages in typescript of recollections of her work as a member of the Committee of Selection.

The committee met once a month to make its choice from books submitted in galley proof from publishers. Harry Scherman and Robert K. Haas, who organized the Book-of-the-Month Club, remained in the background as the five committee members discussed the new books available and made their selection, usually a unanimous one. Dorothy reported that the committee was never pressured to pick a book because it might be "popular" over one of higher quality. Their job was to select the book they liked best and thought was best from those available. "Harry Scherman had a maxim," she reported,

which he repeated innumerable times at ever so many meetings, and I think it's a very valuable one for critics to remember. Every once in a while, some one of us would be led into this kind of comment on some book under consideration: "Well, I liked it — very much indeed — I think it's a splendid book. But I think it might be a little bit over the head of the average reader."

Harry Scherman never let the snobbish remark pass. He always — it was one of the few comments he made during meetings — he always used to say, and we found it very true: "If you like it, you will find that American readers are just like you. They're not any different."

And we have certainly, during these long, long years of choosing books for the American readers, come to feel that the little coterie of people that formerly were supposed to be the only ones that cared about books of good quality is simply nonexistent.[14]

The work of the Committee of Selection involved a tremendous amount of reading. One of the questions the interviewer asked Dorothy was how she managed to do it all. This was her answer: "How did I do all that reading? I just ruined my eyes. My eyes are very dim now, but then I'm seventy-six years old now, it's about time to have dim eyes. But I read much too much. At one time, many years before my retirement, I found my eyes were giving out. They became very bloodshot and very painful, so that I had to keep them shut with cold compresses on them in order not to suffer too much."[15] She discovered that one of the difficulties lay in the length of galley proof. Her oculist pointed out that the lenses he prescribed were for a certain reading distance, but that galley proof, about three times as long as a regular page, far exceeded the capacity of the eyes to adjust comfortably. Everyone on the committee was having the same difficulty, so the publishers went through the galley proof sheets, cutting each into three pages. "From that time on," Dorothy said, "we practically never read galley proof. It was a sort of imitation page proof. (They call them Book-of-the-Month Club proofs.)"[16]

To get the reading done Dorothy seized every available moment. She told the interviewer how she "discovered" Pearl Buck's *Good Earth* almost accidentally on the train:

I did my reading wherever I was. I did a good deal on the train. I especially remember one book I read on the train. Galley proof, cut up, is only printed on one side, so when it's stapled together it makes a book twice as thick as the book will be. The natural human tendency is to put off the big thick books for something that looks more manageable. This month, I was reading for dear life here and everywhere I went, but I had saved one thick book to read on the train going down to New York. I'd looked into it a little, and it seemed to be about agriculture in China. I thought, "Oh, well, that probably is nothing that would be of general interest anyhow," so I could look at that then.

As the train pulled out of Arlington, I opened it, and by the end of the first twelve pages I was sitting up just electrified by the quality of it, and read it, nearly putting my eyes out, all the way to New York. I hadn't begun to finish then — sat up in the hotel bedroom until I had finished it. And early in the morning, long before any New York office was really open, I went around — found nobody but the janitor, languidly sweeping out in the Book-of-the-Month Club office—and left a note saying, "I think this book is of first importance and I think every effort should be made to hold it over to next month, because it may be that it hasn't been thoroughly read."

Then I went back, later on, having had my breakfast and put hot and cold water on my eyes, as you do after a strain. I found that sure enough, it hadn't been really read. . . . So it was held over until the next month, and then it was chosen unanimously. And that was *The Good Earth*. . . . When I first read the first ten or twelve pages and saw the quality of it, I looked back. I said, "Who's writing this? Pearl Buck?" I'd never heard the name, nor had anybody else. She'd never been in this country, not since her childhood. It was her first book.[17]

Dorothy was also responsible for giving a start in America to the Danish author, the baroness Karen Blixen who wrote under the pen name Isak Dinesen. Karen Blixen was the niece of Dorothy's friend Mary Westenholz, whom she called "one of the finest women I've ever known, and whom I've known nearly all our lives."[18] When Karen Blixen's brother sent some of her stories to Dorothy in typescript to see if they could be published in America, his aunt was much upset at what she regarded as misuse of her friendship. Dorothy, however, "thought they were very fine, highly colored like a new kind of fruit or a new kind of wine," and said, "I'd never seen anything like them."[19]

Dorothy sent Karen's stories to Paul Reynolds to see if he could place them separately in American magazines or perhaps together with a book publisher. In her accompanying letter she said, "They seem to me most original, strange, interesting and rich in texture."[20] Reynolds was from the first pessimistic—he did "not think they could be published in any magazine" and was doubtful about book publication—but promised to "try some publishers and see what they say."[21] What they said was, in Dorothy's report, "Why they're just crazy, you can't make anything out of them, there's no story at all. How strange. What do they mean?"[22]

Two months later the stories were back with Dorothy, ready to be returned to Denmark, when Robert Haas of Random House, who was one of the founders of the Book-of-the-Month Club and a Vermont summer neighbor, dropped in to visit. "I brought out these," she recalled later,

and I perfidiously did not tell him that I'd already tried them on several other publishers. I said, "here is a batch of manuscripts sent to me by the nephew of my dear Mary Westenholz." . . . Bob Haas took it back to read, and he was as puzzled by them as everyone else had been, but he was interested in the personal side of it, and said. "I'll take it back and see what the other people at Random House think." And I assume that he didn't tell them any more than I had told him, that he had been stumped by them. And they had a singular experience there. Everybody at Random House — all the readers, and even all the salesmen — was crazy about them. They felt, just as I did, that they were something new and different in quality, and that their strangeness was something precious.

So with great enthusiasm they were published by Random House. And we picked them as a choice in 1934. . . . The other judges were carried away by the exotic flavor, and also encouraged by the fact that they had been accepted by Random House, and were very much liked. You know, it takes a little courage to bring out something so different from anything that has ever been done before. . . . It was sent out with considerable trepidation, and was received with tremendous critical acclaim.[23]

A book that took even more courage to select was Richard Wright's *Native Son.* "It was the first book of that kind which had come out," Dorothy recalled,

telling with savage frankness not only what it meant to be poor and downtrodden in the industrial world, but a Negro. And it did not spare the reader any of the tragedy, horror, fear which the true depiction of a human being, forced into a situation of hopelessness, always creates in the reader. . . . there had been very little crack in the solid crust of prejudice against the Negro, and we were not sure that the book would be at all acceptable, because it wasn't — and by its nature couldn't be — the kind of book which could be given to my seventeen year old daughter.[24]

When the question came up in discussions, the committee took the stand that they "were not sending out books suitable for inexperienced young people to read . . . you can't cover human experience, and keep it within the bounds which are going to be profitable for inexperienced young people to read."[25] In the case of *Native Son,* however, Dorothy remembered, "the publishers began to get alarmed too, fearing that it would be taken as just horror for its own sake. And they asked me — I suppose, a respectable old lady — if I would write an introduction to it, which I was very glad to do and very much honored to have had the chance to do."[26]

After the worries of the committee and the publishers, it was an anticlimax, but a welcome one, to have the first reviews full of "unalloyed praise of the power and vigor of this new voice."[27] Dorothy recalled that "we felt very much like people going upstairs in the dark who think there's one more step than there is! We had taken an attitude, so to speak, of mild heroism — of risking the utter condemnation of the reading subscribers — and nothing of that kind occurred."[28] Of her own part, Dorothy said:

> Perhaps my introduction helped, but I didn't pretend it was a book for young people. My feeling is that there are many aspects of human life which require experience of life to understand, and if there's one quality which even the brightest teenager doesn't have, it's experience. So he gets it all wrong. And he shouldn't read that kind of book. Although, for many of them, it's a form of introduction to experience which isn't quite so violent as experience itself.[29]

Sometimes Dorothy disagreed with her fellow committee members over the choice of a book. She was the only woman and the only country dweller in the group. When *The Last Adam* was chosen over her protests, she had a fantastic dream the following night. She described it in a letter to Merle Haas, Robert Haas's wife:

> The night I came home from the meeting that had chosen that book, I dreamed a long conversation between some country people and a city person about a book centering around an elevator man in the city. He was a jovial, foul-mouthed, coarse old fellow whose custom it was to kiss and hug every woman he had in his elevator before he let her out. Of course the city person (in my dream) protested loudly and said the story couldn't be true to life. The country people answered, "Of you just don't like realism, that's all! You like to have your stories prettified." The city person wildly cried, "It *isn't* realism! Such a man couldn't hold his job a minute." (N.B. this was what I had kept saying about The Last Adam — that perhaps such a doctor could exist, all right, but he would not in any New England community in the country go on holding the job of health officer for two years let alone thirty, and would not have any practice at all among anybody who could possibly get anybody else. The "values" of that book were absolutely all wrong. The details were right enough, but their relation to each other was preposterous). The country people asked "How do you know it isn't possible. You don't pretend to know every elevator man in New York do you?" The city person cried out "But *no* business would go on hiring a man like that." The country people then pointed out (in an amusing caricature of Henry Canby over The Last Adam) how perfectly the details were done — the elevator was described so perfectly, and the expression on the faces of the women kissed and hugged was so well done, and the sound the elevator made going up was almost as though you heard it etc. etc. To which the city person "But that hasn't anything to do with the truth of the situation — it's a false situation well

described, that's all." And the country people "I guess you're a little old-fashioned and don't like any sex in your books etc. etc." Lots more. I woke up laughing my head off and quite eased of my wrath over the choice.[30]

In spite of occasional disagreements, the work with the Book-of-the Month Club was on the whole a happy and rewarding experience for Dorothy. The founders, Harry Scherman and Robert K. Haas, remained her lifelong friends, and at Christmas 1941 Dorothy wrote to Harry, "What wonderful years these have been — are — in a working comradeship of such warm, absolutely trusting friendship as cynics — the poor fish! — could never imagine."[31] The joy Dorothy found in meeting with this stimulating group of fellow authors and critics is reflected in her anguish at retiring from the board. In 1950 she wrote to Harry Scherman, "Oh, dear Harry, I'm so shaken by this drawing-to-a-close — it doesn't seem possible! But I can't see but that it is just plain inevitable!"[32]

Did work for the Book-of-the-Month Club interfere with her writing? "No," Dorothy said, "I never felt any collision at all. They seemed to be going along on parallel rails. One was so entirely different from the other. You know, the act of creating something out of nothing is so different from just watching somebody else perform it. Why, it's just the difference between playing a game of tennis and watching a game of tennis!"[33]

21
Drama: *Tourists Accommodated*

The Fishers were very much part of the little village of Arlington where they lived, and Dorothy frequently put her special skills to use for the benefit of the community. In 1915 she wrote a historical sketch for the stage, which was put on to raise money for the school. She wrote to Paul Reynolds about this project:

> Last autumn, wanting to make some money for improvements to our district school, the people of our neighborhood (under my leadership) got together and presented a historical play—that is sort of play, which I wrote, and which was merely a presentation of life in Arlington in 1791, the year Vermont was admitted to the Union. All the people in it were plain farmer-folk, who had never had any experience before in that sort of thing. Nothing was bought for the costumes, although there were over thirty people, men, women and children, on the stage, all in correct colonial costume; and the proceeds were clean gain for the school. The "acting" was excellent because all the players were required to do was to live a bit on the stage as their own great-grandfathers had lived, and the play interested the village beyond words. The development of the "historical instinct" both in the players and the audience was remarkable, and everybody who had anything to do with it has had a livelier sense of the continuity of human life ever since.[1]

Dorothy subsequently described this community historical experience in an article entitled "Growing a Play."[2]

In 1934 another local dramatic presentation became Dorothy's only published play. *Tourists Accommodated* has the long explanatory subtitle: "Some scenes from present-day summer life in Vermont, Written by Dorothy Canfield Fisher out of experiences, cheerful and otherwise, of her neighbors in the North District of Arlington, Vermont." The play was first copyrighted by the author in 1932 and was published in 1934 "as part of the publication program of The Committee for the Conservation of Vermont Traditions and

Ideals of the Vermont Commission of Country Life."[3]

The Introduction tells how the play came to be written:

One cold, sunshiny January afternoon, three or four years ago, we women who live in the North District of our Vermont town were sewing together in a farmhouse living-room, making an outfit of clothes for an expected and (to tell the truth) not especially welcome baby in one of the poorer families of town. That is not very enlivening work, but because we are all old friends and kinsfolk as well as neighbors, we always enjoy getting together for any purpose, and as we cut and basted and stitched on those familiar tiny garments, we also talked and laughed a good deal.

Several of the farm families represented there — in fact a majority of them — had in the years just preceding this meeting begun to take in automobile tourists overnight, or for meals. This was a strange, revolutionary venture for reticent, solitary-minded New England mountain people. Before long, the lively talk, ranging here and there over neighborhood affairs, turned to this subject, and to the accompaniment of shouts of laughter, became an experience-meeting about the ways of travelers. As one funny story followed another, every incident something that had really happened, one of the group exclaimed as she wiped the mirthful tears from her eyes, "We ought to make a play out of all this."

So we did.

Then and there we began to talk over what kind of a play it might be. First of all, if we were to act in it, it must be simple and natural, to keep it within our untrained abilities. The best way to manage that was, of course, to have in it only characters familiar to us. We began to recall such people to mind. By the time the tea and cookies were being passed around, we were asking each other, "Well, which kind of a person would *you* like to be in the play?" . . . The plot — if you can call it that — of the struggle to pay the expenses of a promising daughter in Normal School needed only to be picked up out of anybody's life around us. And the tourists — oh, there were more funny stories about them than we had time to use!

Of course, being New England women, with (I suppose we must admit it) an especial liking for the satiric and tart, at first we thought of nothing but the ridiculous absurdities of the city-folks who had come our way (at least they seemed absurdities to us). But by and by our fun was interrupted by the quiet voice of one of the neighbors, well known for her gentle ways. "See here," said she, meditatively stirring her tea, "if we're going to have this natural, and the way it is in real life, why, we'll have to put in one *nice* city family, For we've all had them, as nice as folks can be. You know it."

Of course we knew it, and being reminded of it, we put our heads together to remember exactly in what ways some of the nice city people who had passed through had shown their niceness. . . . Then, going further, somebody else said, "But we're just as ridiculous as anybody. Why not show up some of *our* funny ways too?" . . . During the next week I set down on paper a sketch of this material and called a meeting of all the North District neighbors at the schoolhouse. I read my sketch aloud then, and we women were much encouraged by the loud laughter of the men and children who were our first audience. Then everybody began to make suggestions — chiefly as to the ways of saying things. You see, we wanted the country people on our stage to be real country people, not as they are usually portrayed by city actors with stuck-on chin-whiskers, stiff new overalls and a grotesque accent such as nobody on earth — north, south, east, or west — ever heard. We wanted to show a little piece of country life just as it looks and feels to country people. So everybody was told to read his part over several times before he began to learn it by heart, and to change the wording of it as he wished, if he could think of any phrases or expressions that would make what he had to say seem more natural to him. . . .

Now finally do you ask what gives us courage to present our innocuous homespun production to the formidable general public? Well, because ever since we gave it here for the first time in our Town Hall (and were obliged to keep repeating it till we were worn out) so many people from all over the state have written to ask us to send them our "play" so that they could produce it in their Town Halls. And because as time goes on, such requests keep coming in from other rural communities farther and farther afield outside of the state. And not only from country people. I look at the calendar as I write and see that this very evening "Tourists Accommodated" is being produced by a company of amateur actors in a suburb of New York City — of all places![4]

Dorothy's "innocuous homespun production" appeared on the Arlington stage in 1932, but the lasting appeal of the piece is evident in the inclusion of a scene from it forty years later, in 1973, in the anthology *The Literature of Vermont: A Sampler*.[5]

22

World War II:
The Children's Crusade and *Our Young Folks*

In 1939 the war threat that had been smouldering in Europe burst into flame. Dorothy and John again felt a need to help, as they had in an earlier European conflict. The practical result of their concern was again work for the innocent victims of oppression and conflict. A steady stream of Jewish refugees from Hitler's Germany found temporary refuge in the little log cabin John had built for the Harcourts years before, and Dorothy wrote letters to help find a place for these people to use their intellectual and artistic gifts in America.

In the summer of 1939, Dorothy organized and found money for a project that brought sixty German and Austrian refugee children to spend the summer in farm and village homes in Bennington County. That September she began work on a project of national scope, writing and speaking almost continuously to urge the children of America to contribute their pennies to help the children of Europe who were victims of war.

The "Children's Crusade" was sometimes misunderstood and criticized, but Dorothy campaigned wherever she might be heard to get the chance to involve the children of America in a gesture of help and sympathy. In October she spoke in Grand Rapids to the State Commissioners of Education convention. In February she was in St. Louis, where she addressed 12,000 persons at the meeting of the Association of Officers of Administration. In April she was speaking in Philadelphia. When the crusade ended on April 30, 1940, $130,000 had been given by American children to help children of other lands who had suffered because of war.

This public campaigning took a heavy toll of Dorothy's vital energy. She wrote to Edward Post that she had "worked on that as I had worked once before in my life, in France 1916–1919. I don't enjoy this kind of organized relief work," she confessed, "in fact I suffer acutely when engaged in it, and in both cases took it on only because I seemed at the time the only one near enough the sudden need who was able to struggle with it."[1] And to Harry

Scherman she recalled a line her father used to quote: "No man can effect great benefits for his country without some sacrifice of the minor virtues!"[2]

The Fisher family was in a time of transition. In 1939 Governor George Aiken appointed John to serve as chairman of the Vermont State Board of Education for a term of ten years, and he was immediately called away from home to speak on various platforms throughout the state. Dorothy also continued her active circuit of public speaking and gave a series of lectures at Miami University in Florida. That year, too, their son graduated from Harvard Medical School and began service as an intern in Massachusetts.

Dorothy had for some time been troubled by an enlarged thyroid gland. "The long steady effort of the Children's Crusade which I used to think of as an attempt to push a glacier along, was too much," she reported in January 1941. "The thyroid was affected and from being what the doctors quaintly call 'benign,' it became toxic, pushing me over the edge into real sickness such as I'd never known. An operation last autumn, long and complicated, the usual weeks in the hospital, the usual weeks of slow convalescence, in which I'm still immersed."[3]

Although Dorothy blamed her illness on the Children's Crusade, that was only a fraction of her productive work in this period. Somehow, in the midst of her hectic schedule, she found time to publish two books for children and to serve on the American Youth Commission of the American Council on Education. In her own report, "It was a group of American citizens, mature in age, seasoned in life-experience, of varied professions, invited by one of the great Foundations of our country to give their time and thought to an endeavor to find out in general what the facts are about the situation of young people in our industrial democracy."[4] The commission had funds to employ a staff of professional scholars and statisticians to make a survey of the facts; "this took five years of effort on the part of the staff and frequent, lengthy meetings of the Commission itself."[5] Another year was devoted to the preparation of the report, *Youth and the Future,* which appeared in January 1942.

The members of the commission were representative of "one or another special group of citizens of our country—for those engaged in education, in the professional care of delinquents and criminals, in industrial production, in labor unions, in corporations supplying electricity and other needed services, and so on."[6] She saw herself as " 'representative' only of the general public."[7]

When the report of the commission was issued, it was "stately, dignified, and admirable,"[8] "a historic document,"[9] but Dorothy felt the need for an informal report to the constituency she represented. In *Our Young Folks* she wrote this account "as of one citizen to others."[10] "What is in it," she said, is just about what you yourself would have known and felt after six years' contact with admirably trained specialists and intelligent and experienced citizens if you too had been present at those long meetings. What passed over my untutored head without my taking it in is probably about what you too would have missed if, like me, you had had only an ordinary background of general information. What was caught and understood by my amateur but intense interest as an American mother and grandmother in the welfare of our younger generation is probably approximately what you would have grasped of the vast accumulation of reports, graphs, statistics, and special research projects.[11]

In *Our Young Folks,* which appeared in 1943, the economic and social issues that have played background roles in most of Dorothy's novels come directly to the fore as they affect young people. The situation of the past, the changes that have made the past an inadequate predictor of the future, the special problems of girls, and the dangers and opportunities created by the increase of leisure time — all are considered here.

Dorothy found the task of putting all the material in a form where it could be understood in its full significance by ordinary people a difficult one. Afterward, she wrote to an appreciative reader:

It takes a great deal of time (at least that's my experience) to do decent work. Endless revision is necessary, and the passage of time over the head of the author seems to have something magical about it. That you revise an article as best you can, lay it aside, and a month later you can see ever so many more ways to improve it. You speak with generous appreciation of "Our Young Folks." If you could just know the years I spent on that book, writing and rewriting, in despair often about the whole proposition, taking it up again because I was under contract and must finish it, tearing up pages which represented many days of work and starting all over again — you would think there is nobody except himself who can help an author.[12]

Dorothy suffered acutely during World War II. Again her French friends were in constant danger, she had little or no news of them for the long period of German occupation, and she relived in her mind the horrors of the earlier conflict.

At home matters were hardly more reassuring. On the completion of his internship in 1942, Jimmy volunteered for service with the Medical Corps. Dorothy had called medicine "the finest profession known to humanity," and she was immensely proud of Jimmy. While he was in training in Pennsylvania in the fall, John and Dorothy went to visit him, but on the way home John suffered a heart-block fainting spell. The following March John had a coronary thrombosis and spent ten weeks in bed.

Only one important piece of fiction comes from this period, a short narrative "The Knot-Hole," which was published in *The Yale Review* in 1943. It is the story of French prisoners of war, and it is so realistic that Dorothy's cousin, Arthur Canfield, asked her if it was based on real events. She answered, "I am very much pleased that you read 'The Knot-Hole' with sympathy. No, there is no foundation in literal fact for the story. I'm not a reporter of facts you know, ever—but a real sure-enough fiction writer. It is all fact, as I know from the comments on it from many French people since it has appeared. But not literal facts. You'll know very well what the difference is."[13]

When Dorothy sent "The Knot-Hole" to Paul Reynolds, she wrote, "I think it will be good for Americans to read—if I have succeeded at all in communicating some of the deep feeling with which I wrote it."[14] She later wrote, I think it is as good a work as I have ever done, from a literary point of view."[15] Her own estimate of the quality of the story was borne out when it was included in the 1943 O. Henry Prize Stories and won second prize among the narratives in the volume.

As the war drew to a close in Europe, Dorothy began to feel that it might be possible for her to write a novel again, or at least some shorter fiction. In a long report on her feelings about the writing of fiction and nonfiction, she said:

Now this return-to-fiction idea—there is so much to be said on that point! Since the invasion of France, I have not—until the other day—written anything in the way of fiction except "The Knot-Hole" and that was more like a groan of anguish than a story. I have written incessantly, articles and statements, in which I have tried to uphold the civilized decent attitude towards life. Articles and statements can be produced by the single effort of will, purpose, concentration.

But fiction—that's more like falling in love, which can't be done by will-power or purpose, but concerns the *whole* personality, which includes vast areas of the unconscious and subconscious, as well as those processes within the control of purposefulness. This element of the unknown puts into the writing of fiction an element of the uncontrollable. And fiction written *without* the whole personality is not fiction (that is, re-created human life, interpreted) but only articles or statements in narrative *form.*

Now that the war has progressed to the point where we can be *sure* that the Nazis will not actually, literally invade and hold our country, now that we are *sure* that none of us will ever be tortured to make us betray our friends, not to speak of the lessening of the unbearable burden on the heart of horrified sympathy for Europeans who *were* still under that threat, that grim reality, I feel an immense lessening of emotional tension. And the other day, sitting down at my desk to write yet another of the stream of articles, I felt the old impulse, buried so long beneath the great deposit of anxious moral concerns, to write something because I *wanted* to, because I felt like making one of those comments on human life by *implication,* which, if successful, turn out to be creative fiction.[15]

A month after Dorothy wrote so optimistically of the future, she learned that her son's battalion had been transformed to a Ranger Commando unit. The following February, while freeing American prisoners of war in the Philippines, Jimmy was severely wounded and died the following day. Letters of sympathy poured into the Fisher home in Arlington. To one of these Dorothy responded, "I can't write to you yet — not in words. My son is still being torn from me. The giving him up to death is as agonizing physically as bringing him into life. But I will survive — and go on to try my best to stand for righteousness through thick and thin. But now there is only intolerable pain."[17]A poignant note is struck by another letter, written by Dorothy's secretary, to a sympathetic friend: "Mrs. Fisher's oculist has told her to use her eyes as little as possible for the time being, because they have become so inflamed from the long periods of weeping."[18]

A year and a half later, Dorothy wrote, "I am using work as an opiate — and like all opiates, it is dangerous when abused, when too big doses of it are taken. Just now I am staggering from a huge overdose. All sorts of things, book-reviews, articles (these mostly of the help-good-causes variety), letters, letters (many of these of the same kind as the articles) are piled in formidable masses on my desk."[19]

The first memorial that the Fishers established to the memory of their son was to bring to America for graduate study the two Philippine doctors who had cared for him after he was wounded, Dr. and Mrs. Carlos Layug. Dorothy wrote to Edward Post about them:

They were with our darling lost son, in his last hours, and risked their lives to try to save his. He had told them, just before the attack on the Cabantuan prison began, in which he was mortally wounded, that if they all lived through the desperate undertaking, he would certainly help them come to this country for some post-graduate study. You can imagine that when we heard that — from some of the rescued prisoners in the Cabantuan prison, who came to see us here — we had but one idea, to try to find those two fine people, and carry out our son's wishes.

It is done, over and around innumerable obstacles, too long to set down. They are now actually at the Harvard Medical School, studying for a year. . . . They are splendid young people (just our son's age, in the early thirties) especially interesting because — highly trained cultivated professional people as they are, they are still Orientals, from the Pacific area, and hence see life from a different angle from ours. We find them singularly interesting, and lovable. . . .

Everybody is being very kind to them at the Harvard Medical School where their presence is regarded (as we regard it) as a sort of living memorial to the Harvard Medical School graduate, who died and is buried in their far Oriental country. There are only sixty, carefully picked doctors in that graduate course — we were much touched that the Trustees, or the Faculty Committee or whoever is in charge of admissions, made room for these two, as their part of a memorial to our Jimmy.[20]

23
The Small Town:
American Portraits and
Memories of Arlington, Vermont

Dorothy had written to Edward Post after her son's death that she would continue "to stand for righteousness through thick and thin." Her postwar books were all, each in its own way, a keeping of that pledge.

Among the refugee couples that came to the log cabin on the Fisher place in Vermont were a Viennese lawyer and his artist wife, Edward and Enit Kaufman. Enit Kaufman had been a highly successful portrait painter in Vienna and Paris, and she decided to show her appreciation to the land that gave her shelter in a characteristic way. She would make a series of portraits of eminent Americans, all the leaders of America who would sit for her, and then she would make a gift of the collection to an American museum, from which it could be loaned for exhibit in other parts of the country.

Money for the project ran low when the series was only partially completed, so Dorothy suggested that Enit have the pictures reproduced and printed in a book. Publishers, it turned out, would be interested in such a collection of portraits only if they were accompanied by biographical sketches written by some well-known author. Dorothy volunteered to write the sketches, and the volume, *American Portraits,* was published by Henry Holt and Company in 1946.

Although Dorothy undertook the task from humanitarian motives, as she worked with the biographical material her mind mulled over the accumulating evidence of the background of greatness in characteristic fashion. The subjects for the portraits had been chosen as "a sampling of the army of Americans who have, in one walk of life and another, achieved success far beyond the average."[1] Behind the achievement of eminence Dorothy began to discover surprises.

"Like many authors," she reported,

I am given to plaguing the family circle with talk about the particular piece of writing on which I am working. I used to try out these biographical sketches by reading them aloud to any member of the home circle available as I finished a first draught. At first this was very well received. Although the search for biographical facts had, with intention, not gone beyond records and publications open to anyone's inspection, there was an almost looking-through-the-keyhole interest in finding out little-suspected or long-ago-forgotten facts about the early background of scientists, philosophers, men of politics, generals, public servants, now of first rank. . . . But it was not long before I heard another sort of comment: "Why, it's the same story, over and over. Sounds as though you were making it up, to prove something."

I reminded my listeners that neither Enit Kaufman nor I had had any preconceived idea whatever about the early years of these people, now renowed leaders in their chosen fields. To no avail. The biographies written later did not profit by family advice, valuable because of its uninhibited frankness. "No, I do not want to hear about Vannevar Bush. I suppose you'll be saying that his father too was one of those small-church ministers?" Well, yes, so he was.

And so — really, who would have thought it — was Thomas Lamont's.

So much was said, sceptically, by the family circle about the improbable similarity in many of these life-stories that I was daunted, and I wondered whether, because of some special personal slant, I was departing from sacred objectivity. . . . the pattern is a recurring one, to a degree nobody beforehand would have guessed. It was not, literally could not have been, "made up to prove something." But perhaps it did prove something, or at least suggest something. [2]

After considering and rejecting a variety of hypotheses, ranging from inherited intelligence to absence of wealth, Dorothy comes to a "tentative hypothesis" about the environmental background that is most favorable to growth to later success:

It is my guess that the great preponderance, in this sampling of Americans who have achieved success, of people whose youth was spent in rural and small communities, comes quite simply from the day-by-day closeness in such places to "managerial responsibility" and is due to the remoteness from such responsibility of those who are brought up in the midst of larger numbers. Those local free high schools twenty-five or thirty or forty years ago were certainly not better educational institutions in themselves than the expensive prep schools, as one might at first think.

But the boys and girls who went to those small semi-rural high schools were saturated to the marrow of their bones by constant contract with the feeling of communal responsibility for understanding the workings of local institutions and for helping to keep them working.[3]

She contrasts this attitude of responsibility with "the private-soldier mentality, which waits to be told what to do by a leader whose actions are not to be questioned except at peril of endangering the effectiveness of the group's action."[4] She concludes that "most of the pre-eminently successful and fulfilled people in the typical sampling of eminent Americans in this book were brought up — whatever other conditions around them may have been — as working members of human groups small enough in number to have something of the old town meeting quality."[5]

Among the portraits in the collection is one of Dorothy herself. For it she wrote the "first and only autobiographical note I have ever written."[6] It is significant of her sense of herself as part of a larger life stream that she spends half of her sketch describing her ancestral heritage and concludes by saying, "I have lived, ever since my marriage in 1907, within a stone's throw of where my great-greats of 1764 slid off their horses, at the end of the long trip from Connecticut up over the Indian trails, and, because the water of our brook is soft, decided that here they would make their home. I am, a hundred and eighty years later, drinking water from that same brook. Maybe that is symbolical of something."[7]

The illustrator Norman Rockwell was a neighbor of the Fishers in their narrow Vermont valley, and one of his most charming pictures is a portrait of John and Dorothy Fisher. Dorothy was glad to write an introduction to a book about him and his work, and she used this introduction as a vehicle for some trenchant remarks about artistic creation in general, many of them as applicable to the creator with words as to the artist with color and line. She wrote:

I have recently written a defense of those serious and sincere modern authors who attempt to understand and portray what they see in American life, even if their report is shocking to those who have never come in contact with filth and moral degradation. My argument is that if, in American life, such sordidness and misery are often found, nothing is gained by pretending in books that things in our country are different from what they are.

Having gone on record publicly with this claim of the right of an honest portrayer of human life to give us his report, even if it sickens us, I think I have the right to make the same claim for another honest portrayer of human life even if his report cheers and comforts us.

Just at present the one is up on the see-saw of aesthetic fashion and the other is down. This is, I think, an especial reason for calling the attention of Americans to the story of Norman Rockwell's work. . . . If he had painted in the mid-Victorian period of hush-hush about the ugly and ignoble aspects of human life, a comment on what he gives us should, perhaps, have contained a reminder that . . . he does not look at death, failure, defeat. But we have in these last decades supped deep of portrayals of frustration and defeat. Such portrayals give but one aspect of real life. Another aspect has the right to our recognition. . . . In a period when wormwood and vinegar are the fashionable flavorings, it is genuine originality for Rockwell to dip his brush into the honey-pot of lovableness and zest in living.

His originality (it must take some courage, too) in thus painting an aspect of the truth which he chooses to paint, is shown again by his swimming against the current of fashion—in ignoring what is known as "natural" beauty. Just as he does not portray misery and malicious wrongdoing . . . , so he resolutely does not paint landscapes. . . .

In the case of a man so transparently sincere, so honestly earnest as Norman Rockwell, does it take "courage" to go against a fashionable aesthetic convention? Probably not. Probably he has no time to think whether he is going against what the knowing ones of his period accept. It is obvious from the story of his life and work that he is single-heartedly focused on what makes up the life of any kind of creative personality, the long, desperate struggle with his own limitations. But if we are to understand him, we will do well to remember that it does not make sense to think that his elimination of tragedy and cruelty can be laid to a wish to please the people who look at his work, because he leaves out, firmly and consistently, something else that would please them, something which moderns love to look at—the beauty of Nature.

In both instances it is plain that he purposefully makes his own choice from an inner necessity. Every artist learns early, or he is no artist, that he must drink out of his own cup, must cultivate his own half-acre, because he never can have any other.[8]

When Dorothy chose to find her own "half-acre" in Arlington, she accepted its traditions as her own, and in 1955 the Arlington Historical Society published a volume of her reminiscences under the title *Memories of My Home Town,* "as part of the effort of our local Historical Society to preserve a reasonable amount, not only of the facts of our communal past, but of its human color, too."[9] The book was sold out almost immediately, "before we could draw our comfortably slow, rural breath," and "became a collector's item before it was off the printing press."[10]

The publishing house of Duell, Sloan and Pearce decided the following year to bring out a series of books under the general heading, "Memories of My Home Town," and the firm asked Dorothy to expand the little volume that she had assembled for the Arlington Historical Society. The result was *Memories of Arlington, Vermont,* a series of local stories, grouped under the chronological headings "Eighteenth Century," "Early Nineteenth Century," and "Later Nineteenth Century and Twentieth Century."

Dorothy saw the book as a contribution to neighborliness in a nation grown so large that it was impossible to get to know the other people in it as neighbors without help. In her informal introduction, entitled "The Purpose of This Series," she concludes, "If we are all to be fully fellow-countrymen, we'd better set about knowing each other more humanly. The purpose of this series of home-town memories is a move in this direction. Each one of the books in this series has as its intention — to give the reader some informal glimpses of the homely human life of a region not his own."[11]

Dorothy had always been keenly aware of the tradition lying back of her. As she became old she leaned, as old people will, more and more heavily on that past and drew spiritual sustenance from it. In her small town she found the past inextricably interwoven in the present. "In Arlington, as in most small, old, close-knit communities," she wrote, "everyday chat between neighbors is not limited to the present. The past is part of today. Especially if a piece of the past is, as old stories often are, an explanatory footnote from 1810, or 1799, or 1862, or 1955, to gossip of the day marked on your calendar as now."[12] She added, "The surface has changed greatly from time to time. The people, and their way of taking life, have not changed much."[13]

24
History Books for Children:
Paul Revere and the Minute Men, Our Independence
and the Constitution, A Fair World for All,
And Long Remember

In 1949 Bennett Cerf, the president of Random House, asked Dorothy to write the first two books of a new series to be known as "Landmark Books." "We envisage," he wrote, "in due course, a series that will embrace sixty to seventy titles and cover the whole scope of American ideology and progress. The slogan we are going to use for the series is 'Landmarks of American History Told for American Boys and Girls.' "[1] The series was to start with a story of Paul Revere, to be followed by a book on the writing of the Declaration of Independence and the Constitution.

In April 1950 *Paul Revere and the Minute Men* was complete. After reading the manuscript Bennett Cerf wrote enthusiastically, "Dorothy, this is so exactly what I wanted for our Landmark Series that if you had been anywhere around when I finished the last page, I would just have taken you into my arms and hugged the life out of you. If the rest of our books can come anywhere close to this one, this series is going to be more important and more successful than even our wildest dreams for it."[2] A month later, the second book was also finished and in the publisher's hands, and again the reception was enthusiastic. Dorothy's old friend Robert Haas, the vice-president of Random House, wrote to her: "I read 'Our Independence and the Constitution' last night, and all I'll say — for the simple reason that it is all I *can* say — is that it thrilled me even more than 'Paul Revere.' "[3]

In these two volumes for children Dorothy brings the history-book heroes of American independence to life again and invites modern young people to share with them the difficult decisions, the exciting adventures, and the often sobering successes of their times. Dorothy does not forget that the struggle and the privations attending the nation's birth were experienced by children as well as by their elders. The half-grown son of Paul Revere and the little daughter of a Philadelphia patriot have important parts in the events she relates.

Dorothy's success in interpreting history for young people brought her another assignment, this time one of international scope. At the request of the United Nations, Dorothy wrote a small volume entitled *A Fair World for All* "to explain in everyday language the Universal Declaration of Human Rights."[4] In an introduction to the book, Eleanor Roosevelt, who had served on the Commission on Human Rights from its beginning, wrote:

> At first it was hoped that this Declaration could be made short enough to be memorized by everybody, but as the work progressed it was found difficult to omit any of the thoughts finally included. The rights of human beings, as well as the responsibilities that go with them, are indeed very numerous and very great. . . . It is good for young people to have this responsibility in terms that they can understand, since here are standards which they must consider in their relationship with the peoples of the world.[5]

The complete Universal Declaration of Human Rights is printed at the beginning of the volume, and then each clause of the declaration is taken separately and explained by means of illustrations. To these explanatory chapters Dorothy adds one more, "What of It?" She begins this chapter by saying:

> Well, there it is.
> And what is it now we have it? It is building material for the only bridge which will let us keep on along the human road, the road which our forefathers have been laying out, section by section, and then building, section by section, ever since there were any human beings.
> That road has led us now to the brink of a dreadful, black chasm, so deep that if we fall into it that fall will be the end of us. The name of the chasm is war — total world war. If we can get a bridge made across that, we can go on building our human road into the future.[6]

She goes on to say, "But a heap of even the best material isn't a bridge — isn't anything. Not yet. . . . All of us will be needed to put it into shape so that we can use it to get across the great chasm — the danger of war — into world peace, which is the only place we can all go on living."[7]

The first suggestion for Dorothy's last book, *And Long Remember,* came from Helene Frye, the Junior Books editor of Whittlesey House. In 1953 she wrote to Dorothy, suggesting a "heart to heart little book for the young people of America. They are our only hope — they face terrific problems and they are so confused. I have been thinking for a long time of the great service such a book by you would be."[8]

Dorothy saw in Helene's suggestion one more opportunity to share the help she had received from the past with young Americans who were going on into the future. The book was to contain biographical sketches of those Americans whose lives had been an inspiration to Dorothy, and it was to have the subtitle "Some Great Americans Who Have Helped Me." The title, taken from the Gettysburg Address, contains by implication the sentence of which it is a part: "The world will little note nor long remember what we say here, but it can never forget what they did here."

In the Introduction, Dorothy wrote:

> At times, during the last forty-odd years of hot wars and cold wars interspersed with periods of truce which were not peace, I might have lost the courage needed to face the bad news of today and the worse news threatening tomorrow if I had not remembered the life-giving ideas spoken or acted out by the long line of great citizens who have proved that human existence is not fated to be only a mad scramble of grab and guzzle. So now I want to share these memories with young people today, and to make the last book I shall ever write a collection of true, *true* stories about real people who have given us all a reason to feel proud that we too are Americans.[9]

All through the year 1958 Dorothy worked on this "last book." Her strength was steadily failing, and she found it increasingly difficult to put her ideas into words, to manage what she once called "that terrific struggle with making ideas concrete."[10] She leaned heavily on Helene Frye and wanted the volume dedicated to her in gratitude for her patience and understanding.

Dorothy was able to complete only twelve of her list for *And Long Remember*; her completed sketches include those on George Washington, Thomas Jefferson, Old Dr. Franklin, John Paul Jones, Patrick Henry, Nathan Hale, David Farragut, Dorothea Dix, Robert E. Lee, Ulysses S. Grant, George Washington Carver, and John Woodward Phillip. Among the essays planned but not completed for publication were ones on Henry David Thoreau, Ralph Waldo Emerson, President and Mrs. Franklin D. Roosevelt, and President Dwight D. Eisenhower. A draft of the Emerson essay, which is among Dorothy's unpublished papers, recalls one of her early novels *The Bent Twig,* for it centers on the same Emersonian quotation that plays a large role in that book: " 'What will you have,' quoth God. 'Take it and pay for it.' "[11]

The series of biographical sketches is introduced by two essays. The first, "Knowing the best of the past . . . ," explains the purpose of the collection. In it Dorothy gives her own definition of greatness:

In the future as in the past, a few will rise far above the general average, a few will carry on the great tradition handed down to them by those earlier men and women whose main motive was not to seek advantage for themselves, who actually forgot themselves most of the time because their minds were entirely occupied with something bigger — perhaps organizing a working government to provide liberty and justice for all, perhaps finding a cure for diphtheria, protesting against slavery, or puzzling out as best they could the reasons for the tides, the trade winds, and eclipses of the sun and moon.[12]

In the universal admiration for such persons, Dorothy finds reason for optimism about the future of the human race: "This tells us something about what we human beings really care for deep down in our hearts, that in the long run the vast majority of people all over the world have come to believe such unselfish actions are worthwhile, that they are expressions of intelligence and character at its highest level."[13] She concludes the introduction with the assertion that "Knowing the best of the past, you can face the future resolute and unafraid."[14]

The second introductory essay is entitled "The Man Who Heard Lincoln." This is the story of a Vermont boy who was chosen to serve in the honor guard when President Abraham Lincoln delivered the Gettysburg Address. His place was directly in front of the president, and he stood there hardly an arm's length from the Great Emancipator as he spoke the moving phrases of that address. Yet this young soldier was so intent on his own personal part in the ceremony that he was almost totally insensible to the words being spoken into his ear, to the proximity of greatness. In answer to later inquiries he could only reply, "Well now I can't rightly recollect them words. You see it was all over so quick . . . and all the while I was holding myself up still and straight so as to be a credit to the regiment like the sergeant said I should."[15] Dorothy sees in his performance the parable of a man who is so wrapped in himself that he misses what is really important, the greatness that could inspire him: "He didn't even try to hear and understand the glorious message which was going past his ears."[16]

In this book of sketches of "a few examples of great Americans who have set a high standard of citizenship for us to follow,"[17] each of the biographies contributes a different part to the composite picture of greatness, but for Dorothy true greatness always contained the element of selflessness. In writing of Nathan Hale she asks rhetorically, "What do we mean by success in life? Isn't it to be honest, kind, and brave, to follow the truth as we see it, to care less for our own comfort than for the good of others?"[18]

25
Vermont Tradition

During her long writing career Dorothy's work had proceeded constantly along two separate paths, fiction and nonfiction. Sometimes she had treated the same subject both directly in nonfiction and by implication in a parallel book of fictional narrative. It was not, however, until her last major work that the two paths converged in one volume, *Vermont Tradition, The Biography of an Outlook on Life.*

The original plan for the book was quite modest. In 1938 Roger L. Scaife, the vice-president of Little, Brown and Company, wrote to Dorothy to suggest that she write a book on Vermont. In answer to her question about what sort of a book it should be, he replied, "in some way, your own of course, you should convey your love for the State. That should be the heart and soul of the book. Your methods of conveying this impression, what has led you to have this fondness for one little section of our country and its people only you know how to express."[1] He added, "My suggestion is to take your time in making your decision with the understanding that you can also take your time in writing the book."[2]

Dorothy's interest in the project was real, but many matters intervened, and it was 1950 when she finally began serious work on it. In 1951 she resigned from the Board of Selection of the Book-of-the-Month Club, and she wrote, "I find before me more free time than for the last quarter of a century, for writing. And the Vermont book will be one of the first things I take up."[3]

Dorothy had a lifelong interest in studying what constituted the essence of Vermont. It is evident in her first collection of stories, *Hillsboro People,* which appeared in 1915. In 1933 she wrote an introduction to a book of poetry by a fellow Vermonter, *A Mountain Township* by Walter Hard. Here she told the reader what Vermont meant to her and suggested the Vermont qualities to be found in the verses of the volume. She wrote:

Vermonters are mountaineers, yes, but not Celtic or picturesque ones. . . . Rigorous understatement rather than exuberant overstatement is their native idiom. Their poetry is implicit. Their passion is too concentrated an essence to dilute with many words. . . . Above all they are Anglo-Saxons in ruling out self-pity from among the permissible emotions. In their code it is too far beneath contempt to deserve expression; . . . there is, in addition to self-pity, one other emotion you will not find expressed. This is boredom. It does not thrive in the Vermont climate, kept down as it is by the necessity to work hard, and by the habit (common to most mature human beings *when the daily routine of their lives leaves them time for reflection*) of trying to extract from each particular which comes into personal life some light about the general of which it is a manifestation . . . the tendency of the Vermonter . . . is to try to see how the isolated detail that comes before his eyes in the daily round is related to larger matters."[4]

One of these "larger matters" is historical context. In some remarks recorded for the 1954 meeting of the Vermont Historical Society, Dorothy spoke of the importance of knowing the past and said, "The stubborn, slowly developing human intelligence cannot but be shaped, encouraged and developed by adding to our consciousness of the present, the deep, vital, other-dimension of a realization that we are one in purpose with our human forefathers."[5]

On the title page of *Vermont Tradition* is a quotation from Henri Bergson: "The present contains nothing more than the past. And what is found in the effect was already in the cause." This book then was not to be a history in the usual sense of the word but a story of the development of a particular type of character. In very much the same way as she had developed the lives of her fictional people, Dorothy proposed to write of the development of the Vermont "outlook on life."

Her first task was to define that outlook on life, so that she had a firm hold on her theme. As she had with so many of her books, she talked this over with her friend Sarah Cleghorn and asked for her help in revising the manuscript. Dorothy knew that Sarah would not be wholly in sympathy with the point of view she intended to stress, but she counted on Sarah's loyal friendship and was not disappointed.

As she began work, Dorothy wrote to her friend:

I mean of course to have as my theme, that Vermont tradition is concerned *first* with the conduct of human life, and then (according to individual temperament and taste) with the arts or sciences or mystic religion — whereas the artists, scientists and mystics are concerned *first* with their special interest, and add to it, in varying degrees, a concern with everyday human conduct. And then I mean to say that the Vermont tradition grapples energetically with the basic problem of human conduct (as it is in reality and everyday experience) how to reconcile the needs of the *group* of which every man or woman is a member, and responsible to the group for any conduct of his which may affect them — with the craving for individual freedom to be what he really is, without getting disapproved of, for it. The Vermont method of doing this is the opposite . . . [of that] which undertakes to say how the individual shall feel, and believe *in* his individual soul and mind. The Vermont effort is to leave the individual alone in his own world as much as is possible when the welfare of the group is taken into consideration, so that, alone in his own world, the individual can have more than the pin-point of freedom which is all that Amiel sadly says can be allowed him by society. The Vermonter ideal, is to have that pin-point considerable bigger than Amiel thinks possible — big enough to swing a cat in, so to speak.

Then I'll take up the economic and other history which has made it possible for Vermont tradition to keep to this idea, more than urbanized, industrialized regions.

I don't believe this will appeal especially to you personally, who (I think) idealize the group element in human life somewhat — but you're a good editor and can revise the English of a presentation you're not especially interested in.[6]

Sarah Cleghorn's help in editing the manuscript was to Dorothy invaluable. A letter from Dorothy reads:

Your comments on these roughly flung down lumps of clay which arrive at your desk are priceless, apples of gold in pitchers of silver, no less. I am struck — as so often — by the way our minds run along similar (not identical but similar) channels. Many times I exclaim to myself, on seeing a marginal note of yours "Of, of course! I was just *about* to make that change when the telephone rang" Or "when I was called to lunch," or "that's just my idea, only I hadn't got around to it!" . . . *Such* relief — unimaginable — that you are taking on those two "literary chores" I wished on to you![7]

The organization of the book is basically chronological. After "Preliminary Remarks," in which the author defines what she means by the Vermont tradition and enumerates the unique charcteristics that set it aside from other types of heritage, she begins with the earliest settlers and traces her theme to the present day.

This development is divided into six parts. Of the first settlers she writes, "They were young. They were surrounded by friendly neighbors, near enough to dance with, to exchange work with, to call on for help, not near enough to break the blessed freedom of every family to live as it thought best."[8]

Part II describes the land-grant dispute between New York and New Hampshire and what this meant for Vermont's part in the American Revolution. Dorothy's method in this section is to take a fictional squirrel-hunting Connecticut boy and let him wander casually over the border into New York. "He would have stepped from one world into another, out of a world with social ideals looking towards the future of our American nation, into one where the social ideals were based on acceptance of the British past."[9] To back up this fictional account, Dorothy appended to the volume a complete statement of the factual basis on which it rested, which she titled "The Gentry's Last Stand."

This section ends with an account of Ethan Allen, the most colorful of the early Vermont heroes, a man who was "passionate about an idea—the ancient idea that men and women live best and most fruitfully in as much freedom and equality as is possible. He was the voice of Vermont. He still is."[10]

Part III brings Vermont up to and through the Civil War. In this section Dorothy makes an interesting attack on "the despair-and-frustration literary fashion"[11] current in the first half of the twentieth century that was based largely on technological unemployment. Her thesis is that such despair has no part in the Vermont tradition, and to support it she traces the varying fortunes of Vermonters through a number of technological changes. She sees the capacity of Vermonters to weather such economic storms as resting on their classless society, on the fact that economic wealth has never made any Vermonters feel that they belonged to a superior class, and so the loss of it did not cause them despair.

In a direct attack on the tendency in modern literature to see human beings as the victims of economic change, Dorothy writes:

We can quite understand that many people (novelists especially perhaps) would be repelled by the rude lack of hereditary social gradations in our kind of life, would think it dull and monotonous. We don't find it so. In our personal and human relations we live through all the drama, all the emotional ups and downs we can stand. We can see for ourselves that for many temperaments life would be dreary without social institutions which provide the joy of excluding others from what they would like to have. That joy does not taste very sweet on our tongues. But for those who feel that without it life would be tiresome and boring—well, there are any number of other places in our nation, on the globe, where (of course if they are well-to-do) they will find it easily available.[12]

Dorothy goes on to draw another distinction that she feels is typically Vermont in the perception of tragedy. She writes: "Personal grief breaks hearts here as everywhere. And here as elsewhere, those who grieve come after long suffering to a vision of sorrow as beauty because it grows out of love. But yes, Vermont is prosaic and dry in refusing to see any putrescent beauty or poetry in decay. It is not part of our tradition to drape emotional crape around a lost bank account."[13]

Part IV describes the century following the Civil War and shows in four successive chapters how the fears and forebodings of the disheartened older Vermonters did not come to reality. The four areas in which they saw the future of Vermont most seriously threatened were financial ruin through war debts; emigration of the most vigorous young people to the newly opened lands of the West; the flood of illiterate immigrants of "foreign" stock; and the feeling that the Civil War, which had cost so heavily, had been fought for the freeing of a people who were (perhaps) only fit to be slaves.

In the four chapters each fear is examined and is shown not to be borne out by subsequent events. The war debts of a million and a half dollars, which had seemed overwhelming to the thrifty Vermont farmers, were all paid fourteen years later. The emigration to the West took those who wanted to go, and those who wanted to stay remained, with a resultant easing of those tensions which come from a feeling of being trapped in uncongenial surroundings. The new immigrants from other countries became Americanized and settled into the communities as useful citizens. To answer the last question, whether the Negro slaves of the South had been worth the Vermont lives spent in freeing them, Dorothy reports on a packed hall listening to the great Negro diplomat Ralph Bunche: "His audience was made up of the grandchildren of men many of whom had risked, some of whom had given, their lives to strike the chains from his grandfather. A cloud, a twilight shadow which had hung over one aspect of the Vermont Tradition, blew away to nothingness—forever."[14]

There is one other chapter in the section on the growth of Vermont since the end of the Civil War. It is descriptive rather than historical. Under the title "One-way Social Street," Dorothy describes a significant difference between the social organization of Vermont and that of other sections of America. She writes of America: "We boast that no American is a slave, a serf, or even a vassal to the class into which he was born. We tell the world that our nation leaves him free to move out of it, if he wishes. That is true only if he moves one way. The son of a blacksmith can become President of the United States."[15] "Almost everywhere in our America, our nation has done wonderfully in laying out and hard-surfacing one lane of its inter-job highway. But one lane only. The sign on the other, which leads from white-collar to

Overalls, still reads, 'Road Closed. Proceed at Your Own Peril.'

"In Vermont we are proud to post the notice—and to try to live up to it, 'Open for Traffic in Both Directions.' "[16]

Part V is a series of brief biographies of leaders produced by Vermont: Justin Morrill, Warren Austin, John Dewey, and Robert Frost. In the presence of educators and statesmen, and in the absence of painters, actors, multimillionaires, and abstract scientists, Dorothy sees an indication of the type of human product fostered by the Vermont tradition. "Peaches and pomegranates do not, you see, grow on apple trees. But apples do."[17]

Part VI contains a discussion of the extent to which the Vermont tradition persists today. After citing a number of legal and legislative decisions that indicate that the tradition is still an important force in the lives of Vermonters now, as in the past, Dorothy retells a story about a town meeting. This tale, under the title "Let the Bridges Fall Down!" was written for the *Reader's Digest* in 1945, just after word of her son's death had reached Dorothy.

The question before the town meeting was whether to build badly needed bridges over the local stream or to build a high school in the town (the nearest one at that time was twelve miles away over roads often impassable in winter and early spring). It seemed that "the tangible needs of the body" were about to triumph over "the impalpable needs of the mind and spirit,"[18] when Patrick Thompson, the local grocer, sprang to his feet to say, "What kind of a town would we rather have, fifty years from now—a place where nitwit folks go back and forth over good bridges? Or a town with brainy, well-educated people capable of holding their own in the modern way of life? You know which of those two is really wanted by every one of us here. I say, '*Let the bridges fall down!*' "[19]

This story, written down so soon after the sacrifice of her son, is a fitting conclusion, for in *Vermont Tradition* Dorothy has written between the lines that her Jimmy, and all the other young men whose lives have been given for American ideals, did not die in vain.

On the wall of the statehouse in Montpelier are inscribed these words of Calvin Coolidge: "If the spirit of liberty should vanish in the United States, and our institutions should languish, it could all be restored by the generous store held by the people in this brave little state of Vermont." At the close of *Vermont Tradition* Dorothy asks the question: "Can the whole of the [human] family ever learn to act for the good of the whole, for that whole made up of ordinary men and women who have in common only that they are human?"[20] She answers her question with the guardedly optimistic answer: "Anyone who has been part of such solidarity, not as an ideal, a theory, something in a book, a spiritual aspiration, but as a living fiber in everybody's heart—he knows that we have a chance. A fighting chance. Enough. What more is needed for any heart with courage in it?"[21]

Dorothy was more than seventy years old when she wrote *Vermont Tradition*. She leaned heavily on Sarah Cleghorn for help in wording and for encouragement, but she poured her own waning vitality unstintedly into the work. The writing of the book involved much more exacting research than any of her novels. When it was done Dorothy wrote to her publishers:

> What an absorbing piece of work this has been! I've worn myself out, physically, with the intent focussing on it of all my faculties for so long: the financial cost has been rather ruinous, as I have had to pay for much more research, historical and economic, than I had dreamed of; and as for the never-ending cost of typing a long book, the pages of which have been revised as many times as this book—the less said the better.
>
> And yet—I wish I could reach Mr. Scaife and thank him for pushing me into this by main force and persistence. I don't regret all this expenditure of time, money and vitality. The effort has turned out just what he thought it might be—something written from very deep within the subject. As he used to say "really from the very inside." His idea was that of a *creative* publisher.[22]

The book contains no dedication. Dorothy wrote: "I'd like to dedicate this to my husband without whose sympathy and help I could never have written any books. But he comes of a Quaker family background, has quiet retiring Quaker tastes and has never been willing to have his name appear. So I'll just leave the fly leaf empty."[23]

Vermont Tradition is an important adjunct to Dorothy's novelistic work because it proves an important point. Critics often said that the world which she described did not actually exist in any geographical location. In *Vermont Tradition* she shows that she was, as surely as any realistic urban writer, describing fictionally the world that she experienced in real life. When the heroine of *The Bent Twig* or *The Brimming Cup* goes from an acquisitive, competitive, urban society to the socially constructive rural setting of Vermont, this geographical ending is not an imaginary utopia for the author, but the world as she saw it around her. Urban readers and critics might doubt its existence, but Dorothy maintained that it was really there, and she drew her strength from this knowledge. Not until this last long book, however, a work that is neither novel nor history but both, does Dorothy use her novelist's perceptive sensitivity and narrative skill to explore the meaning behind her observations, to develop the reasons for and the background of her Vermont experience.

When Dorothy wrote, early in 1953, that she had "worn myself out, physically, with the intent focussing on it of all my faculties for so long," this was more basically true than she perhaps realized. On the morning of December 1 of that year she suffered a cerebral hemorrhage. As she lay with one arm and one leg paralyzed, she thought of the members of her family who had also had the "family stroke" and had died of it—her father, her grandmother, and various other Canfield relatives.

> But then, along with these older members of the family, I saw at that moment, quite plainly, an irascible old man, his thick white hair all tousled, Andrew Jackson-style, leaning out of bed and shouting angrily, "*Give me that cane!*" That was great-uncle Zed. He, too, had had the family "stroke" when he was about my age, 75, and had been paralyzed—but to everyone's surprise, he slowly recovered enough to walk around with two canes. The family felt sure he would drop dead at every step and tried their best to keep him bedridden. I suppose the rural doctors didn't know as much then as the medical profession does now about the different degrees of cerebral hemorrhages. I remember very well taking long walks with Uncle Zed after he had had his first stroke. Then, after a couple of years, he was laid low with another one, and fiercely insisted again, after a month or so in bed, on getting up. And he walked around again and lived the normal life of an old man for some years and had another stroke and got up again and so on till one killed him at the age of—oh, I don't know, 83 or 84, old enough for anybody. . . . I've no idea, of course, what's before me now. Who does know what's before him? But as you can see, it hasn't been a very violent or melodramatic experience. Uncle Zed stood by, as he has in many another experience of my life.[24]

Dorothy Canfield Fisher died on Sunday, November 9, 1958, of what she called the "Canfield stroke." John Fisher wrote afterward to Edward Post:

> During the past ten months her physical strength weakened but not her intense interest in people, the complexity of their characters—above all their capacity for growth. . . . Death came quickly and without warning. On that Sunday we sat a while on the porch talking together in the sunshine. Then it grew colder and we went into the house. She was barely across the threshold when she stumbled. I caught her before she fell, and her body went limp in my arms. I laid her on the floor trying to rouse her from what I hoped was only a fainting spell. It was no use, she never breathed again. But she could not have suffered much for her face as she lay there was serene as always.[25]

Her associates on the editorial board of the Book-of-the-Month Club summed up her meaning for them and for the world:

She was more than an American of great ability. She was one of the rarest and purest character. In her completely unself-conscious integrity, her courage, her humor and her practical good sense (the last almost always used to help other human beings) she harked back to and lent new luster to our highest pioneer traditions. A confirmed Vermonter, she was also a cosmopolitan in both space and time. All who knew her felt at once this combination of deep-rootedness and broad humanity; and felt themselves the larger for it. Her death leaves our country poorer. Her life enriched it.[26]

Dorothy Canfield was born the child of a crusader and an artist. All through her long life she carried the two conflicting natures of her parents within her own personality and wrestled with them to create meaning out of their differences. It was a struggle that often wrung from the author anguished expressions of inadequacy and despair, even while she was producing works that won international acclaim.

Yet she never withdrew from the challenge or abandoned the fight to reconcile her opposing creative forces and to find and transmit an understanding large enough to include both the artist and the crusader. After her death a note was found on her desk, affirming the belief that supported her. It read simply, "Hope and faith in the possibilities of human nature."[27]

Notes

In these notes the author's name Dorothy Canfield Fisher has been abbreviated to her initials DCF. Published works by Dorothy Canfield (Fisher) are referred to by title only; publisher and date of publication are given in the list of works on page 249. The most important collections of letters and other unpublished materials are in the Wilbur Collection of the University of Vermont (UVM), Columbia University (CU), and Princeton University (PU), with a few items primarily relating to her grandfather in the Hay Library of Brown University (Brown). The location where unpublished material may be found is indicated in parentheses after each item.

Introduction

1 DCF to Anna Pettit Broomell, Sept. 8, 1944 (UVM). The italics is the author's.
2 DCF to David Baumgardt, Feb. 13, 1957 (UVM).
3 The quotations in this paragraph are taken from the Preface by Dorothy Canfield Fisher to *Norman Rockwell, Illustrator,* by Arthur L. Guptill (New York: Watson-Guptill Publications, 1946).

Chapter 1
Parents and Other Ancestors

1 *Vermont Tradition,* p. 3.
2 *American Portraits,* p. 147.
3 Note by DCF on back of photograph in unpublished papers (UVM).
4 *The Real Motive,* pp. 249–50.
5 Ibid., pp. 250–52.
6 Ibid., pp. 252–53. A typed copy of a letter from Albert Camp in California dated Aug. 21, 1949, is among the unpublished papers (UVM).
7 Marginal note to "Hop-picking Song," unpublished papers (UVM).
8 Eli H. Canfield, "Recollections of a Boyhood in Vermont 1817–1856," written to his son James in the 1870s, unpublished. The original handwritten manuscript and a typescript are in the Hay Library, Brown University. This quotation is from p. B-19 of the typescript.
9 Ibid., p. B-17.
10 In *A History of Bristol Borough* by Doren Green (Bristol, Pa., 1911), pp. 72–73, is found the following description of the location and buildings of the college: "On the banks of the

Delaware, three miles below Bristol, stands what is known as Bristol College. About 1778, the farm belonged to one Benger, an Irish sporting gentleman. . . . He sold it to Andreas Evarandus Van Braam Honchgust, the governor of an East India island, who retired to this country on the island being taken by the British. He erected an elegant mansion and called it China Retreat. The marble used in the construction of this building was brought up the river by Samuel Hibbs, of Bensalem, in a shallop. In 1798 he sold the property, containing 361 acres and thirty perches, to Captain Walter Sims. . . . China retreat was turned into a seat of learning in 1833, and organized as Bristol College, with the Rev. Chauncey Colton, D.D., president, and under the patronage of the Episcopal Church. Additional buildings were erected, and at one time as many as eighty or one hundred students were in attendance. It ran its course in a few years, and was succeeded by a classical school. In 1842 the late Captain Alden Partridge, one of the earliest superintendents at West Point, opened a military school in the China Retreat Building, which was kept up for about three years. During the late civil war the buildings were occupied as a military hospital, and later were used for a state school for the education of colored soldiers' orphans. Subsequently the land was used as a picnic grounds and known as College Park. Today the property is occupied as a private residence."

[11] Eli H. Canfield, "Recollections," p. B-17.

[12] Ibid., pp. B-18 to B-19.

[13] Seventh in a list of "7 Practical Duties of a Christian," in a letter to parishioners, Delaware, Ohio, Easter 1849 (Brown).

[14] *Raw Material*, p. 245.

[15] Ibid., pp. 241–42.

[16] James A. Canfield, "Biographical Sketch of the Rev. Eli H. Canfield by his Grandson," pp. 2–3 (Brown). Dorothy disagrees with her brother in *Memories of Arlington, Vermont*, p. 86, where she says, "My brother and I both remember hearing the story ever so many times when we were young. He remembers it quite distinctly as having taken place inside St. James Church. And I remember with equal distinctness that it was told as taking place in the Town Hall. I consider that I have some real proof on my side, in that the door at the end of the aisle in St. James through which she had to pass to go out is a swinging door and she couldn't slam it! Whereas the Town Hall door always slammed with a resounding, satisfying clangor."

[17] *Memories of Arlington, Vermont*, pp. 84–85.

[18] *A Harvest of Stories*, pp. 61–62.

[19] Ibid., p. 63.

[20] Ibid.

[21] Unpublished papers (UVM).

[22] *Memories of Arlington, Vermont*, p. 83.

[23] James Hulme Canfield, *Taxation, A Plain Talk for Plain People* (New York: The Society for Political Education, 1883).

[24] James A. Canfield, "Biographical Sketch of the Rev. Eli H. Canfield by his Grandson," p. 3 (Brown).

[25] *The Class of Sixty-Eight. Williams College after Thirty-Five Years* (New York, 1903).

[26] George S. Hibbard, *Rupert, Vt., Historical and Descriptive 1761–1898* (Rutland, Vt., 1899).

[27] Jonas Wilder to James Hulme Canfield, Dec. 14, 1868 (UVM).

[28] *The Interstate Schoolman* 7, no. 6 (June 1909), p 5.

[29] James Hulme Canfield, *The College Student and His Problems* (New York: The MacMillan Company, 1902), p. 177.

[30] Ibid., p. 70.

Chapter 2
Home and School

[1] DCF to Pearl Buck, June 22, 1943 (UVM).

2 As reprinted in the *Nashville* (Tenn.) *American,* July 20, 1889.
3 *Columbia* (Mo.) *Herald* clipping, no date (UVM).
4 James Hulme Canfield to Eli H. Canfield, Oct. 2, 1889 (UVM).
5 Unpublished papers (UVM).
6 *American Portraits,* pp. 147–48.
7 DCF to Sarah Cleghorn, Jan. 23, no year (UVM).
8 *The Nebraska Alumnus,* Feb. 1938.
9 Ibid.
10 Ibid.
11 Ibid.
12 Reprinted from National Education Association, *Volume of Proceedings,* Denver, Colo., July 5, 1909.
13 James Hulme Canfield to Mr. Musz, Nov. 15, 1891 (UVM).
14 DCF to Henry Carter, July 27, 1953 (UVM).
15 Ibid.
16 The typescript for this article has this marginal note by DCF at the top of the first page: "This was written (about 1951) at the request of an undergraduate at the University of Chicago, who wrote me saying 'I am a Vermont boy and hence feel I can ask you for "something" ' and signed his letter Michael Filosa. It is for the undergraduate magazine at the Univ. of Chicago." (UVM) Another version of this article appeared in *The Educational Forum* 16, no. 3 (Mar. 1952).
17 Ibid. (typescript), p.3.
18 Ibid., p. 8.
19 Ibid., pp. 9–11.
20 DCF to Fraser Drew, Dec. 7, 1949 (UVM).
21 This story is also available in *Willa Cather's Collected Short Fiction 1892–1912* (Lincoln, Nebr.: University of Nebraska Press, 1965), pp. 505–13.
22 Willa Cather and Dorothy Canfield, *The Fear That Walks by Noonday* (New York, Phoenix Book Shop, 1931), with a foreword by Ralph Allan.
23 James E. Pollard, *History of the Ohio State University, The Story of Its First Seventy-Five Years 1873–1948* (Columbus, Ohio: The Ohio State University Press, 1952), p. 135.
24 Ibid., pp. 137–38.
25 Ibid., p. 162. The internal quotation is from Cope, the secretary of the Board of Trustees.
26 Ibid., pp. 148–49.
27 Dorothy Canfield Fisher, "A Librarian's Creed," *Columbia University Columns,* 2, no. 1 (Nov. 1952), p. 4.
28 DCF to Pearl Buck, July 10, 1942 (UVM).
29 Unpublished papers (UVM).
30 Ibid.
31 Dorothy Canfield, *Émile Augier, Playwright–Moralist–Poet, A Study* (Columbus, Ohio: The Ohio State University, June 1899). Printed for private circulation.
32 Ibid., p. 51.
33 Cf. p. 103.
34 *Émile Augier,* p. 22.
35 Cf. p. 131.
36 *Émile Augier,* pp. 23–24.
37 Pollard, *History of the Ohio State University, p. 164.*
38 Unpublished papers (UVM).
39 Ibid.
40 "Mrs. Flavia Canfield, Mother of the Famous Writer," *Delineator,* Feb. 1928.
41 *A Harvest of Stories,* p. xv.
42 Ibid., p. xvi.
43 Ibid.
44 Ibid., pp. xvi–xvii.

[45] Ibid., p. xx.

[46] Ibid.

[47] Ibid., p. xxvi.

[48] Ibid., pp. xxvi–xxvii.

[49] Unpublished papers (UVM).

Chapter 3

Transitions

[1] Dorothy Canfield Fisher, "A Librarian's Creed," *Columbia University Columns, 2, no. 1* (Nov. 1952), p. 3.

[2] Ibid., p. 6.

[3] Ibid., p. 8.

[4] Ibid., p. 9.

[5] Ibid., p. 10.

[6] Ibid., p. 12.

[7] Ibid., p. 11.

[8] National Education Association, *Volume of Proceedings,* Denver, Colo., July 5, 1909.

[9] Reported in *New York City Evening Post,* Mar. 31, 1909.

[10] Alfred Harcourt, *Some Experiences* (Riverside, Conn., 1951), p. 23.

[11] Unpublished papers (UVM).

[12] Dorothy Canfield, *Corneille and Racine in England: A Study of the English Translations of the Two Corneilles and Racine, with Especial Reference to Their Presentation on the English Stage* (New York: Columbia University Press, 1905). This dissertation was republished with the title *Corneille and Racine in English,* in *Columbia University Studies in Romance Philology and Literature* 5 (New York: AMS Press, 1966).

[13] DCF to Céline Sibut, no date, trans. from French (UVM).

[14] DEF to Céline Sibut, May 11, 1904, trans. from French (UVM).,

[15] DCF to Céline Sibut, May 9, 1905, trans. from French (UVM).

[16] Printed copy, but no indication of source, in unpublished papers (UVM).

[17] Unpublished papers (UVM).

[18] DCF to Céline Sibut, May 11, 1906, trans. from French (UVM).

[19] Quoted in letter of May 11, 1906.

[20] "Fisher Chronology" — among unpublished papers (UVM).

[21] DCF to Céline Sibut, Oct. 4, 1905, trans. from French (UVM).

[22] DCF to Céline Sibut, no date, trans. from French (UVM).

[23] Ibid.

[24] DCF to Alfred Harcourt, Mar. 1, 1932 (UVM).

[25] DCF to Paul Reynolds, Sept. 2, 1907 (CU).

[26] DCF to Paul Reynolds, Feb. 1916 (CU).

[27] Quoted in DCF to Paul Reynolds, Oct. 29, 1919 (CU).

[28] These stories appeared in the following magazines:
"Romance Is Dead" in *Harper's Bazaar,* Jan. 1905; "A Philanthropic Honeymoon" in *Munsey's Magazine,* May 1906; "The Rejected Suitor" in *Everybody's Magazine,* Aug. 1906; "The Story of Ralph Miller" in *Munsey's Magazine,* 1906; "The Pants-Button" in *Munsey's Magazine,* 1907; "The Bedquilt" in *Harper's Magazine,* Nov. 1906; "A Man of Ideas" in *Munsey's Magazine,* 1908; and "A Dweller in the Wilderness" in *Munsey's Magazine,* 1909.

[29] "The Awakening" appeared in *Munsey's Magazine,* 1907.

[30] "The Last of the Garrison" appeared in *Everybody's Magazine,* July 1906.

[31] DCF to Mr. Streit, July 30, 1946 (UVM).

[32] Ibid.

[33] "The Piano" appeared in *Munsey's Magazine,* 1906; "A Pyrrhic Victory," in *Everybody's Magazine,* 1907.

[34] DCF to Mrs. Reynolds, July 31, 1918 (CU). "A Good Fight and the Faith Kept" was first published as "The Conqueror" in *American Magazine,* Mar. 1916.
[35] *Outlook,* 1905, p. 441.
[36] DCF to Céline Sibut, May 11, 1906, trans. from French (UVM).
[37] Ibid.
[38] Ibid.
[39] Ibid. in trans. by Malcolm D. Daggett (UVM).
[40] Ibid.

Chapter 4
Serious Writing

[1] Dorothy Canfield, "At the Foot of Hemlock Mountain," *Scribner's Magazine* 44, no. 6 (Dec. 1906), pp. 748–53; also in *Hillsboro People,* pp. 3–18.
[2] *Hillsboro People,* p. 6.
[3] Ibid., p. 8.
[4] Ibid., pp. 9–10.
[5] Ibid., p. 10.
[6] Ibid., pp. 12–14.
[7] *A Harvest of Stories,* p. xxvii.
[8] Typed copy among unpublished papers (UVM).
[9] Ibid.
[10] Ibid.
[11] DCF to Frederick A. Pottle, Aug. 22, 1945 (UVM).
[12] Ibid.
[13] Ibid.
[14] DCF to Alfred Harcourt, Jan. 28, 1920 (UVM).
[15] Dorothy Canfield, "How 'Flint and Fire' Started and Grew," in *Americans All,* ed. B. A. Heydrick (New York: Harcourt, Brace and Company, 1920), p. 210.
[16] Ibid., pp. 211–14.
[17] Ibid., pp. 217–20.
[18] John Fisher to Bradford Smith, Feb. 10, 1959 (UVM).

Chapter 5
Gunhild

[1] DCF to her family, July 30, 1905 (UVM).
[2] *Gunhild,* p. 317.
[3] Ibid., p. 319.
[4] Ibid., pp. 2–3.
[5] Ibid., p. 324.
[6] *Christian Intelligencer,* Feb. 26, 1908.
[7] *Montreal Star,* Feb. 29, 1908.
[8] *New York Nation,* no date on clipping (UVM).
[9] Sarah Fisher Scott to author, Aug. 20, 1973.
[10] "How 'Flint and Fire' Started and Grew," p. 219.

Chapter 6
The Squirrel-Cage

[1] Louis M. Starr, "An Interview with Dorothy Canfield Fisher," *Columbia University Oral History Collection,* typescript (UVM), 1956, pp. 32–33.
[2] DCF to Blanche Sibut, Feb. 12, 1920 (UVM).
[3] DCF to Sarah Cleghorn, no date, postmarked July 1, 1922 (UVM).
[4] DCF to Henry Holt, Sept. 14, 1915 (PU).
[5] DCF to Alfred Harcourt, Nov. 3, 1929 (UVM).

[6] Comments on Dorothy's home life based on an interview with Pearl Buck, summer 1971.

[7] DCF to Mother, no date (UVM).

[8] Ibid.

[9] *The Squirrel-Cage,* pp. 50–51.

[10] Ibid., p. 336.

[11] Ibid., p. 338.

[12] Ibid., pp. 352–54.

[13] Ibid., p. 22.

[14] Ibid., p. 73.

[15] *Philadelphia Press,* June 8, 1912.

[16] *Washington* (D.C.) *Star,* May 11, 1912.

[17] *Chicago Evening Post,* May 24, 1912.

[18] Elizabeth Wyckoff, "Dorothy Canfield: A Neglected Best Seller," *The Bookman* 44, no. 1 (Sept. 1931).

[19] *The Squirrel-Cage,* p. 274.

[20] DCF to Alfred Harcourt, Apr. 20, 1911 (PU).

Chapter 7
The Bent Twig and *Understood Betsy*

[1] *A Montessori Mother,* pp. v–vi.

[2] *The Squirrel-Cage,* p. 273.

[3] *The Bent Twig,* pp. 12–13.

[4] Ibid., p. 13.

[5] Ibid.

[6] Ibid., p. 17.

[7] Ibid., p. 106.

[8] Ibid.

[9] Ibid., p. 268.

[10] Ibid., p. 267.

[11] Ibid., p. 370.

[12] DCF to Arthur Canfield, Dec. 14, no year (UVM).

[13] *The Bent Twig,* p. 301.

[14] Ibid., p. 99.

[15] Ibid., p. 449.

[16] Ibid., p. 344.

[17] DCF to Paul Reynolds, Oct. 20, 1915 (CU).

[18] Henry Holt to DCF, Sept. 10, 1915 (PU).

[19] DCF to Henry Holt, Sept. 14, 1915 (PU).

[20] Henry Holt to DCF, Sept. 13, 1915 (PU).

[21] Ibid.

[22] Ibid.

[23] DCF to Henry Holt, Sept. 17, 1915 (PU).

[24] Henry Holt to DCF, Sept. 15, 1915 (PU). Henry Holt, an enthusiast for simplified spelling, consistently used "yu" for "you" in his letters.

[25] DCF to Henry Holt, Sept. 17, 1915 (PU).

[26] DCF to Henry Holt, Sept. 16, 1915 (PU).

[27] John Fisher to Alfred Harcourt, no date (PU).

[28] Ibid.

[29] DCF to Henry Holt, Sept. 16, 1915 (PU).

[30] Ibid.

[31] Ibid.

[32] Ibid.

[33] DCF to Henry Holt, Sept. 16, 1915 (PU).

[34] John Fisher to Alfred Harcourt, no date (PU).

[35] Alfred Harcourt to John Fisher, on back of preceding letter, labeled "from longhand letter to J.R.F., Sept. 20, AH" (PU).

[36] DCF to Henry Holt, Sept. 17, 1915 (PU).

[37] John Fisher to Alfred Harcourt, no date (PU).

[38] *The Bookman,* Jan. 1916.

[39] *Chicago Daily News,* Dec. 23, 1915.

[40] *The Bookman,* Jan. 1916.

[41] *The Rochester Herald,* Nov. 10, 1915.

[42] Mentioned in a review of *Bonfire* in the *Dayton News,* Oct. 13, 1933.

[43] DCF to Alfred Harcourt, no date (UVM).

[44] Sarah N. Cleghorn, *Threescore: The Autobiography of Sarah N. Cleghorn,* with an Introduction by Robert Frost (New York: Harison Smith and Robert Haas, 1936), pp. 179-80.

[45] Alfred Harcourt, *Some Experiences,* p. 99.

[46] DCF to Paul Reynolds, Apr. 26, 1916 (CU).

[47] *Understood Betsy,* p. 5.

[48] Ibid., p. 6.

[49] Ibid., p. 251.

Chapter 8
World War I and Its Aftermath: *The Deepening Stream*

[1] DCF to Céline Sibut, Dec. 9, 1912, trans. from French by Malcolm D. Daggett (UVM).

[2] DCF to Céline Sibut, Mar. 8, 1916, trans. from French by Malcolm D. Daggett (UVM).

[3] Ibid.

[4] Ibid.

[5] Ibid.

[6] Ibid.

[7] DCF to Céline Sibut, Mar. 19, 1916, trans. from French by Malcolm D. Daggett (UVM).

[8] DCF to Blanche Sibut, Mar. 14, 1916 (UVM).

[9] Quoted in letter from DCF to Céline Sibut, Apr. 2, 1916, trans. from French by Malcolm D. Daggett (UVM).

[10] Ibid.

[11] DCF to Céline Sibut, Apr. 12, 1916, trans. from French by Malcolm D. Daggett (UVM).

[12] Ibid.

[13] DCF to Céline Sibut, May 11, 1916, trans. from French by Malcolm D. Daggett (UVM).

[14] DCF to Alfred Harcourt, no date (PU).

[15] Ibid.

[16] DCF to Céline Sibut, June 13, 1916, trans. from French by Malcolm D. Daggett (UVM).

[17] DCF to Paul Reynolds, June 24, 1916 (CU).

[18] DCF to Céline Sibut, July 8, 1916, trans. from French by Malcolm D. Daggett (UVM).

[19] Ibid.

[20] DCF to Céline Sibut, May 11, 1916, trans. from French by Malcolm D. Daggett (UVM).

[21] DCF to Céline Sibut, July 23, 1916, trans. from French by Malcolm D. Daggett (UVM).

[22] DCF to Paul Reynolds, Nov., 24, 1916 (CU).

[23] DCF to Paul Reynolds, June 11, 1917 (CU).

[24] DCF to Paul Reynolds, July 20, 1917 (CU).

[25] DCF to Paul Reynolds, June 13, 1918 (CU).

[26] DCF to Alfred Harcourt, May 26, no year (PU).

[27] Ibid.

[28] *Threescore,* p. 178.

[29] Ibid., pp. 178-79.

[30] "A Pyrrhic Victory," *Everybody's Magazine,* 1907.

[31] DCF to Sarah Cleghorn, May 2, 1918 (UVM).

[32] DCF to Sarah Cleghorn, Apr. 8, 1918 (UVM).

[33] DCF to Sarah Cleghorn, May 2, 1918 (UVM).

[34] Ibid.
[35] Ibid.
[36] Alfred Harcourt to DCF, July 12, 1918 (PU).
[37] DCF to Alfred Harcourt, June 5, 1920 (UVM).
[38] Alfred Harcourt to DCF, June 13, 1933 (UVM).
[39] DCF to Mr. and Mrs. Alfred Harcourt, Nov. 10, 1920 (UVM).
[40] Ibid.
[41] DCF to Mr. and Mrs. Alfred Harcourt, Feb. 21, 1920 (UVM).
[42] DCF to Alfred Harcourt, Apr. 19, 1920 (UVM).
[43] John Fisher to Alfred Harcourt, Aug. 3, 1920 (UVM).
[44] Ibid.
[45] DCF to Alfred Harcourt, Nov. 10, 1920 (UVM).
[46] DCF to Sarah Cleghorn, postmarked July 1, 1922 (UVM).
[47] DCF to Paul Reynolds, January 24, 1923 (CU).
[48] "J. S. H." in the *Brattleboro Reformer,* Nov. 14, 1958 (UVM).
[49] Sue Harcourt to DCF, Feb. 12, 1923 (UVM).
[50] DCF to Alfred Harcourt, no date (UVM).
[51] DCF to Céline Sibut, Sept. 4, 1923 (UVM).
[52] *The Deepening Stream,* p. 23.
[53] Ibid., p. 4.
[54] Letter to Shirley and Harriet at the University of Connecticut, Apr. 20, 1943, in private collection of Professor Eric W. Carlson.
[55] *The Deepening Stream,* p. 41.
[56] Ibid.
[57] Ibid., p. 42.
[58] Ibid., p. 103.
[59] Ibid., p. 128.
[60] UVM.
[61] DCF to Alfred Harcourt, Easter Sunday, 1926 (UVM).
[62] *The Deepening Stream,* p. 219.
[63] Ibid., p. 221.
[64] Ibid., p. 388.
[65] Ibid., p. 392.
[66] Ibid., p. 392.
[67] Ibid., p. 393.
[68] Remarks reported by Pearl Buck in an interview, summer 1971.
[69] DCF to Alfred Harcourt, Aug. 6, 1927 (UVM).
[70] DCF to Alfred Harcourt, no date (UVM).
[71] DCF to Alfred Harcourt, no date (UVM).
[72] Ibid.
[73] Alfred Harcourt to DCF, May 8, 1929 (UVM).
[74] Alfred Harcourt to DCF, Apr. 2, 1930 (UVM).
[75] DCF to Alfred Harcourt, Nov. 14, 1930 (UVM).
[76] Harry Scherman to DCF, Jan. 15, no year (CU).
[77] Ibid.
[78] Ibid.
[79] Ibid.

Chapter 9
The Brimming Cup and *Rough-Hewn*

[1] DCF to Paul Reynolds, Sept. 3, 1918 (CU).
[2] DCF to Blanche Sibut, Feb. 12, 1920 (UVM).
[3] DCF to Sarah Cleghorn, Mar. 3, 1917 (UVM).

[4] DCF to Paul Reynolds, Jan. 9, 1920 (CU).
[5] Ibid.
[6] Ibid.
[7] DCF to Paul Reynolds, Jan. 29, 1920 (CU).
[8] DCF to Paul Reynolds, Feb. 9, 1920 (CU).
[9] Ibid.
[10] DCF to Paul Reynolds, Apr. 24, 1920 (CU).
[11] Ibid.
[12] Ibid.
[13] John Fisher to Alfred Harcourt, Aug. 3, 1920 (UVM).
[14] DCF to Alfred Harcourt, Nov. 10, 1920 (UVM).
[15] DCF to Alfred Harcourt, Nov. 16, 1920 (UVM).
[16] Ibid.
[17] *The Brimming Cup,* pp. 13-14.
[18] Notes on Martha Hulme Canfield for a History of St. James Church, Arlington (UVM).
[19] *The Brimming Cup,* pp. 266-67.
[20] DCF to Alfred Harcourt, Nov. 10, 1920 (UVM).
[21] William Lyon Phelps, writing in the *Literary Review,* Mar. 19, 1921.
[22] William Allen White, "The Other Side of Main Street," *Collier's Weekly,* July 30, 1921.
[23] Ibid.
[24] Ibid.
[25] Alfred Harcourt, *Some Experiences,* p. 58.
[26] DCF to Paul Reynolds, Aug. 14, 1920 (CU).
[27] DCF to Paul Reynolds, Oct. 22, 1920 (CU).
[28] DCF to Paul Reynolds, Jan. 31, 1921 (CU).
[29] Bradford Smith's Notes (UVM).
[30] DCF to Alfred Harcourt, Apr. 6, 1921 (UVM).
[31] DCF to Alfred Harcourt, Nov. 18, 1922 (UVM).

Chapter 10
The Feminist Novels: *The Home-Maker* and *Her Son's Wife*

[1] DCF to Helen K. Taylor, Feb. 8, no year (UVM).
[2] DCF to Céline Sibut, Mar. 5, 1922, trans. from French by Malcolm D. Daggett (UVM).
[3] *The Home-Maker,* pp. 62-63.
[4] Ibid., pp. 287-88.
[5] Ibid., p. 301.
[6] Ibid., pp. 307-8.
[7] Ibid., pp. 310-12.
[8] Ibid., p. 316.
[9] Ibid., p. 319.
[10] Ibid., p. 318-19.
[11] DCF to Alfred Harcourt, Oct. 4, 1924 (UVM).
[12] DCF to Alfred Harcourt, Dec. 14, 1923 (UVM).
[13] DCF to Alfred Harcourt, June 17, 1923 (UVM).
[14] DCF to Alfred Harcourt, Oct. 28, 1923 (UVM).
[15] DCF to Alfred Harcourt, May 19, 1924 (UVM).
[16] DCF to Alfred Harcourt, Jan. 8, 1924 (UVM).
[17] DCF to Alfred Harcourt, June 7, 1924 (UVM).
[18] DCF to Alfred Harcourt, Mar. 11, 1925 (UVM).
[19] *Her Son's Wife,* p. 24.
[20] Ibid., p. 69.
[21] Ibid., p. 26.
[22] Ibid., p. 27.
[23] Ibid., p. 26.

24 Ibid., pp. 60–61.
25 Ibid., p. 190.
26 Ibid., p. 194.
27 Ibid., p. 195.
28 Ibid., p. 193.
29 Ibid., p. 195.
30 Ibid., p. 194.
31 Ibid., p. 199.
32 Ibid., p. 197.
33 Ibid., p. 200.
34 Ibid., p. 204.
35 Ibid., p. 205.
36 Ibid., p. 224.
37 Ibid., p. 245.
38 Ibid., p. 251.
39 Ibid., p. 255.
40 Ibid., p. 257.
41 Ibid., p. 256.
42 Ibid.
43 Ibid.
44 Ibid., p. 294.
45 Ibid., p. 302.
46 DCF to Paul Reynolds, stamped received Sept. 2, 1924 (CU).
47 DCF to Paul Reynolds, Sept. 3, 1924 (CU).
48 DCF to Paul Reynolds, Sept. 19, 1924 (CU).
49 DCF to Paul Reynolds, Sept. 23, 1924 (CU).
50 DCF to Paul Reynolds, Sept. 29, 1924 (CU).
51 DCF to Alfred Harcourt, Dec. 12, 1924 (UVM).
52 DCF to Paul Reynolds, Mar. 28, 1925 (CU).
53 CDF to Alfred Harcourt, Apr. 28, 1926 (UVM).
54 DCF to Paul Reynolds, Jan. 1, 1926 (CU).
55 DCF to Paul Reynolds, Jan. 8, 1926 (CU).
56 DCF to Alfred Harcourt, Nov. 27, 1925 (UVM).
57 Quoted in letter from Alfred Harcourt to DCF, Aug. 25, 1926 (UVM).
58 DCF to Alfred Harcourt, Aug. 4, 1926 (UVM).
59 DCF to Alfred Harcourt, no date (UVM).
60 William Lyon Phelps, *Selected Readings from Much Loved Books* (Chicago: The University of Knowledge, Inc., 1940), p. 303.
61 *Her Son's Wife,* pp. 43–44.
62 Ibid., p. 275.
63 Maria Gleit, writing in *Der Bund* (Bern, no. 184, Apr. 21, 1946), trans. from the German.
64 *Güte, Wissen, Verstehen: Drei Lebensbilder grosser amerikanischer Erzieher,* ed. Friderike Maria Zweig (Esslingen: Bechtle Verlag, 1949), p. 96, trans. from the German.
65 Edward A. Post, "The Neo-Puritanism of Dorothy Canfield," *Christian Register,* Boston, Aug. 17, 1933.
66 In correspondence with Merle Haas (UVM).
67 Mary Westenholz to DCF, Sept. 10, 1938 (UVM).
68 DCF to Arthur Canfield, June 15, no year (UVM).

Chapter 11
Two Views of a Vermont Village: *Bonfire* and *Seasoned Timber*

1 DCF to Alfred Harcourt, May 27, 1933 (UVM).
2 *Harcourt, Brace News,* Jan. 10, 1934, p. 1 (UVM).

[3] *Bonfire,* p. 52.
[4] Ibid.
[5] Ibid.
[6] Ibid.
[7] Ibid.
[8] DCF to Alfred Harcourt, Oct. 5, 1933 (UVM).
[9] Alfred Harcourt to DCF, May 1, 1933 (UVM).
[10] DCF to Alfred Harcourt, May 3, 1933 (UVM).
[11] DCF to Alfred Harcourt, Oct. 5, 1933 (UVM).
[12] DCF to Alfred Harcourt, no date (UVM).
[13] DCF to Paul Reynolds, no date, stamped received Feb. 8, 1932 (CU).
[14] DCF to Edward A. Post, Jan. 24, no year (UVM).
[15] Ibid.
[16] DCF to Alfred Harcourt, Apr. 22, 1933 (UVM).
[17] DCF to Edward A. Post, Jan. 24, no year (UVM).
[18] DCF to Edward A. Post, no year (UVM).
[19] DCF to Edward A. Post, Jan. 24, no year (UVM).
[20] Alfred Harcourt to DCF, May 1, 1933 (UVM).
[21] DCF to Alfred Harcourt, May 3, 1933 (UVM).
[22] Review of British edition, signed G. L. C. Newspaper name not given on clipping (UVM).
[23] Quoted in letter from DCF to Arthur H. Quinn, Sept. 5, 1938 (UVM).
[24] Ibid.
[25] DCF to Alfred Harcourt, Nov. 8, 1935 (UVM).
[26] DCF to Alfred Harcourt, Nov. 2, 1935 (UVM).
[27] DCF to Alfred Harcourt, no date (UVM).
[28] DCF to Alfred Harcourt, Feb. 6, 1938 (UVM).
[29] DCF to Alfred Harcourt, July 1938 (UVM).
[30] DCF to Alfred Harcourt, Sept. 22, 1938 (UVM).
[31] DCF to Alfred Harcourt, Sept. 28, 1938 (UVM).
[32] Ibid.
[33] DCF to Alfred Harcourt, no date (UVM).
[34] Unpublished papers (UVM).
[35] DCF to Edward A. Post, Oct. 26, no year (UVM).
[36] Pauline Corley in the *Miami* (Fla.) *Herald,* Mar. 5, 1939 (UVM).
[37] DCF to Paul Reynolds, stamped received Nov. 28, 1927 (CU).
[38] DCF to Alfred Harcourt, Dec. 16, 1933 (UVM).
[39] *Seasoned Timber,* p. 111.
[40] Unpublished papers (UVM).
[41] *Seasoned Timber,* p. 10.
[42] Ibid., p. 457.
[43] Ibid., p. 435.
[44] Ibid., p. 457.
[45] Ibid., p. 161.
[46] Ibid.
[47] Ibid., p. 462.
[48] Ibid., pp. 463–64.
[49] DCF to Paul Reynolds, no date, stamped received Oct. 10, 1938 (CU).
[50] Harry Scherman to DCF, no date (UVM).
[51] Harry Scherman to DCF, Feb. 15, 1939 (UVM).
[52] Ibid.
[53] Alfred Harcourt to DCF, Nov. 17, 1938 (UVM).
[54] DCF to Paul Reynolds, Aug. 4, 1938 (CU).
[55] *The Election on Academy Hill* (New York, 1939).
[56] *Ce Coeur a tant de Peine* (Paris, no date).

[57] John R. Fisher to Bradford Smith, Feb. 10, 1959 (UVM).
[58] John Wright Buckham, "Dorothy Canfield Fisher: Interpreter of Life and Character," *The Educational Forum,* Mar. 1943.
[59] *Seasoned Timber,* p. 7.
[60] Ibid., p. 468.
[61] Pauline Corley interview.
[62] *Seasoned Timber,* p. 484.

Chapter 12
Early Collaborations: *Hillsboro People, The Real Motive,*
Fellow Captains, The Sturdy Oak

[1] Sarah N. Cleghorn, *Threescore: The Autobiography of Sarah N. Cleghorn,* with an Introduction by Robert Frost (New York: Harrison Smith and Robert Haas, 1936), p. ix.
[2] Ibid., p. 132.
[3] Ibid., p. 148.
[4] Ibid., pp. 132–33.
[5] Ibid., p. 161.
[6] Ruth Stark of Henry Holt and Company to DCF, Feb. 28, 1952 (UVM).
[7] DCF to Paul Reynolds, Feb. 25, 1916 (CU).
[8] Paul Reynolds to DCF, Feb. 26, 1916 (CU).
[9] Henry Holt to DCF, July 15, 1911 (PU).
[10] DCF to Sarah Cleghorn, Mar. 25, 1919 (UVM).
[11] DCf to Alfred Harcourt, Feb. 3, 1916 (PU).
[12] DCF to Paul Reynolds, May 15, 1914 (CU).
[13] DCF to Paul Reynolds, Mar. 7, 1913 (CU).
[14] Paul Reynolds to DCF, Dec. 28, 1915 (CU).
[15] Alfred Harcourt to Sarah Cleghorn, June 12, 1916 (PU).
[16] *Fellow Captains,* p. 3.
[17] Ibid., p.2.
[18] Ibid., p. 3.
[19] This story had been published in *Everybody's Magazine* in 1907.
[20] *The Sturdy Oak: A Composite Novel of American Politics by Fourteen American Authors,* ed. Elizabeth Jordan (New York: Henry Holt and Company, 1917).
[21] Ibid., p. ix.

Chapter 13
From World War I:
Home Fires in France, The Day of Glory, Basque People

[1] DCF to Paul Reynolds, Feb. 26, 1918 (CU).
[2] DCF to Paul Reynolds, Feb. 9, 1918 (CU).
[3] William Almon Wolff to DCF, no date (UVM).
[4] DCF to Mother, no date (UVM).
[5] Alfred Harcourt to DCF, July 12, 1918 (PU).
[6] DCF to Paul Reynolds, June 7, 1918 (CU).
[7] DCF to Paul Reynolds, June 27, 1918 (CU).
[8] DCF to Alfred Harcourt, June 28, no year (PU).
[9] DCF to Paul Reynolds, May 22, 1918 (CU).
[10] DCF to Paul Reynolds, Sept. 3, 1918 (CU).
[11] DCF to Paul Reynolds, Oct. 8, 1918 (CU).
[12] *The Day of Glory,* p. 103.
[13] Robert Frost, "From Robert Frost," in *Dorothy Canfield Fisher, In Memoriam* (New York: Book-of-the-Month Club, Inc., 1958).
[14] *Vermont Tradition,* pp. 10–11.

15 DCF to Paul Reynolds, June 25, 1925 (CU).
16 *Basque People,* pp. 3-4.
17 Ibid., p. 7.
18 Ibid., p. 39.
19 DCF to Alfred Harcourt, Apr. 24, 1931 (UVM).
20 *Basque People,* pp. 4-5.
21 DCF to Alfred Harcourt, Apr. 24, 1931 (UVM).
22 DCF to Alfred Harcourt, no date (UVM).
23 DCF to Paul Reynolds, Nov. 16, 1925 (CU).
24 DCF to Adriano Tilgher, May 1, 1932 (UVM).
25 Adriano Tilgher, "Books and Authors: Dorothy Canfield," *Il Popolo di Roma,* Jan. 30, 1932, p. 4 (trans. by Vergilio Zanin) (UVM).

Chapter 14
Two Do-It-Yourself Collections: *Raw Material* and
Made-to-Order Stories

1 *Raw Material,* pp. 17-18.
2 Ibid., pp. 9-10.
3 Ibid., p. 10.
4 Ibid., pp. 11-12.
5 Ibid., pp. 12-13.
6 Ibid., pp. 13-15.
7 Ibid., pp. 22-23.
8 DCF to Paul Reynolds, Nov. 11, 1921 (CU).
9 DCF to Céline Sibut, Mar. 12, 1925, trans. from French (UVM).
10 DCF to Paul Reynolds, July 21, 1921 (CU).
11 DCF to Paul Reynolds, Jan. 25, 1922 (CU).
12 DCF to Paul Reynolds, Jan. 28, 1922 (CU).
13 DCF to Alfred Harcourt, Mar. 12, 1924 (UVM).
14 DCF to Alfred Harcourt, May 6, 1924 (UVM).
15 *Made-to-Order Stories,* Introduction.
16 Ibid., p. 25.

Chapter 15
The Educator: *Fables for Parents, Nothing Ever Happens and
How It Does, Tell Me a Story*

1 Alfred Harcourt to DCF, Apr. 26, 1937 (UVM).
2 Ibid.
3 DCF to Alfred Harcourt, May 10, 1937—description of book for advertising purposes enclosed with letter (UVM).
4 DCF to Paul Reynolds, May 28, 1931 (CU).
5 Paul Reynolds to DCF, July 14, 1931 (CU).
6 Ibid.
7 John R. Fisher to Bradford Smith, Feb. 10, 1959 (UVM).
8 DCF to Paul Reynolds, July 18, 1931 (CU).
9 DCF to Paul Reynolds, Jan. 25, 1935 (CU).
10 Ibid.
11 DCF to Paul Reynolds, stamped received Feb. 27, 1935 (CU).
12 DCF to Alfred Harcourt, no date (UVM).
13 DCF to Alfred Harcourt, June 29, 1935 (UVM).
14 Harry Scherman to DCF, no date (UVM).
15 Judge Ben Barr Lindsey and Wainwright Evans, *The Companionate Marriage* (New York:

Boni and Liveright, 1927).
[16] DCF to Paul Reynolds, July 31, 1928 (CU).
[17] Ibid.

Chapter 16
The Last Anthologies: *Four-Square* and *A Harvest of Stories*

[1] DCF to Donald Brace, July 13, 1949 (UVM).
[2] *Four-Square,* p. vii.
[3] DCF to Paul Reynolds, Dec. 1, no year, stamped received Dec. 1, 1925 (CU).
[4] DCF to Donald Brace, July 10, 1949 (UVM).
[5] *A Harvest of Stories,* p. xiii.
[6] Ibid., p. xxvi.
[7] Ibid., p. xxix.
[8] Ibid.
[9] DCF to Edward A. Post, Dec. 26, 1956 (UVM).
[10] DCF to Edward A. Post, Jan. 11, 1956 (UVM).
[11] DCF to her family, July 30, 1905 (UVM).
[12] DCF to Mr. McCallum and Miss McCarthy, May 15, 1956 (UVM).
[13] Ibid.

Chapter 17
The Writing of Nonfiction

[1] DCF to David Baumgardt, Feb. 13, 1957 (UVM).
[2] DCF to Paul Reynolds, Oct. 10, 1920 (CU).
[3] DCF to Paul Reynolds, Dec. 11, 1925 (CU).
[4] DCF to Paul Reynolds, stamped received Aug. 23, 1919 (CU).
[5] DCF to Alfred Harcourt, Dec. 15, 1924 (UVM).
[6] DCF to Paul Reynolds, Sept. 1, 1919 (CU).
[7] Ibid.
[8] DCF to Paul Reynolds, Oct. 29, 1919 (CU).
[9] DCF to Alfred Harcourt, June 5, 1923 (UVM).
[10] DCF to Alfred Harcourt, Nov. 10, 1933 (UVM).

Chapter 18
The Montessori Books

[1] *A Montessori Mother,* p. 127.
[2] Ibid., p. 132.
[3] Ibid., pp. 132–40.
[4] *Public,* Mar. 5, 1913.
[5] Two of Dorothy's books on the Montessori method were reissued in 1965: *A Montessori Mother* (under a new title *Montessori for Parents*) and *The Montessori Manual* (both Cambridge, Mass.: R. Bentley, 1965). Educational theories in the United States had gone full cycle and come back to interest in the Montessori method again. Dorothy's firsthand report of what she had seen in Rome was again relevant to the American scene.
[6] *New York Evening Post,* no date on clipping (UVM).

Chapter 19
Translations: Papini's *Life of Christ* and Tilgher's *Work*

[1] Translator's note at beginning of *Life of Christ* by Giovanni Papini, freely trans. from the Italian by Dorothy Canfield Fisher (New York: Harcourt, Brace and Company, 1923).
[2] DCF to Arthur Canfield, Dec. 14, no year (UVM).
[3] DCF to Donald Brace, Nov. 23, 1922 (UVM).
[4] DCF to Alfred Harcourt, Jan. 28, 1922 (UVM).

5 DCF to Paul Reynolds, Nov. 27, 1922 (CU).
6 DCF to Paul Reynolds, Dec. 3, 1922 (CU).
7 DCF to Alfred Harcourt, Apr. 10, 1923 (UVM).
8 DCF to Merle Haas, June 10, 1931 (UVM).
9 DCF to Alfred Harcourt, no date (UVM).
10 DCF to Alfred Harcourt, July 28, 1930 (UVM).
11 DCF to Mr. Chase, Jan. 21, 1931 (UVM).
12 DCF to Alfred Harcourt, Jan. 28, 1931 (UVM).
13 *Work, What It Has Meant to Men through the Ages,* p. x.
14 Ibid., p. vi.
15 Ibid., p. vii.

Chapter 20
Adult Education and the Book-of-the-Month Club

1 Louis M. Starr, "An Interview with Dorothy Canfield Fisher," p.1.
2 Ibid., p. 2.
3 DCF to Paul Reynolds, Dec. 30, 1925 (CU).
4 DCF to Paul Reynolds, Dec. 17, 1925 (CU).
5 DCF to Alfred Harcourt, no date (UVM).
6 Ibid.
7 DCF to Alfred Harcourt, May 1, 1926 (UVM).
8 DCF to Alfred Harcourt, Dec. 12, 1929 (UVM).
9 *Why Stop Learning?,* pp. 293–94.
10 Dorothy Canfield Fisher, "Book-Clubs," in *The Bowker Lectures on Book Publishing,* 3d ser. (New York 1948), pp. 89–90.
11 Ibid., p. 90.
12 Ibid., pp. 91–95. This account of joining the Book-of-the-Month Club board, given many years later, places invitation and acceptance in the spring. The acceptance letter to Robert K. Haas (UVM) is, however, dated Dec. 22, 1925, and refers to "your prospectus and letter of December 15th." Whether the discrepancy is one of deliberate fictionalizing of events or just of faulty memory is difficult to determine. A warm Saturday in the Christmas shopping season could certainly have produced the phenomena she describes.
13 Ibid., pp. 95–96.
14 Interview, p. 43.
15 Ibid., pp. 16–17.
16 Ibid., p. 18.
17 Ibid., pp. 18–20.
18 Ibid., p. 60.
19 Ibid., p. 61.
20 DCF to Paul Reynolds, Dec. 5, 1932 (CU).
21 Paul Reynolds to DCF, Dec. 8, 1932 (CU).
22 Interview, p. 61.
23 Ibid., pp. 61–63.
24 Ibid., pp. 88–89.
25 Ibid., pp. 89–90.
26 Ibid. p. 90.
27 Ibid.
28 Ibid.
29 Ibid., p. 91.
30 DCF to Merle Haas, Jan. 28, no year (UVM).
31 DCF to Harry Scherman, Christmas Day 1941 (CU).
32 DCF to Harry Scherman, Oct. 4, 1950 (CU).
33 Interview, p. 33.

Chapter 21
Drama: *Tourists Accommodated*
[1] DCF to Paul Reynolds, Mar. 27, 1916 (CU).
[2] "Growing a Play," *Delineator,* Nov. 1916.
[3] *Tourists Accommodated,* title page.
[4] Ibid., pp. 1–9.
[5] *The Literature of Vermont: A Sampler,* ed. Arthur W. Biddle and Paul A. Eschholz (Hanover, N.H.: University Press of New England, 1973).

Chapter 22
World War II: The Children's Crusade and *Our Young Folks*
[1] DCF to Edward A. Post, Jan. 13, 1941 (UVM).
[2] DCF to Harry Scherman, Jan. 12, 1940 (CU).
[3] DCF to Edward A. Post, Jan. 13, 1941 (UVM).
[4] *Our Young Folks,* p. xiii.
[5] Ibid.
[6] Ibid., pp. xii–xiii.
[7] Ibid., p. xiii.
[8] Ibid.
[9] Ibid., p. xiv.
[10] Ibid.
[11] Ibid.
[12] DCF to Mrs. Sherwin, June 13, 1944 (UVM).
[13] DCF to Arthur Canfield, May 29, 1943 (UVM).
[14] DCF to Paul Reynolds, Sept. 4, 1942 (CU).
[15] DCF to Paul Reynolds, stamped received Oct. 9, 1942 (CU).
[16] DCF to Anna Pettit Broomell, Sept. 8, 1944 (UVM).
[17] DCF to Professor and Mrs. Edward A. Post, no date (UVM).
[18] (Mrs.) Jane T. Wunderley to Mrs. Arthur Guiterman, Mar. 28, 1945 (UVM).
[19] DCF to Edward A. Post, Sept. 20, 1946 (UVM).
[20] Ibid.

Chapter 23
The Small Town: *American Portraits* and
Memories of Arlington, Vermont
[1] *American Portraits,* p. 9.
[2] Ibid., pp. 15–17.
[3] Ibid., p. 23.
[4] Ibid., p. 26.
[5] Ibid., p. 27.
[6] Ibid. p. 147.
[7] Ibid., p. 148.
[8] Arthur L. Guptill, *Norman Rockwell, Illustrator,* Preface by Dorothy Canfield Fisher, pp. viii–xi (New York: Watson Guptill Publications, 1946).
[9] *Memories of Arlington, Vermont,* p. vii.
[10] Ibid.
[11] Ibid., p. viii.
[12] Ibid., p. 3.
[13] Ibid., p. 5.

Chapter 24
History Books for Children: *Paul Revere and the Minute Men,*
Our Independence and the Constitution, A Fair World for All, And Long Remember

[1] Bennett Cerf to DCF, Dec. 12, 1949 (UVM).

[2] Bennett Cerf to DCF, Apr. 19, 1950 (UVM).
[3] Robert K. Haas to DCF, Apr. 26, 1950 (UVM)
[4] *A Fair World for All,* p. 5.
[5] Ibid., p. 6.
[6] Ibid., p. 157.
[7] Ibid., p. 158.
[8] Helene Frye to DCF, May 27, 1953 (UVM).
[9] *And Long Remember,* p. 13.
[10] DCF to Anne Ross of Bobbs-Merrill, July 7, 1954 (UVM).
[11] Unpublished papers (UVM).
[12] *And Long Remember,* p. 10.
[13] Ibid., p. 13.
[14] Ibid., p. 13.
[15] Ibid., p. 17.
[16] Ibid., p. 18.
[17] Ibid.
[18] Ibid., p. 67.

Chapter 25
Vermont Tradition

[1] Roger L. Scaife to DCF, June 23, 1938 (UVM).
[2] Ibid.
[3] DCF to Ned Bradford, Feb. 3, 1950 (UVM).
[4] Walter Hard, *A Mountain Township* (New York: Harcourt, Brace and Company, 1953), Introduction by Dorothy Canfield Fisher, pp. xvii–xviii.
[5] Reprinted in *Vermont History* 23, no. 2, (Apr. 1955), pp. 85–91.
[6] DCF to Sarah Cleghorn, Jan. 12, no year (UVM).
[7] DCF to Sarah Cleghorn, Mar. 12, no year (UVM).
[8] *Vermont Tradition,* p. 52.
[9] Ibid., p. 57.
[10] Ibid., p. 153.
[11] Ibid., p. 163.
[12] Ibid., p. 208.
[13] Ibid.
[14] Ibid., pp. 315–16.
[15] Ibid., p. 320.
[16] Ibid., p. 338.
[17] Ibid., p. 392.
[18] *Vermont Tradition,* p. 412.
[19] Ibid., p. 413.
[20] Ibid., p. 414.
[21] Ibid., p. 415.
[22] DCF to Ned Bradford, Feb. 19, 1953 (UVM).
[23] DCF to Ned Bradford, Mar. 6, 1953 (UVM).
[24] Round-robin letter from DCF, Jan. 8, 1954, among letters to Edward A. Post (UVM).
[25] John R. Fisher to Edward A. Post, Nov. 21, 1958 (UVM).
[26] *Dorothy Canfield Fisher, In Memoriam* (New York: Book-of-the-Month Club, Inc., 1958).
[27] *News and Notes,* Vermont Historical Society, vol. 10, no. 4 (Dec. 1958), p. 31.

List of Works

Dorothy Canfield Fisher published works of fiction under the name Dorothy Canfield and nonfiction under the name Dorothy Canfield Fisher. The following list of her published books keeps this division.

DOROTHY CANFIELD

Gunhild. New York: Henry Holt and Company, 1907.
The Squirrel-Cage. New York: Henry Holt and Company, 1912.
Hillsboro People. New York: Henry Holt and Company, 1915.
The Bent Twig. New York: Henry Holt and Company, 1915.
The Real Motive. New York: Henry Holt and Company, 1916.
Fellow Captains (with Sarah N. Cleghorn). New York: Henry Holt and Company, 1916.
Understood Betsy. New York: Henry Holt and Company, 1917.
Home Fires in France. New York: Henry Holt and Company, 1918.
The Day of Glory. New York: Henry Holt and Company, 1919.
The Brimming Cup. New York: Harcourt, Brace and Company, 1921.
Rough-Hewn. New York: Harcourt, Brace and Company, 1922.
Raw Material. New York: Harcourt, Brace and Company, 1923.
The Home-Maker. New York: Harcourt, Brace and Company, 1924.
Made-to-Order Stories, New York: Harcourt, Brace and Company, 1925.
Her Son's Wife. New York: Harcourt, Brace and Company, 1926.
The Deepening Stream. New York: Harcourt, Brace and Company, 1930.
Basque People. New York: Harcourt, Brace and Company, 1931.
Bonfire. New York: Harcourt, Brace and Company, 1933.
Fables for Parents. New York: Harcourt, Brace and Company, 1937.
Seasoned Timber. New York: Harcourt, Brace and Company, 1939.
Four-Square. New York: Harcourt, Brace and Company, 1949.
A Harvest of Stories. New York: Harcourt, Brace and Company, 1956.

DOROTHY CANFIELD FISHER

A Montessori Mother. New York: Henry Holt and Company, 1912.
A Montessori Manual. Chicago: The Richardson Company, 1913.
Mothers and Children. New York: Henry Holt and Company, 1914.
Self-Reliance. New York: The Bobbs-Merrill Company, 1916.
Life of Christ by Giovanni Papini, freely trans. from the Italian by Dorothy Canfield Fisher. New York: Harcourt, Brace and Company, 1923.
Why Stop Learning? New York: Harcourt, Brace and Company, 1927.
Work: What It Has Meant to Men through the Ages by Adriano Tilgher, trans. from the Italian by Dorothy Canfield Fisher. New York: Harcourt, Brace and Company, 1931.
Tourists Accommodated. New York: Harcourt, Brace and Company, 1932.
Nothing Ever Happens and How It Does (with Sarah N. Cleghorn). Boston: The Beacon Press, 1940.
Tell Me a Story. Lincoln, Nebr.: University Publishing Company, 1940.
Our Young Folks. New York: Harcourt, Brace and Company, 1943.
American Portraits. New York: Henry Holt and Company, 1946.
Paul Revere and the Minute Men. New York: Random House, 1950.
Our Independence and the Constitution. New York: Random House, 1950.
A Fair World for All. New York: Whittlesey House, 1952.
Vermont Tradition. Boston: Little, Brown and Company, 1953.
Memories of Arlington, Vermont. New York: Duell, Sloan and Pearce, 1957.
And Long Remember. New York: Whittlesey House, 1959.

Index